THEORY AND INTERPRETATION OF NARRATIVE

James Phelan, Peter J. Rabinowitz, and Robyn Warhol, Series Editors

Narrative Sequence in Contemporary Narratology

Edited by RAPHAËL BARONI and FRANÇOISE REVAZ

The Ohio State University Press • Columbus

Copyright © 2016 by The Ohio State University.
All rights reserved.

Library of Congress Cataloging-in-Publication Data

Names: Baroni, Raphaël, editor. | Revaz, Françoise, editor.
Title: Narrative sequence in contemporary narratology / edited by Raphaël Baroni and
    Françoise Revaz.
Other titles: Theory and interpretation of narrative series.
Description: Columbus : The Ohio State University Press, [2015] | 2016 | Series: Theory and
    interpretation of narrative | Includes bibliographical references and index.
Identifiers: LCCN 2015036743 | ISBN 9780814212967 (cloth : alk. paper) | ISBN 0814212964
    (cloth : alk. paper)
Subjects: LCSH: Narration (Rhetoric) | Discourse analysis, Narrative.
Classification: LCC PN212 .N3785 2015 | DDC 808/.036—dc23
LC record available at http://lccn.loc.gov/2015036743

Cover design by Thao Thai
Text design by Juliet Williams
Type set in Minion Pro
Printed by Thomson-Shore, Inc.

Cover image: *Broadway Boogie-Woogie* was painted in 1942 by Piet Mondrian after he
reached New York to escape the war in Europe. The Dutch painter was impressed by the
movement of cars on the intersecting avenues of the city and the syncopated dynamism
of jazz music. In this work, he reinterprets his visual language, made of horizontal and
vertical lines and flat areas in primary colors, to increase the rhythm and movement of the
composition. Like contemporary narratology, this work reflects a quest for a more dynamic
form of expression.

∞ The paper used in this publication meets the minimum requirements of the American
National Standard for Information Sciences—Permanence of Paper for Printed Library
Materials. ANSI Z39.48-1992.

9 8 7 6 5 4 3 2 1

CONTENTS

List of Illustrations   vii

Introduction: The Many Ways of Dealing with Sequence
    in Contemporary Narratology   1
    RAPHAËL BARONI

Part I   Theorizing Sequence

  1 On Narrative Sequence, Classical and Postclassical   11
     GERALD PRINCE

  2 The Configuration of Narrative Sequences   20
     JOHN PIER

  3 The Eventfulness of Non-Events   37
     PETER HÜHN

Part II   Rhetorical Perspectives on Narrative Progression

  4 Privileged Authorial Disclosure about Events: Wolff's
     "Bullet in the Brain" and O'Hara's "Appearances"   51
     JAMES PHELAN

  5 Ending Twice Over (Or More): Alternate Endings in Narrative   71
     EYAL SEGAL

  6 Virtualities of Plot and the Dynamics of Rereading   87
     RAPHAËL BARONI

Part III   Sequences in Nonliterary Narratives

  7 Intrigue, Suspense, and Sequentiality in Comic Strips:
     Reading *Little Sammy Sneeze*   107
     ALAIN BOILLAT and FRANÇOISE REVAZ

8 Musical Narrativity   130
   MICHAEL TOOLAN

9 Narrativizing the Matrix   151
   EMMA KAFALENOS

Part IV *Unnatural and Nonlinear Sequences*

10 Unusual and Unnatural Narrative Sequences   163
   BRIAN RICHARDSON

11 Sequence, Linearity, Spatiality, or: Why Be Afraid of Fixed
   Narrative Order?   176
   MARIE-LAURE RYAN

Conclusion: Epistemological Problems in Narrative Theory:
   Objectivist vs. Constructivist Paradigm   195
   FRANCO PASSALACQUA and FEDERICO PIANZOLA

   Contributors   219
   Index   223

ILLUSTRATIONS

Figure 6.1	Dynamics of known and unknown plot	94
Figure 6.2	Virtualities of Peter's Promise	99
Figure 6.3	Virtualities of Prayer at Gethsemane	100
Figure 7.1	Winsor McCay, *Little Sammy Sneeze*, September 25, 1904	108
Figure 7.2	Peter Newell, *The Naps of Polly Sleepyhead*, 1906	110
Figure 7.3	The Lumière brothers, *L'Arroseur arrosé*, 1895	112
Figure 7.4	Winsor McCay, *Little Sammy Sneeze*, April 2, 1905	114
Figure 7.5	Winsor McCay, *Little Sammy Sneeze*, 1904–6	115
Figure 7.6	Winsor McCay, *Little Sammy Sneeze*, 1904–6	118
Figure 7.7	Winsor McCay, *Little Sammy Sneeze*, March 12, 1905	118
Figure 7.8	Winsor McCay, *Little Sammy Sneeze*, January 29, 1905	119
Figure 7.9	Roba, *Aventures de Boule et Bill*, 1999	121
Figure 7.10	Winsor McCay, *Little Sammy Sneeze*, October 23, 1904	123
Figure 7.11	Winsor McCay, *Little Sammy Sneeze*, January 15, 1905	124
Figure 7.12	Winsor McCay, *Little Sammy Sneeze*, October 16, 1904	126
Figure 11.1	Types of networks: (a) distributed network, (b) tree, (c) complete graph	179
Figure 11.2	Generative network for the sample stories	185

Figure 11.3	The linear discourse structure of Robert Coover's "The Babysitter"	188
Figure 11.4	What the reader's mental map of "The Babysitter" could look like	189
Figure 11.5	Structure of a typical computer game	192

INTRODUCTION

The Many Ways of Dealing with Sequence in Contemporary Narratology

RAPHAËL BARONI

SINCE ARISTOTLE, poeticians and, more recently, semioticians, linguists, and narratologists have debated many basic features of narrative first identified in the *Poetics*. Among them, we find the common assumption that narrative is an "imitation" or "representation" of actions (*mimesis praxeos*); that this "representation" aims to elicit emotions, such as fear and hope; and that "well-formed" stories are organized as a "whole" (*holos*), meaning that they possess a beginning, a middle, and an end. These three aspects of narrative are related to temporality, since actions told unfold in time, fear and hope orient the attention of the audience toward an uncertain resolution, and the unity of representation is assured by the cataphoric function of the beginning and the anaphoric function of the ending.

Since then, however, there have been many ways to deal with the nature, role, and relative importance of each of these components of narrative sequences. Indeed, as stated by Hilary Dannenberg: "Many key definitions of narrative hinge on the aspect of temporal sequentiality, and the repeated attempts to redefine the parameters of plot reflect both the centrality and the complexity of the temporal dimension of narrative" ("Plot" 435). Based on the duality of *fabula* and *sjuzhet* emphasized by Boris Tomachevsky, conceptualizations of narrative sequence can be linked either to the chronology of the events, to its reorganization by the narrative representation, or to the interplay between these two sequential dimensions.[1] Derived from Aristotle's *muthos,* the concept of plot—not necessarily synonymous with sequence—is even more polysemic, since it can be related to each of these aspects and can also describe additional properties: for example, "plot" can be understood as the causal relation between the events told (Forster) or as a rhetorical device whose primary function is to arouse a "cognitive desire" for a possible ending (Brooks 37; Dannenberg, *Coincidence and Counterfactuality* 6; Baroni 18), while "emplotment" is sometimes viewed as a configuration conferring meaning and unity on the endless and chaotic flow of time (Ricœur). This has led H. Porter Abbott to state that plot "is an even slipperier term than narration, both more polyvalent and more approximate in its meanings, indeed so 'vague in ordinary usage' that narratologists often avoid it altogether" (43). Hence, while it is necessary to distinguish between the slippery notion of plot and a more precise conceptualization of narrative sequences—with a focus on *fabula* and/or *sjuzhet*—, there is a need to clarify the relation between the two concepts, because it is obvious that plot is connected in some ways with the sequential nature of narratives. In a recent survey, Karin Kukkonen suggests distinguishing between "three basic ways of conceptualizing plot":

(1) Plot as a fixed, global structure. The configuration of the arrangement of all story events, from beginning, middle to end, is considered.
(2a) Plot as progressive structuration. The connections between story events, motivations, and consequences as readers perceive them are considered.
(2b) Plot as part of the authorial design. The author's way of structuring the narrative to achieve particular effects is considered. (§2–§5)

In this volume, while some authors, like Prince or Hühn, focus more specifically on the configuration of the story events, others, like Eyal Segal or James Phelan, are more focused on the progressive structuration of the story by the reader and the authorial design of the narrative discourse. Indeed, the history of narratology provides an interesting insight on how various epistemological frameworks influence the way "slippery" objects are seized. While formalists and structuralists mainly focused their attention on the logical organization of fully formed stories in order to describe their immanent (and more or less invariant) sequential organization, more recent paradigms—including reception theory (Eco), psychoanalysis (Brooks), rhetoric (Phelan, Sternberg), and cognitive science (Herman, Ryan, Fludernik)—have privileged

---

1. On this specific aspect, see Sternberg, *Expositional Modes and Temporal Ordering.*

a more dynamic perspective, highlighting the moving configuration of narrative sequences in the reader's mind while they progress through the story. As discussed by Franco Passalacqua and Federico Pianzola in the conclusion of this volume, this "shift"[2] can be also described as an epistemological tension between an objectivist conception, centered on a reified and/or idealized *fabula*, and a constructivist conception, focusing on the interaction between the objective features of narrative representations and the subjective experience of the audience. This shift stood out clearly when Umberto Eco wrote, in 1979, that *fabula* "is not produced once the text has been definitely read: the *fabula* is the result of a continuous series of abductions made during the course of the reading. Therefore, the *fabula* is always experienced step by step" (31). This conception is far removed from the formalist description of narrative functions found in Vladimir Propp's highly influential *Morphology*, since, as noted by David Herman, "[Propp's] approach gave an overly deterministic coloration to narrative sequences.... Part of the interest and complexity of narrative depends on the merely probabilistic, not deterministic, links between some actions and events" (*Story Logic* 94). In 1984, Peter Brooks described this change of focus by highlighting the dynamics of plots in connection with the reader's affective experience:

> I am convinced that the study of narrative needs to move beyond the various formalist criticisms that have predominated in our time: formalisms that have taught us much, but which ultimately—as the later work of Barthes recognized—cannot deal with the dynamics of texts as actualized in the reading process. (35–36)

Twenty years later, Emma Kafalenos, offering a panorama on contemporary narratology, insisted on the new importance conferred on the interaction between the reader and the representation:

> What I see new is the specificity of the analysis of how readers' decisions contribute to the construction of the narrative world.... Further developments along this path, if it occurs, will bring us an increasingly precise account of sites where indeterminacy can enter a narrative representation, and of conditions that heighten the interactivity between representation and reader in constructing narrative worlds. (114)

---

2. We should rather speak of "shift" instead of "evolution" since, as stated by Sternberg, functionalist paradigms existed long before and even contemporaneously with formalist and structuralist theories (see "Reconceptualizing Narratology"). This is the reason why Sternberg also rejects the opposition between "classical" and "postclassical" narratologies.

More recently, Hilary Dannenberg proposed a definition of plot aimed at encompassing the logical configuration of the *fabula*—which constituted the main focus of interest in formalist and structuralist paradigms—and the "dynamics of texts" related to the reader's progression through the text. To do so, she considers "cognitive desire" to be in possession of the "final configuration" of the story, but this "coherent and definitive constellation of events" can be revealed only at the closure of the narrative, while "plot in its unresolved aspect" is described as "an ontologically unstable matrix of possibilities" (*Coincidence and Counterfactuality* 13). Capitalizing on older concepts, but also opening up new perspectives embracing questions that include narrative interest, narrative progression, and the cognitive and emotional engagement of the reader, we see that, at least in Dannenberg's conception, the evolution of narrative theory over the past forty years does not necessarily lead to a clash of paradigms. As stated by David Herman: "Rethinking the problem of narrative sequences can promote the development of a postclassical narratology that is not necessarily poststructuralist, an enriched theory that draws on concepts and methods to which the classical narratologists did not have access" ("Scripts, Sequences, and Stories" 1048–49).

In this volume, Gerald Prince's opening chapter offers a broad overview of the various ways classical and postclassical narratologies have repeatedly tried to (re)define narrative sequence. Prince points out the tensions but also the convergences and relations between these definitions, especially by discussing the relative importance of text and context. In his chapter, John Pier then sets forth a configurational approach to narrative sequence that is both prototypical and intersequential. Prototypically, narrative sequence is a form of "diagrammatic iconicity" (Peirce) for patterning chronological-causal relations into a transformation from an initial to a final state. As such, sequence is not characterized by narrativity. Viewed intersequentially, the sequence is the product of the relations between "the absolute dynamics of the causally propelled action" and "the variable dynamics of the reading-process" (Sternberg) and thus emerges from the dynamic forces of narrativity. As for Peter Hühn, he shows how the notion of "eventfulness," which plays a central role in the dynamics of plots and the definition of narrativity, is closely linked to cultural and historical contexts, since the perception by the reader of "something meaningful happening" is necessarily linked to a situated interpretation. He also distinguishes between two types of "events," since something can happen in the story but remain pointless or insignificant in the narrative economy, while some "non-events" can become highly "eventful" when they are seen as an alternative to specific expectations.

While the first chapters deal primarily with the question of the relation between narrative sequence and narrativity, the second section illustrates more specifically the rhetorical paradigms that have improved our understanding of the narrative functions shaping the reader's progression through the text, thus marking an important revision of "classical" models of narrative sequence. As stated by Wayne C. Booth, the rhetoric of plot that originated in Aristotle's reflections on catharsis was neglected by the New Criticism under the allegations of "plot heresy" and the "intentional" and "affective" fallacies (84). Over the last forty years, however, we have witnessed the emergence of a "second generation rhetorical theory" helping to recontextualize narrative structures in the light of the relationship between an "implied author" and its "authorial audience" (Shen). James Phelan's contribution to this volume offers an exemplary case of this new rhetorical approach centered on narrative progression. In this case, he analyzes different kinds of "privileged authorial disclosures" and their effects on the reader. In the next chapter, Eyal Segal, following the perspective opened up by Meir Sternberg, examines various characteristics of alternative endings, the two major ones being the relations between the endings' degree of (un)happiness and of (un)conventionality (e.g., in terms of closure/openness). Raphaël Baroni, meanwhile, argues that unactualized virtualities of the story may preserve their emotional impact on the reiteration of a narrative, especially when they belong explicitly to the *fabula* and are associated with specific value-laden alternatives.

In a survey dealing with the recent evolutions in narrative studies, Jan Christoph Meister signals "a shift in focus from text-based phenomena to the cognitive functions of oral and non-literary narrative, thus opening a new chapter in the narratological project" (340). Meister insists particularly on studies that "explore the relevance of narratological concepts for the study of genres and media outside the traditional object domain of text-based literary narrative" (340). The studies gathered in this volume offer an opportunity to illustrate the challenge raised by narratives that depart from the canonical stories we find in classical literary works. Highlighting a phenomenon similar to the paradoxical suspense analyzed in the previous chapter, Alain Boillat and Françoise Revaz study the narrative interest of comics series, where multiple variations around a single motif are able to captivate the audience. As for Michael Toolan, he takes up the controversial issue of musical narrativity, showing how a sequential art, while being apparently nonreferential, can be related to some kind of narrative experience. In the last chapter of this section, Emma Kafalenos introduces the concept of "matrix" in order to explain how specific groups of people interpret differently the same event (and therefore its causal configuration) according to the order of the information conveyed by media. By doing so, she also shows the applicability of concepts forged in the rhetorical analysis of literary works for the understanding of political events.

Another challenge for contemporary narratology emerges from the analysis of experimental and/or unnatural narratives. Opening the last section of this volume, Brian Richardson illustrates a very lively branch of contemporary narratology that deals with unusual narrative configurations. For Richardson, unnatural narratives force us to denaturalize and rethink basic concepts—in this case, sequence or plot. In a chapter that can be regarded as a reply to the unnatural narratology, Marie-Laure Ryan considers that, despite the many attempts to challenge the linearity of narrative sequences, experimental stories, such as interactive stories or video games, do not do away with the fundamental linearity of narratives and that, consequently, most narratological concepts remain unaltered despite some spectacular but ultimately only apparent transgressions. The contrasting conclusions drawn by Richardson and Ryan show that the impact of unnatural narratology on the general theory of narrative sequence remains a contested issue.

The studies gathered here illustrate the many critical and complex issues surrounding the age-old concepts of narrative sequence and plot as well as the new epistemological and methodological challenges they have encountered in contemporary narrative research. In the conclusion of this volume, Franco Passalacqua and Federico Pianzola reconsider the ontological status of narrative sequence in various paradigms that they label "objectivist" and "constructivist." While the authors argue in favor of the latter paradigm, they conclude, quoting Mieke Bal, that the most responsible activity for theorists is "to challenge concepts that seem either obviously right or too dubious to keep using as they are, in order to revise instead of reject them" (Bal 44). It is the ambition of this volume to participate in this debate and contribute to the dynamic evolution of narrative theory.

We hope that these contributions, emanating from some of the most influential scholars in the field of narrative studies, offer further insight into developments in contemporary narratology, and, in particular, into the study of narrative sequences in all the diversity of their semiotic manifestations, forms, and functions.[3]

---

3. The ideas developed in this book were based on discussions that followed the First International Conference of the Narratological Network of French-Speaking Switzerland held in Fribourg in May 2011. Many thanks to Marine Borel and Jean-Philippe Faure for their assistance with the index, and to John Pier: his editorial skills and multicultural knowledge in narrative theory were essentials in the elaboration of the volume.

WORKS CITED

Abbott, H. Porter. "Story, Plot, and Narration." In *The Cambridge Companion to Narrative*, edited by David Herman, 39–51. Cambridge: Cambridge Univ. Press, 2007.
Aristotle. *Peri Poetikés / Poetics*. In *Aristotle's Theory of Poetry and Fine Art*, edited and translated by Samuel H. Butcher, 1–111. New York: Dover Publications, 1951 (1895).
Bal, Mieke. *Travelling Concepts in the Humanities: A Rough Guide*. Toronto: Univ. of Toronto Press, 2002.
Baroni, Raphaël. *La tension narrative: Suspense, curiosité, surprise*. Paris: Seuil, 2007.
Booth, Wayne C. "*The Rhetoric of Fiction* and the Poetics of Fiction." In *Towards a Poetics of Fiction*, edited by Mark Spilka, 75–89. Bloomington and London: Indiana Univ. Press, 1977.
Brooks, Peter. *Reading for the Plot: Design and Intention in Narrative*. Cambridge and London: Harvard Univ. Press, 1992 (1984).
Dannenberg, Hilary P. *Coincidence and Counterfactuality: Plotting Time and Space in Narrative Fiction*. Lincoln and London: Univ. of Nebraska Press, 2008.
———. "Plot." In *The Routledge Encyclopedia of Narrative Theory*, edited by David Herman, Manfred Jahn, and Marie-Laure Ryan, 435–37. London: Routledge, 2005.
Eco, Umberto. *The Role of the Reader: Explorations in the Semiotics of Texts*. Bloomington: Indiana Univ. Press, 1979.
Fludernik, Monika. *Towards a 'Natural' Narratology*. London: Routledge, 1996.
Forster, Edward M. *Aspects of the Novel*. New York: Harcourt, Brace, 1927.
Herman, David. "Scripts, Sequences, and Stories: Elements of a Postclassical Narratology." *PMLA* 112, no. 5 (1997): 1046–59.
———. *Story Logic: Problems and Possibilities of Narrative*. Lincoln: Univ. of Nebraska Press, 2002.
Kafalenos, Emma. "Editor's Column." Special issue. "Contemporary Narratology." *Narrative* 9 (2001): 113–14.
Kukkonen, Karin. "Plot." In *The Living Handbook of Narratology*, edited by Peter Hühn, John Pier, Wolf Schmid, and Jörg Schönert. Hamburg: Hamburg Univ., 2014. http://www.lhn.uni-hamburg.de/article/plot.
Meister, Jan Christoph. "Narratology." In *Handbook of Narratology*, edited by Peter Hühn, John Pier, Wolf Schmid, and Jörg Schönert, 329–50. Berlin and New York: de Gruyter, 2009.
Phelan, James. *Reading People, Reading Plots: Character, Progression, and the Interpretation of Narrative*. Chicago: Univ. of Chicago Press, 1989.
Propp, Vladimir. *Morphology of the Folktale*. Translated by Laurence Scott. Austin: Texas Univ. Press, 1968.
Ricœur, Paul. *Time and Narrative*. Translated by Kathleen McLaughlin and David Pellauer. Chicago: Univ. of Chicago Press, 1984 (1983).
Shen, Dan. "Implied Author, Authorial Audiences, and Context: Form and History in Neo-Aristotelian Rhetorical Theory." *Narrative* 21, no. 2 (2013): 140–58.
Sternberg, Meir. *Expositional Modes and Temporal Ordering in Fiction*. Bloomington and Indianapolis: Indiana Univ. Press, 1978.
———. "Reconceptualizing Narratology: Arguments for a Functionalist and Constructivist Approach to Narrative." *Enthymema* 4 (2011): 35–50.
Tomachevsky, Boris. "Thematics" (1925). In *Russian Formalist Criticism: Four Essays*. Translated with an introduction by Lee T. Lemon and Marion J. Reis, 61–98. Lincoln: Univ. of Nebraska Press, 1965.

PART I

Theorizing Sequence

CHAPTER 1

On Narrative Sequence, Classical and Postclassical

GERALD PRINCE

THERE ARE MANY different kinds of sequence, of ordered or connected series of elements. For many (classical or postclassical) narratologists, the characterization of narrative sequences—which are (usually taken to be) component units of narratives that are themselves capable of functioning as narratives—constitutes one of the primary and necessary tasks of narrative theory.[1] Varying with the proposers' views about narrativity and their answers to the question, "What do all and only narratives have in common?" numerous proposals have been presented. Gérard Genette, for instance, who was less interested in story than in discourse or in the relations between story and discourse and who was discussing minimal narratives rather than narrative sequences (but the difference is not essential since any narrative sequence satisfies the necessary and sufficient conditions of narrativity), wrote in *Narrative Discourse Revisited*: "For me, as soon as there is an action or event, even a single one, there is a story because there is a transformation, a transition from an earlier state to a later and resultant state" (19). William Labov, who defines

---

1. On the distinction between classical and postclassical narratology, see Herman ("Scripts, Sequences, and Stories" and *Narratologies*). See also Fludernik ("Histories of Narrative Theory" and "Beyond Structuralism in Narratology"); Nünning and Nünning ("Von der strukturalistischen Narratologie zur 'postklassischen' Erzähltheorie"); and Gerald Prince ("Classical and/or Postclassical Narratology").

11

a minimal narrative as a sequence of two propositions, one of which refers to a "before" and the other to an "after," would perhaps agree (*Language in the Inner City*). So would Claude Bremond (*Logique du récit*), even if he prefers to speak of triads corresponding to the three fundamental stages in the unfolding of any process (a situation opening a possibility, an event actualizing the possibility, and a situation resulting from this event); or Jim Phelan, at least with regard to the number of events (rather than units or elements) required, since he describes narrative as "someone telling someone else on some occasion and for some purposes that something happened" (*Living to Tell about It* 18); or Marie-Laure Ryan, since she seemingly endorsed the view that "a narrative text is the representation of a number of events in a time sequence" (*Possible Worlds* 109). Or so would I, at least in one of my many "incarnations" (*Grammar of Stories*). In another incarnation, and in order to distinguish narrative from mere event description, I insisted on a minimum of two asynchronous events, neither of which presupposes or entails the other (*Narratology*). Vladimir Propp also, when it comes to minimal sequences (which he calls "moves"), hesitates in *Morphology of the Folktale* between one event (the liquidation of a lack) and two (a villainy and its reparation). But Tzvetan Todorov, even as he makes clear in a footnote that it is purely a matter of convention and that stories could be defined as comprising one and only one event (*Introduction to Poetics* 52), opts for at least two events (a destabilizing one and a restabilizing one). Presumably, Meir Sternberg, who speaks of sequential representations of sequential events, does, too ("How Narrativity Makes a Difference"), like Brian Richardson, who defines narrative as the "representation of a causally related series of events" (*Unlikely Stories* 105). Paul Larivaille, however, likes three events—provocation, action, and sanction ("L'Analyse (morpho)logique")—although he would probably grant that the three are one (constituting one transformation), not unlike Jean-Michel Adam in *Le Texte narratif* (complication, action, resolution), or Françoise Revaz in *Les Textes d'action*. As for Emma Kafalenos (*Narrative Causalities*), she might, like some story grammarians, require as many as four (destabilization, decision to intervene, and initial and main interventional acts).

In spite of these variations, it is safe to add that narratologists agree that narrative sequences represent linked series of situations and events and further agree that these sequences can be expanded or summarized, that they can be combined with other sequences in specifiable ways such as conjunction, embedding, or alternation, and that they can be extracted from larger sequences.

Now, as I have just suggested, characterizations of narrative sequences include more than just the number of events: temporal links, for example, initial and final states or situations, transformational relations, and more, much more. Indeed, from the Russian formalists on (and even before the Russian formalists: think of Aristotle), from Boris Tomashevsky, who saw conflicts of interests at the core of any *fabula*; or Vladimir Propp and any of his thirty-one functions; or A. J. Greimas and his contracts, competencies, tests, successes, and failures; to most, not to say all, of the narratologists I mentioned earlier—students of narrative, when discussing sequences, have tended not only to specify numbers of states and events or possible modes of combination between them but also to make explicit and even abundant room for the semantic dimension of their object (purposes, destabilizations, interventions, complications). Even those narratologists who would prefer to characterize sequences in syntactic or "formal" terms often do not altogether avoid recourse to semantic or "content" features (entailed by relevance and causal relations, contraries or contradictories).

Some narratologists have also made room for pragmatic features in their characterization of narrative sequences and have, at times, given those features pride of place. Once again, the tendency goes back to Aristotle, with his discussion of good plots, fear, pity, and catharsis. More recently, it is found in William Labov's description of so-called "complete sequences" and his emphasis on evaluation and point. It is also manifest, as the name more than indicates, in rhetorical narratology, which views narratives not merely as representations but as purposive acts of communication, and which stresses the experience of these acts. Similarly, in texts like *S/Z* or "Textual Analysis of a Tale by Edgar Allan Poe," Roland Barthes insists on narrative as a unit of exchange, on narrating as a mercantile act, on narrative situation as contractual, and he argues that narrative texts are organized in terms of (at least) two kinds of sequence: proairetic ones involving the articulation of situations and events but also hermeneutic ones involving a trajectory from enigma to solution. Most recently, in his exploration of narrative tension, Raphaël Baroni argues that the latter structures narrative and, indeed, constitutes a fundamental dimension of narrativity.

There is no doubt that pragmatic concerns play a role in shaping narrative sequences, that narratives are communicative acts, that evaluative passages emphasizing the pointedness of a narrative give the latter a particular form, or that narrative tension is an important narrative element. However, this does not mean that these concerns represent essential traits of all and only narrative sequences. After all, many communicative acts are not narrative and, unfortunately, too many narratives turn out to be pointless. It seems to me that, rather than relating to the distinctive nature of narrative sequences and helping to characterize it, such pragmatic concerns relate to a different, though no less significant, narratological problem—the reasons for which narratives are produced and consumed. Rather than answering questions like "What is narrative?" or "What is a narrative sequence?" or "What are the features constitutive of all narrative sequences?" they ultimately help answer questions like "Why narrative sequences?" or "Why narratives?"

A third narratological task that is equally important consists in answering still another narratological question: "What does it mean to understand a narrative sequence or a narrative?" It need hardly be said that understanding is difficult and perhaps impossible to define. Even an operational definition, such as "understanding a narrative sequence is being able to answer correctly relevant questions about its meaning," might well be inadequate, ultimately, and, in any case, raises further definitional obstacles. For instance, the notion of relevance calls for some explanation. A proposition (P) is relevant in a context (C) if and only if it implies at least one proposition (Q) in that context, that is, if and only if the union of P and C logically and nontrivially implies Q, and P does not logically imply Q, and C does not logically imply Q.[2] Given a context like "Mary always attends the Narrative Conference," a proposition like "The Narrative Conference will be in Las Vegas next year" has relevance in it since we can derive the important contextual implication, "Mary will be in Las Vegas next year." A relevant question, then, is a question whose possible answer (or answers) yields at least one new contextual implication in the context of the propositions that have already been extracted as well as the implications that have already been yielded. So that a question whose answer is already known—already part of the context—will not be relevant since it will not yield new implications. A question that has little or nothing to do with the extraction of meaning will not be relevant either: to ask how many consonants there are on the first page of a given novel and to find the answer will not prove very helpful for understanding that page. A question that has little if anything to do with the textual propositions expressed will also prove irrelevant, as the following riddle illustrates: "John lives in a studio apartment and has a sister. How old is John?" Of course, all other things (like semantic complexity or context size) being equal, a question whose answer yields relatively many or few implications will be relatively more or less relevant. As for the notion of "correct answer," needless to say, it is easily as problematic as that of "relevant question."

That said, I think that understanding a narrative even superficially does involve the ability to answer questions regarding what happened in the world represented, to whom (or to what), where, when, how, why; the ability to

---

2. On relevance, see Sperber and Wilson.

summarize and expand the narrative without contradicting the answers to these questions; and the ability to paraphrase it.

One will have noted, perhaps, that my examples of questions leading to understanding as well as my list of abilities testifying to it do not include or evoke elements like fear and pity, surprise and suspense, configuration and evaluation. I realize that emotion and cognition are difficult to disentangle and that the former affects the latter (and vice versa). But I think that one can answer a question like "What finally happened to Little Red Riding Hood" without considering uncertainties and anxieties about her ultimate fate and without examining the *raison d'être* of its recounting. Still, it is not easy (or even possible) to set aside all pragmatic factors or operations when assessing the nature and structure of narrative sequences and their understanding as distinct from their functioning, however much one might want to do it. In fact, though many contextual elements might not affect the nature or meaning of given sequences, and though interpretation is not equivalent to understanding and might not lead to understanding, the ability to answer questions about the what, where, or when of narrated elements does depend, to some extent at least, on pragmatics.

Texts do not convey explicitly all the information needed for their understanding, and in discussions of textual content, it is often difficult to keep the information stated apart from the information implied. As a matter of fact, the exact wording of written texts, for example, is often quickly forgotten. Narrative sequences, in particular, are semantic and not semiotic in nature. Contrary to signs, they are not recognized but rather apprehended as such. In other words, one of the steps taken when addressing questions about a narrative's content is the establishment or reconstitution of the implicit information that the narrative provides. Now, a good deal of implicit textual information is, of course, algorithmically retrievable. For instance, "John is good" is predictably recoverable from "All men are good and John is a man," because it is logically entailed by it. Likewise, "Jane got here at five o'clock" is entailed by "Jane left her place at four o'clock, and it took her an hour to get here." Hypernymic, hyponymic, holonymic, meronymic, and troponymic relations and operations similarly underlie the mechanical retrieval of information. "The door was open" implies the existence of a building, just as "Misty is a dog" implies "Misty is a canine" or "Misty is an animal." Furthermore, the presentational order of situations and events can govern certain aspects of a sequence's meaning. Unless the sequence explicitly indicates otherwise, and as William Labov and Joshua Waletzky emphasized in their study of spontaneously occurring narratives, two narrated (sets of) events or situations are taken to occur at different times if "their order cannot be changed without changing the inferred sequence of events in the original semantic interpretation," but they would be taken to occur at the same time if their order could be changed without modifying the original interpretation (21). The events in "John saw Peter and ran" are not simultaneous, whereas the events in "Mary drank a lot, but she ate very little" are. Moreover, given two (sets of) events (A and B) that are not simultaneous, and unless the text indicates otherwise, A will be taken to precede B in time if A appears before B. So that with something like "John saw Peter and ran," John's seeing precedes his running instead of the reverse. Other retrievals exploit general principles or laws regulating semiotic systems and pertaining to identity, consistency, coherence, exhaustiveness, and so on. For instance, should events be represented contiguously in the space of the narrative text—and barring any textual counterindication—they are taken to occur in the same (general) setting, as in "Jane drank her scotch, and Mary drank her beer"; should a given proper name designate a given character, it will designate only that character; and should another character be said to have two children, he or she will be taken to have no more than two children.

But the establishment or reconstitution of textual meaning often depends on less mechanical, less conventional, less straightforward, more uncertain and more arguable procedures, operations, and calculations. They are tied not only to linguistic and logical competencies but also to rhetorical and encyclopedic ones, and they rely at least as much on the extra- as the intra-textual, on context as opposed to co-text. Connotations can play an important role, and though they are not mere idiosyncratic sets of meanings evoked by words and things, they are less obvious and less stable than denotations. Figures and tropes modify whatever literal information is conveyed, and irony, closely tied to situation and context, can be particularly "unstable." Features like narrative frequency and narrative speed can affect the relative importance of a situation or event, thus affecting summarization. Similarly, narratorial authority and reliability affect the value of the information provided. This is especially true with narratives that feature not only many characters but also several narrators: the setting up of distinctions between these agents in terms of their authority or reliability and the classification of all the propositions expressed according to their degree of veracity raise a number of vexing problems (the enumeration of which I will spare myself and the reader). Of course, frames, scripts, or schemata used to complete sequences and fill textual gaps are at least partly based on probabilistic assumptions and conclusions rather than on invariant specifications. As for regulative semiotic principles, many of them are also based on typicality, probability, or plausibility, instead of necessity. For example, given two contiguously represented events (A and B) in some text, a causal connection will be taken to exist between them if B temporally follows A and is thought to typically result from it. Thus, in "It rained very hard and John got wet" or "Mary got bored and she left the party," John's wetness will be seen as resulting from the rain and Mary's leaving as caused by her boredom.

The founding fathers of narratology (or at least those among them who explored the narrated and its constituents) recognized the role of factors like knowledge of the world and quasilogical or paralogical operations in narrative understanding. In his celebrated "An Introduction to the Structural Analysis of Narrative," for instance, Barthes argued that "the mainspring of the narrative activity is to be traced to th[e] very confusion between consecutiveness and consequence, what-comes-after being read in a narrative as what-is-caused-by. Narrative would then be a systematic application of the logical fallacy denounced by scholasticism under the formula *post hoc, ergo propter hoc*" (248). Although a few years later Barthes's *S/Z* would dismiss the very attempt to develop a science of narrative and describe narrative *langue* as an exhausting and spurious enterprise incapable of capturing a text's *différence* and value, much of this famous writing of a reading represents a development of Barthes's "Introduction" and its pragmatic disposition, from the emphasis on connotation to the affinity between proairetic description and functional analysis or semic characterization and indicial analysis. Likewise, Claude Bremond's logic of narrative, which was patterned on the logic of action, and his intricate typology of roles were not (and could not be) without pragmatic sympathies. By the early 1980s, it seemed clear to most narratologists that an adequate model of narrative would have to include some kind of pragmatic component.

Put differently, classical narratology, as it is often called, makes room for pragmatics. Where it differs from its postclassical expansive successor is in the kind of room it makes and, what is more immediately relevant to our concerns here, in the location it assigns that room in its house. Classical narratology, though it acknowledges the significance of context, frequently neglects it by (temporarily) bracketing it, (artificially) restricting it, or making it part of the text and (unintentionally) drowning it. On the other hand, postclassical narratology, even though it stresses the importance of the text, can drown it by making it part of the context. Classical narratology likes to distinguish between questions and to set some of them aside. Postclassical narratology sometimes yields to the temptation of asking them all—and at the same time. I have already mentioned a number of questions that I think should be kept distinct, and there are many others that can be (and have been) raised: "How, for example, does one identify narrative sequences?"; "What is the relation between medium of communication and narrative form?"; "What stages do we go through in developing the ability to produce and process various sequences?"; "Why are some types of sequence used more frequently than others?"; "Why are some used more frequently at some times or in some places?" and so on and so forth. Once again, no narratology would necessarily want to ignore them. The role of the context and, in particular, that of the "reader" or receiver must be addressed, whether it be in the measure of authority associated with the various textual voices heard, the identification or resolution of ambiguity, or the tracing of surprise and suspense, but what should also be included are the play and sway of such emotions as hatred, disgust, or admiration; the tracking of tensional rises and falls; or the determining of narrativeness and tellability. But if the reader or receiver has a role in narratological drama, it might not be in every scene. Still, in the final analysis, whatever definition of sequence one adopts, whatever questions one considers pertinent, and whatever priority one assigns them, it is perhaps above all this role and the borders between the universal and the particular, the textual and the lectoral, narrativehood and narrativeness, well-formedness and value, form and force, that narratology should continue to discover and invent, explore and constitute.

WORKS CITED

Adam, Jean-Michel. *Le texte narratif.* Paris: Nathan, 1985.
Baroni, Raphaël. *La tension narrative. Suspense, curiosité, surprise.* Paris: Seuil, 2007.
Barthes, Roland. "An Introduction to the Structural Analysis of Narrative." *New Literary History* 6 (1980): 237–62.
———. *S/Z.* Translated by Richard Miller. New York: Hill & Wang, 1974 (1970).
———. "Textual Analysis of a Tale by Edgar Allan Poe." In *Untying the Text: A Post-Structuralist Reader,* edited by Robert J. C. Young, 133–61. London: Routledge & Kegan Paul, 1981.
Bremond, Claude. *Logique du récit.* Paris: Seuil, 1973.
Fludernik, Monika. "Beyond Structuralism in Narratology: Recent Developments and New Horizons in Narrative Theory." *Anglistik* 11 (2000): 83–96.
———. "Histories of Narrative Theory (II): From Structuralism to the Present." In *A Companion to Narrative Theory,* edited by James Phelan and Peter J. Rabinowitz, 36–59. Oxford: Blackwell, 2005.
Genette, Gérard. *Narrative Discourse Revisited.* Translated by Jane E. Lewin. Ithaca, NY: Cornell Univ. Press, 1988.
Herman, David. *Narratologies: New Perspectives on Narrative Analysis.* Columbus: The Ohio State Univ. Press, 1999.
———. "Scripts, Sequences, and Stories: Elements of a Postclassical Narratology." *PMLA* 112 (1997): 1046–59.
Kafalenos, Emma. *Narrative Causalities.* Columbus: The Ohio State Univ. Press, 2006.
Labov, William. *Language in the Inner City.* Philadelphia: Univ. of Pennsylvania Press, 1972.

Labov, William, and Joshua Waletzky. "Narrative Analysis: Oral Versions of Personal Experience." In *Essays on the Verbal and Visual Arts, Proceedings of the 1966 Annual Spring Meeting of the American Ethnological Society*, edited by June Helm, 12–44. Seattle: Univ. of Washington Press, 1967.

Larivaille, Paul. "L'analyse (morpho)logique du récit." *Poétique* 5 (1974): 368–88.

Nünning, Ansgar, and Vera Nünning. "Von der strukturalischen Narratologie zur 'postklassischen' Erzähltheorie: Ein Überblick über Ansätze und Entwicklungstendenzen." In *Neue Ansätze in der Erzähltheorie*, edited by Ansgar Nünning and Vera Nünning, 1–33. Trier: Wissenschaftlicher Verlag Trier, 2002.

Phelan, James. *Living to Tell about It: A Rhetoric and Ethics of Character Narration*. Ithaca, NY: Cornell Univ. Press, 2005.

Prince, Gerald. "Classical and/or Postclassical Narratology." *L'esprit créateur* 48 (2008): 115–23.

———. *A Grammar of Stories: An Introduction*. The Hague: Mouton, 1973.

———. *Narratology: The Form and Functioning of Narrative*. Berlin: Mouton, 1982.

Propp, Vladimir. *Morphology of the Folktale*. Translated by Laurence Scott. Austin: Texas Univ. Press, 1968 (1928).

Revaz, Françoise. *Les textes d'action*. Metz: Univ. de Metz, 1997.

Richardson, Brian. *Unlikely Stories: Causality and the Nature of Modern Narrative*. Newark: Univ. of Delaware Press, 1997.

Ryan, Marie-Laure. *Possible Worlds, Artificial Intelligence and Narrative Theory* Bloomington: Indiana Univ. Press, 1991.

Sperber, Dan, and Deirdre Wilson. *Relevance: Communication and Cognition*. Oxford: Blackwell, 1986.

Sternberg, Meir. "How Narrativity Makes a Difference." *Narrative* 9 (2001): 115–22.

Todorov, Tzvetan. *Introduction to Poetics*. Translated by Richard Howard. Minneapolis: Univ. of Minnesota Press, 1981.

CHAPTER 2

The Configuration of Narrative Sequences

JOHN PIER

A CONCEPT FORMULATED by the Russian formalists, although with precedents reaching back to Aristotle, *sequence* has played a crucial yet evasive role in the development of modern narrative theory. Numerous researchers have regarded sequence as the *sine qua non* of narrative, constituting its chronological-causal substratum, while others, focusing more on the discoursive qualities of narrative, have devoted less attention to the question. Those concerned with the "content" plane have generally sought to develop some form of model or formalization of sequence in contrast to those whose interest lies in the "expression" plane, where the tendency is to look more closely at questions bearing on narrative communication. More than thirty years ago, Gérard Genette described this situation as the division between two narratologies: a "thematic" narratology devoted to "analysis of the story or the narrative content" and a "modal" narratology devoted to the "analysis of narrative as a mode of 'representation' of stories" (*Narrative Discourse Revisited* 16). Even though the narratological landscape has evolved immensely in the intervening years, and even though the terms of the equation are no longer the same, as Gerald Prince's survey of the various conceptions of sequence attest, exploration of the interface between the two facets of narrative continues to be an important desideratum of research.

In this essay, I will be taking up the question of narrative sequence from a semiotic perspective. Contrary to much reasoning about this narrative category, which tends to frame sequence either as a preexistent or as an immanent structure, the present approach characterizes sequence as *prototypical,* on the one hand, and as *intersequential,* on the other. This means, among other things, that sequences are constituted in the course of narration as a communicative process: rather than a stable entity or a "deep structure" manifested on the textual surface, they play out in a "more-or-less" fashion in relation to other textual and discursive categories but also in relation to the various other instances or exemplifications of discourse. Prototypes, as Jean-Michel Adam (e.g., *Linguistique textuelle* 81–100; *Les textes* 19–59) has argued, are to be distinguished from text types or typologies of texts, for "texts" are too complex and heterogeneous to be adequately classified according to type. With reference, inter alia, to Mikhail Bakhtin's article "The Problem of Speech Genres," which is devoted to the "relatively stable forms" that serve as an interface between *langue* and *parole,* Adam considers that the interaction of texts or discourses with sociodiscursive formations and interactions influences all levels of textualization (compositional, pragmatic, syntactic, semantic) but that this does not yield a typology of texts.[1] He thus proposes a system of five "prototypical sequential schemas" in which a certain number of clauses are grouped together into "macropropositions" and then, through various "preformatted arrangements of propositions," enter into the composition of sequences: descriptive, narrative, argumentative, explicative, dialogal (set out in detail in Adam, *Les textes*). A form of "textual schema," the sequence is "a relational network" which can be broken down into elements constituting a whole, but it is also "a relatively autonomous entity" with an internal organization of dependence and independence in relation to the larger unit of which it forms a part, that is, the text (44; see Adam, *La linguistique textuelle* 161–202). As discourse, however, texts are not the sum total of a certain number of sequences, since in all but the simplest of cases (such as in the so-called minimal narrative) discourses are marked by the presence of various types of sequence. Compositionally speaking, prototypical sequences of different kinds tend to combine in varying distributions and dosages through succession, parallel assemblage, or embedding, and any one of them can serve as the "dominant" of a given discourse, leaving ample space, however, for hybrids and indeterminate cases.[2]

---

1. See figure 1 in Adam, *Les textes* 34.
2. The five prototypical schemas in question are not only sequences, of course, but also relate to genres. The hybrid mixture of genres in discourses—above and beyond the traditional literary genres—is studied under the concept of "genericity" in Adam (*Genres de récits*)

In the following pages, I will be offering a few reflections on the idea that (narrative) sequences, because of their prototypical nature, are a form of what C. S. Peirce called "diagrammatical iconicity" or "diagrams," one of the three types of icon (together with image and metaphor) forming the second trichotomy of signs: icon, index, symbol. Like a grid upon which the days of any month can be indicated or the diagram of an electrical circuit, both of which exist by virtue of an analogy of relations but are restricted to representing no particular month and no specific electrical circuit (cf. the type-token relationship), the prototypical conception of narrative sequence is at the same time diagrammatic: a semiotic postulate, the narrative sequence serves to highlight the patterning of chronological-causal relations of transformation from an initial state to a final state, subsequently configured, in one way or another, to one degree or another, in any given narrative.

Narrative sequence in the sense set out above—prototypical and thus diagrammatic—bears on the textual organization of the events and actions portrayed. This being the case, however, what is the role of reading (or hearing/viewing) in the unfolding of stories, which also takes place sequentially? This is a question of considerable import, for as Meir Sternberg reminds us, narrative is generated out of the "gaps" encountered between two sequentialities: that of "the absolute dynamics of the causally propelled action" (*fabula*, rather than story) and that of "the variable dynamics of the reading-process" (governed by the *sjuzhet*, rather than by plot) (*Expositional Modes* 13). On this basis, sequence in narrative must be regarded through the lens of "intersequential relations, or dynamics, whereby gaps open between the order of the telling/reading ('discourse') and the told ('action')" (Sternberg, "Universals of Narrative" 612). Out of these intersequential relations between "actional and communicative, told and telling/reading sequence," there develops an "interplay between temporalities [which] generates the three universal effects/interests/dynamics of prospection, retrospection, and recognition—suspense, curiosity, and surprise, for short" (Sternberg, "How Narrativity" 117).[3] Triggered by suspense, curiosity, and surprise, the operations of prospection, retrospection, and recognition become so many "strategies" that serve as "basic

---

with regard to narrativity. For a case study, see his chapter 5: "Raconter en co(n)texte dialogal: le monologue narratif au théâtre." A commentary on Adam's discourse analysis can be found in Pier, "Is there a French Postclassical Narratology?" 351–56.

3. In his contribution to this volume, James Phelan maintains that *fabula* is concerned with the chronological sequence of events and *sjuzhet* with sequence in the narrative text; the relation between the two sequences yields "narrative progression." For Raphaël Baroni (also in this volume), referring to Sternberg and Phelan, sequence is related to plot and, like progression, generates "narrative tension."

sense-making operations [for] the construction of rival hypotheses with which to fill in the gaps opened up by the sequence about the world's affairs and whatever attaches to them by nature or art, which in narrative means everything" (Sternberg, "Telling in Time [II]" 531–32). The importance of these operations, which function through inferential reasoning on the part of the reader in response to intersequential relations (assumptions and conjectures about what will happen next, conclusions drawn as to why such-and-such has occurred, a configurational "seeing-things-together," etc.[4]), is such that, for Sternberg, working from a functionalist rather than from an objectivist perspective (most notably that of structuralism), it is these operations that are the defining features of narrative and not (as I would put it, in a synthetic generalization of Sternberg's argument) "the representation of events" or "the recounting of an event or a chain of events by an addresser to an addressee."[5] In this approach, narrative can be defined only in conjunction with narrativity:

> I define *narrativity* as the play of suspense/curiosity/surprise between represented and communicative time (in whatever combination, whatever medium, whatever manifest or latent form). Along the same functional lines, I define *narrative* as a discourse where such a play dominates: narrativity then ascends from a possibly marginal or secondary role ... to the status of regulating principle, first among the priorities of telling/reading. (529)[6]

The crucial and pervasive role attributed to narrativity is reaffirmed in a recent critical overview of research on the topic: "'Narrative' hasn't yet gained a universal *sense* (distinctive features) and *reference* (class membership), which a well-defined concept of narrativity can alone provide" (Sternberg, "Narrativity" 508). In large part, the issue of narrativity flows from the refusal either to predicate it on event sequence or to regard it as a set of "optional features" to be appended to the "essential attributes" of narrative (the objectivist view); the emphasis, rather, is on the need to "conceptualize within narrativity itself the dynamic *intersequence relation* unique to the narrative genre" (634, cf. 507–8). On this view, then, sequence is assimilated into the broader question of intersequentiality and the dynamic relations occurring between the telling/reading and the told.

---

4. Cf. Pier, "After This", esp. 127–31.
5. The numerous variants of the objectivist focus on "the narrated sequence (eventhood, enchainment, experientiality) of the world-in-action" are examined in Sternberg, "Narrativity" 601 passim.
6. Also quoted in Sternberg, "Narrativity" 642.

The systems of sequentiality set out by the two theoreticians diverge in a number of ways but in ways that, I hope to show, throw further light on this pervasive aspect of narrative. Adam's approach to narrative sequence adopts criteria, a number of which have been called into question by Sternberg in his in-depth critique of objectivist accounts of narrative and narrativity, heavily invested in theorizing the content or "what" of narrative. Placing prime importance on intersequential relations, Sternberg, unlike Adam, subscribes to no particular theory or model of the narrative sequence, finding little need to specify the constituents of represented actions and their linkages independently from the discourses in which actions occur. This is because, functionally speaking, "the effect somehow finds or shapes or invents the cause" ("Telling in Time [II]" 529): within the teleological framework in which ends determine or explain means, suspense excites conjecture about "what still lies ahead"; curiosity triggers inferences about "gapped antecedents" in an attempt to "bridge" or "compose" them "in retrospect"; surprise "enforces a corrective reading in late re-cognition" ("How Narrativity" 117). Nevertheless, it is the case that out of the functionalist critique of narrative sequence there emerges a pattern of linkages that serves as an interface between the actional and the communicative. Although this pattern does not coincide with the relations identified by Adam for the narrative sequence, the two perspectives do share some common qualities in terms of their prototypicality.

Among the various intersecting and overlapping angles from which Sternberg examines objectivist positions on the modeling of actional structures, one in particular is of considerable interest in the present context: "*events linked into a causal chain*" ("Narrativity" 546–73; emphasis in original). This mimetic, actional norm dates back to Aristotle's holistic conception of stories as bounded by a "beginning → middle → end":

> A whole is that which has a beginning, a middle, and an end. A beginning is that which does not itself follow anything by causal necessity, but after which something naturally is or comes to be. An end, on the contrary, is that which itself naturally follows some other thing, either by necessity, or as a rule, but has nothing following it. A middle is that which follows something as some other thing follows it. A well-constructed plot, therefore, must neither begin nor end at haphazard, but conform to these principles. (*Peri Poetikés / Poetics* 1450b)

With reference to a "rudimentary generic nucleus" representative of numerous definitions of narrative—"somebody did (and/or underwent) something, with reversal of fortune"—Sternberg identifies "five distinct event-organizing parameters" or "wholeness coordinates" that have developed around Aristotle's holism:

> (vi₁) *Quasi-logical, action-logical (in effect, chrono-logical, because causal) enchainment throughout,* as superior to the looser, additive, "episodic" (in effect, chronological) "A, then B" deployment; or event sequentiality tightened in consequentiality.
>
> . . .
>
> (vi₂) *A minimum of three actional links,* "beginning → middle → end," unlike (say) Forster's two-link minimum plot, "The king died and then the queen died of grief." . . . The "whole," though corresponding to the modern *fabula*, extendible to any length, can also double as an abstract well-formed mini-sequence underlying all (poetic) *fabulas,* and so as the objective condition of narrativity.
>
> . . .
>
> (vi₃) *All three minimum actional links are dynamic,* in that they initiate or sustain or arrest change, exclusive of static (descriptive, "expositional") premises (traits, setups, laws of nature, culture, existence, reality models, in brief). Cause and/or effect, each of those links forwards the action, makes an intelligible difference to the world.
>
> . . .
>
> (vi₄) *A stable endpoint:* the two cutoff points mark a former (un)happy stability undisturbed, to begin with, and established anew at the finish, in antipolar shape [cf. *Peri Poetikés / Poetics* 1450b above].
>
> . . .
>
> (vi₅) *Strongest concatenation.* Throughout, the enchainment unrolls "by necessary or probable sequence": the highest standard of mimetic likelihood, followability, and integrity at once [as in syllogistic logic]. (Sternberg, "Narrativity" 547–51; emphasis in original)

The most frequent of these defining postulates for narrative, from Propp to present and spanning a wide range of theoretical persuasions, has been (vi₅) logical concatenation. Curiously, one of the most radical adherents of this position is Roland Barthes ("Introduction" 10), who, in describing the *post hoc, ergo propter hoc* fallacy as "le ressort de l'activité narrative" [the mainspring of narrative activity], effectively claims that narrative is founded on a "logical error" and that the aim of narrative analysis is to "dechronologize" and "relogify" narrative (a position later abandoned in *S/Z* with the adoption of the "proairetic" and the "hermeneutic" codes). Barthes thus identifies a rich source of reflection on the topic of narrativity but, constrained by the criteria of traditional formal logic, fails to appreciate its implications for the chronological movement peculiar to narrative—a situation I have sought to rectify (Pier, "After This" esp. 109, 114–15).

Where Sternberg finds a potential for resolving some of the issues of the objectivist approach is in (vi$_2$) *a minimum of three actional links*, with its possible extensions to (vi$_1$) *quasi-logical, action-logical enchainment* and/or (vi$_3$) *all three minimum actional links are dynamic*. Revealing difficulties arise with the nature of the links and, more precisely, with what it is that is linked together. According to Gerald Prince:

> A minimal story consists of three conjoined events [e.g., "He was unhappy, then he met a woman, then, as a result, he was happy"]. The first and third events are stative, the second is active. Furthermore, the third event is the inverse of the first. Finally, the three events are conjoined by the three conjunctive features in such a way that (a) the first event precedes the second in time and the second precedes the third, and (b) the second event causes the third. (Prince, *A Grammar* 31; quoted in Sternberg, "Narrativity" 557)

For Aristotle (as Sternberg points out in "Narrativity" 558), the beginning of a story cannot be equated with a self-generated event, much less a "stative" event, but is, more fluidly, "that which does not itself follow anything by causal necessity, but after which something naturally is or comes to be" (*Peri Poetikés / Poetics* 1450b); much the same obtains for the end (once married, the prince and the princess might not of necessity live in a state of happiness ever after). The minimal story thus turns out to be one event poised between two (inverted) states—as subsequently acknowledged by Prince himself in redefining the concept as

> a narrative recounting only two states and one event such that (1) one state precedes the event in time and the event precedes the other state in time (and causes it); (2) the second state constitutes the inverse (or the modification, including the "zero" modification) of the first. (*Dictionary* [revised ed.] 53)[7]

---

7. This definition partially coincides with Genette's definition of the minimal narrative: "For me, as soon as there is an action or an event, even a single one, there is a story because there is a transformation, a transition from an earlier state to a later and resultant state" (*Narrative Discourse Revisited* 19; cf. *Narrative Discourse* 30). Both definitions conflate Aristotle's beginning/end with "states," while Genette adds "action," but without distinguishing it from "event"; moreover, no reference is made here to "recounting" (or "narrating"), thus revealing a gulf in Genette's modal narratology between action/event and narrating and, as a result, leaving unaddressed the question of intersequential relations.

More amenable to narrative logic than *state* or *stative event* are the terms *equilibrium* and *disequilibrium*. Disequilibrium implies (but need not specify) an antecedent (state of) equilibrium and is thus brought about by an intervening, but not necessary, causal intervention; moreover, disequilibrium may be succeeded by a new (state of) equilibrium, but it does not, in itself, cause or logically entail such an equilibrium (an equilibrium which, in any case, remains contingent). Neither equilibrium nor disequilibrium constitutes an event, and consequently the succession equilibrium-disequilibrium-equilibrium proceeds additively, not causally: A, then B, then C. "All three of them," points out Sternberg,

> can be states that differ from one another, but they do not in themselves provide any of the intermediate events necessary for the change of state (A → B) and its changeful arrest (B → C), unless reinforced with these necessities by further stipulations (or in the finished story). ("Narrativity" 560)

Or to put it another way, an equilibrium may be "disturbed" by an external "force," as explained by Tzvetan Todorov (82; also quoted in Sternberg, "Narrativity" 560):

> An ideal narrative begins with a stable situation which is disturbed by some force. From this there results a state of disequilibrium: by a force directed in the opposite direction, equilibrium is re-established.[8]

This definition (which also applies to sequence) confirms the idea that the causative force of change remains distinct from the stable (though potentially unstable or destabilizing) situation, that change is initiated from without. Thus in Shakespeare's *Romeo and Juliet*, for example, the stable situation (the feud between the Capulets and the Montagues) is disturbed by the fortuitous meeting of Romeo and Juliet, producing a disequilibrium (a love affair which is totally taboo between members of the feuding families); a new equilibrium is established (a decision by the families to put an end the feud) as a result of the lovers' tragic death. Seen in this way—and in contradistinction with much theorizing on the topic—the Aristotelian trio is (re)defined not with the inclusion of causes (a causal link binding together beginning, middle, and end) but, dispensing with causal enchainment (ending the feud is neither the necessary nor the probable

---

8. Todorov's definition continues, "The second equilibrium is quite similar to the first, but the two are never identical." Similarity is a relative notion, however, and it can be objected that in many narratives the second equilibrium might be quite dissimilar from the first.

outcome of the lovers' death), constitutes a "three-implying-five" minimum: a sequence in five parts inferable from the actualized text and that applies, to variable degrees, to stretches of discourse varying in length. The imbrication of (states of) equilibrium/disequilibrium and external forces joins up with suspense, curiosity, and surprise, thus with the effects generated between the telling/reading and the told that incite readers to engage in inferencing forward (having fallen in love, what will Romeo and Juliet do next?) and backward (had Friar Lawrence not committed certain blunders, the lovers' death would have been avoided), but also to re-cognize and configure (the realization that the lovers' destiny and reconciliation between the families are inextricable).[9]

The approach to sequentiality adopted by Adam is focused more on the constitution of the sequence itself—a "textual schema"—one variety of which is the narrative sequence. Working within a text linguistic and discourse analytical framework, Adam also draws on Aristotle's beginning, middle, and end, emphasizing, as already mentioned, the prototypical nature of the sequence. Key to his conception of the narrative sequence is Paul Larivaille's quinary model of the narrative sequence, born out of a "double ternary structure" organized into five "functions" combining before, during, and after with the three phases of a transformative process:

> [I.1] *Before* the process [equilibrium], [II.3] the *Process* itself, [III.5] *After* the process [equilibrium], on the one hand, and, on the other, the breakdown of the actual *process:* [2] *Beginning* (also called the "beginning" in Aristotle), [3] *Unfolding* (Aristotle's "middle"), and [4] *End* (also the "end" in Aristotle). (Adam, "Narrative Sequence")

Adam amends this model firstly by reformulating its five "moments" (or "time images") as psycholinguistic text units called "narrative macropropositions" (Np). The second and fourth Nps are renamed, respectively, "complication" and "denouement" (the traditional terms rather than Larivaille's "exciting force" and "sanction"). The middle term, "process/action," is replaced by "(re)action" and "evaluation" (the latter corresponding roughly to the character's mental action).[10] Finally, "state" becomes "situation": initial (orientation or exposition, which can be delayed) and final (the "consequence" of the denouement-Np4).

---

9. Note here that linkages are *inferable,* meaning that while sequences are not constructed as causal necessities or through entailment, nor are they devoid of nontemporal connectedness, as Prince would have it: "Narrative is the representation of *at least two* real or fictive events or situations in a time sequence, neither of which presupposes or entails the other" (*A Grammar* 4; emphasis in original). Prince ("Narrativehood" 19) gives "implies" rather than "entails."

10. Complication-Np2 and denouement-Np4 are associated, respectively, with Tomashevsky's ("Thematics" 72) "exciting force" and "climax," and (re)action/evaluation-Np3 with

It is noteworthy that these three perspectives on sequence are comparable, and in some regards complementary, but that they are not assimilable. Concerned with the textual composition of sequence, Adam distributes the five Nps—each comprising several clauses or, for longer stretches of discourse, representing a hierarchy of propositions—along a single plane. In part, this reflects the historical precedent of sequence in the triad of classical dramaturgy: beginning/exposition → complication/development → conclusion/denouement (cf. Adam, *Genres de récit* 74). The quinary model, by "staggering" the sequence into temporal progression (before, during, after) and the phases of process (initiating, action, closing), opens up a space of negotiation between the temporal and the processual in the unfolding of the actional dimension. Sternberg's "three-implying-five" series is distinguished from the other two schemes in that it is organized around an equilibrium → disequilibrium → equilibrium, closely allied with actional dynamics, in its intersequential relations with the communicative dynamics engaged in the reading process.[11]

Now, it is not insignificant to note that Adam's model of the narrative sequence is, in fact, developed within the scope of two somewhat disparate frameworks: prototypicality and narrativity.[12] A five-part structure in both cases, the prototypical version specifies five criteria for a definition of narrative, followed by the pragmatic features of narrative.[13] Adopted mainly from Bremond, with reference to the relevant passages from Aristotle's *Peri Poetikés / Poetics,* these criteria also correspond to those of the "basic narrative sequence": (1) succession of events, (2) thematic unity (at least one actor-subject [S]), (3) transformed predicates, (4) process (integration of a single action into a whole with a beginning, middle, and end), and (5) causation. To this is added a sixth criterion: final evaluation (explicit or implicit),

---

"peripety"; this trio thus provides the basis for *mise en intrigue* [emplotment] (Adam, *Les textes* 107; *Genres de récit* 75).

11. Raphaël Baroni provides a detailed critique of the quinary model of sequence which he reproaches with being rooted in an actional logic that ignores the relations between the told and the telling and thus the forces of narrative tension experienced in the reading process. Ontologically, the quinary model is trapped in a tautology: "The story structures the narrative which structures the story" (197). To this model he opposes the "récit intrigant" [intriguing narrative] (note that French "intrigue" is "plot" in English). The present essay, by contrast, formulates sequence in terms of prototypicality (diagrammatic iconicity) and intersequentiality between the told and the telling.

12. The first was originally formulated in *Les textes: Types et prototypes* in 1992 and revised in 1997; the revised and augmented edition was published in 2011 (esp. 101–27). The other version of the narrative sequence is presented in *Genres de récits: Narrativité et généricité des textes,* published in 2011 (esp. 66–90). Cf. Adam, *Le texte narratif* 32–33.

13. Adam derives the pragmatics of narrative from Bakhtinian dialogism, Labov and Waletzky's sociolinguistics, conversational analysis, and Umberto Eco's textual pragmatics.

or "evaluative macroproposition" (NpΩ). Not forming part of the sequence as such, the latter criterion nevertheless provides the sequence with a "configuration"—"probably one of the keys to the specificity of narrative" (Adam, *Les textes* 112).

When approaching narrative sequence from the perspective of narrativity, Adam redistributes these criteria, firstly, into the "semantic and compositional bases of narrativity," broken down as follows:[14]

(1) "representation of the becoming [*devenir*] in time of an anthropomorphic actor": this includes the involvement of human interest, the presence of at least one actor, unity of action, change of fortune, and linking together of events according to verisimilitude or necessity (Aristotle's "basis of narrativity");

(2) "a temporal, causal and intentional succession of actions and events": with reference to the temporal nature of human experience (Ricœur) and to the teleology of human action, the idea that temporality (chronology) masks the "retrograde logic" of narrative (cf. *post hoc, ergo propter hoc*); the causal nature of events as opposed to the intentional nature of action;

(3) "the structuring core of the plot: from 'single action' to narrative sequence": this consists of the narrative sequence proper in the form of five narrative macropropositions, distinguished from chronological succession through the structuring force of *mise en intrigue* [emplotment].

Now, between these two conceptions of sequence, it appears to me that the prototypical version is preferable. There are various reasons for this, only a few of which can be singled out here—my point being that there is another way to explore the relevance of sequence as a prototypical concept for narrativity. To the extent that prototypical sequences are "schemas" composed of propositions that are "preformatted" according to various arrangements, there is no question of the narrativity of a narrative sequence, and Adam accordingly makes no mention of narrativity when speaking of sequence in this context; conversely, the second version of narrative sequence associates the concept with narrativity, and the term *prototypical* disappears. In the first case, a prominent role is played by configuration, a notion adopted by Adam

---

14. Not forming part of the narrative sequence, properly speaking, are the "pragmatic components of narrativity," which act as an interface between narrative and sociodiscursive formations and interactions.

from two sources: (1) Louis O. Mink, for whom configuration is the mode of comprehension peculiar to narrative, whereby a series of elements is "seen together" in an act of judgment as a "single and concrete complex of relationships"; and (2) Paul Ricœur (*Time and Narrative* vol. 1, chap. 3; vol. 2, chap. 2), where configuration, inspired partly from Mink, is the second of three forms of mimesis, the locus of textual composition but also of emplotment: a succession of actions is organized into a whole with a beginning and end (cf. Adam, *Les textes* 118).[15] In the version geared to narrativity, sequence is defined as "a transformation of a number of actions into an inclusive [*englobant*] unit, conferring on them, semantically speaking, a relational value of moments m_1, m_2, m_3, m_4 or m_5" (74). Here, however, the principle of configuration does not appear but rather that of emplotment, resulting from the combination of sequences through succession, parallel assemblage, or embedding. Although space does not allow me to develop the question in detail, I contend that while sequence—a sort of "grid" through which a series of utterances is patterned as a narrative, an argument, an explanation, and so on—is pertinent in the sense of textual composition, it is not the locus of configuration as a mode of comprehension such as Mink had in mind.

As suggested earlier in this essay, narrative sequence as prototype can be considered what Peirce called a *diagram*, one of the three types of iconic sign (a sign which "represent[s] its object mainly by its similarity, no matter what its mode of being"; *Collected Papers* 2.276) alongside image and metaphor. The diagram is defined as a form of icon "which represent[s] this relation, mainly dyadic, or so regarded, of the parts of one thing by analogous relations in their own parts" (*Collected Papers* 2.277). I have argued elsewhere ("Versions of the Iconic") that narrative categories in general operate as diagrams, but I would now add that this is the case particularly of sequence. Some of the features specific to the interest of diagrams in this connection that are worthy of further investigation in narrative research are that diagrams are relatively independent in relation to their objects; they are abstractions established according to criteria of relevance; they offer the possibility of generalization; they are conventional; they possess creative potential; they are indispensable in formal reasoning (cf. Johansen 31–33 passim).

Central to the question of sequence is the problem of linkages. Do the five stages of sequence proceed by logical necessity, by cause and effect, randomly, or in some combination thereof? These problems are complex, and the plethora of positions adopted with regard to narrative linkages, ranging from the

---

15. For a brief commentary on configuration in Mink and in Ricœur, see Pier, "Narrative Configurations" 241–42.

formal and syllogistic to the fully deconstructed, have rarely been framed or formulated with an informed view of the underlying logical issues (cf. Sternberg, "Narrativity" 565–73). In one way or another, of course, all of this goes back to Aristotle's dictum that the end must follow "some other thing, either by necessity, or as a rule" (*Peri Poetikés / Poetics* 1450b), subsequently specified when it is stated that "the proper magnitude is comprised within such limits, that the sequence of events, according to the law of probability or necessity, will admit of a change from bad fortune to good, or from good fortune to bad" (1451a).[16] The issues are blurred, however, by the observation that "it is probable . . . that many things should happen contrary to probability" (1456a).[17] This hesitation between the probable (*epi to polu*) as a statistical concept and the verisimilar (*eikos*) resulted, starting in Renaissance and neoclassical poetics, in a certain assimilation of the probable into the verisimilar, with long-lasting effects in the history of literacy theory.[18]

One possible resolution to the difficulties produced by this mixed heritage lies in renouncing the application of the criteria of formal logic to the workings of narrative and to discourse generally as well as in taking account of the inferential nature of the sign and semiosis as developed in Peircean semiotics. Based partly on Eco's adoption of the fact that, for Peirce, the necessary and sufficient elements of the sign—deduction, abduction (hypothesis), inference—form the basis of the abductive reasoning at work in textual communication, I have attempted to show how this system of reasoning constitutes a fundamental departure from a number of the tenets of structuralist narratology ("On the Semiotic Parameters"). In place of the much decried "binarisms" of structuralism, this form of reasoning operates through a variety of intertwining *abductions*: *overcoded abductions* (more or less automatic quasideductive inferences—as when on reading the incipit "Once upon a time . . ." it is assumed that the ensuing story will be a fairytale); *undercoded abductions* (an inferential walk outside the immediately available possibilities in quest of a plausible alternative: "Is *Oedipus Rex* a story of detection, incest, or parricide?"; Eco 28); *creative abductions* (a formulation of new hypotheses to account for the heretofore unexplained); and *meta-abductions* (empirical "testing" of a new hypothesis in light of what is known). I have further argued ("Narrative Configurations") that such abductive reasoning forms a textual basis for what Mink described as the "configurational mode of comprehension" peculiar to

---

16. The Bywater translation proposes "probable or necessary sequence of events."

17. See the French translation of 1451a: "une série d'événements enchaînés selon le vraisemblable ou le nécessaire"; and of 1456a: "il est vraisemblable que beaucoup de choses se produisent aussi contre le vraisemblable."

18. Cf. Dupont-Roc and Lallot 211–12.

stories, whereby the contingencies of forward references are cancelled out by the necessities of backward references: "To comprehend temporal succession means to think of it in both directions at once" ("History and Fiction" 553). These nondeductive, trial-and-error forms of reasoning, in which inferences may be valid with a greater or lesser degree of probability and are thus perfectly conducive to the logic peculiar to narrative, also underlie the process of prospective or "heuristic" reading and retrospective or "semiotic" reading (Pier, "Narrative Configurations" esp. 249–51; "After This" 124–30).

The interest of abductive reasoning for the problems of sequence appears to be at least twofold. First, there is a correlation between the more-or-less quality of sequence in any given text and the various degrees of inferential effort engaged in the four types of abduction outlined above. The more prototypical a sequence is, the less effort it will require to establish linkages so that the sequence will be processed with the use of lower-order (i.e., overcoded or undercoded) abductions; conversely, the less prototypical a sequence is and the less reliable lower-order abductions become, the more higher-order abductions must be entertained (i.e., creative and meta-abductions). The second point of interest of abductive reasoning with regard to the prototypical conception of sequence is that, in line with the principles of Bakhtinian dialogism, it is highly compatible with the processing of various types of sequence that occur heterogeneously in actual texts. Thus, on reading Plato's dialogues, we encounter prototypically dialogal sequences but also argumentative sequences; through the processes of overcoded and undercoded abductions, it will be determined that these dialogues are predominantly arguments and that, functionally speaking, dialogue remains subordinate. The case of conversational storytelling appears to be more ambiguous. Here, the prototypical features of narrative sequence are present, but given the conversational context, so are those of the dialogal sequence, as well as, possibly, those of the argumentative sequence, thus making it necessary to judge abductively, on a case-by-case basis, which sequence represents the dominant.

Now, to return to the question of probability, it will be noted that a special case is to be found in the *post hoc, ergo propter hoc* phenomenon, which is a fallacy in formal logic but which does not mark a fallacy in all cases. In narratives, coincidence between chronology and causality is assumed, if not as a matter of course, as theoretically the most "natural" account of events occurring in time. But once there is reason to think otherwise—as an effect of suspense or surprise, for instance—more intense inferencing and higher orders of abduction come into play with the aim of somehow reconciling the discordances between "forward" references and "backward" references and of configuring the narrative into a complex of relationships. It is this movement that initiates the driving force of narrative—its narrativity: that B comes after A but might not be caused by A or that A is a noncause postulated as a cause does violence to the principle of narrative sequence, particularly when understood in the sense, mentioned above, of the succession of events, thematic unity, transformation of predicates, process, and causation.

The various arguments put forth in this essay are predicated on the idea that sequence is not a "given" of discourse but that, in the case of narrative sequence, at least, it exists by virtue of intersequence—that it is generated in the spaces or gaps opened up between the actional and the communicative. Such a conception differs substantially from the idea that sequences are built up from the smallest units (motifs, functions) that are integrated into successively higher-order structures, subsequently represented at the level of surface manifestation—a key principle and analytical procedure of structuralist narratology. Sequence as prototypical, serving as a diagram in the semiotic sense of an implicit regulating principle rather than as an immanent structure, is bidirectional in two regards, to the extent that, (1) triggered by suspense-driven prospection and curiosity-driven retrospection, (2) it is played out both top-down and bottom-up in the interaction between the actional and the communicative. This dynamic is captured quite neatly by the "three-implying-five" imbrication of states and disturbing external forces. Both prototypical and intersequential, sequence is apprehended through the operations of abductive reasoning with which it correlates, according to degree of prototypicality and intensity of inferencing, while at the same time this form of reasoning also underlies judgments as to the relative weight of various types of sequence in any given text.

WORKS CITED

Adam, Jean-Michel. *Genres de récits: Narrativité et généricité des textes*. Louvain-la-Neuve: Academia Bruylant, 2011.

———. *Linguistique textuelle: Des genres de discours aux textes*. Paris: Armand Colin, 2011 (1999).

———. *La linguistique textuelle: Introduction à l'analyse textuelle des discours*. Paris: Armand Colin, 2011 (2005).

———. "The Narrative Sequence: History of a Concept and a Research Area." Unpublished manuscript.

———. *Le texte narratif: Précis d'analyse textuelle*. New rev. ed. Paris: Nathan, 1994 (1985).

———. *Les textes: Types et prototypes*. Paris: Armand Colin, 2011 (1992).

Aristotle. *On the Art of Poetry: A Revised Text with Critical Introduction*. Translated with a commentary by Ingram Bywater. Oxford: Clarendon Press, 1909.

———. *Peri Poetikés / Poetics*. In *Aristotle's Theory of Poetry and Fine Art*, edited and translated by Samuel H. Butcher, 1–111. New York: Dover Publications, 1951 (1895).

Bakhtin, Mikhail. "The Problem of Speech Genres" (1952–53). In *Speech Genres and Other Late Essays*, edited by Caryl Emerson and Michael Holquist, translated by Vern W. McGee, 60–102. Austin: Univ. of Austin Press, 1986.

Baroni, Raphaël. "Juste une question de *timing*. Du schéma quinaire à la conception post-classique de l'intrigue." In *Théorie, analyse, interprétation des récits / Theory, analysis, interpretation of narratives*, edited by Sylvie Patron, 185–209. Bern: Peter Lang, 2011.

Barthes, Roland. "Introduction à l'analyse structurale du récit." *Communications* 8 (1966): 1–27.

Bremond, Claude. *Logique du récit*. Paris: Seuil, 1973.

Dupont-Roc, Roselyne, and Jean Lallot. "Notes." In Aristote, *La Poétique*. Text, translation, and notes by Roselyne Dupont-Roc and Jean Lallot, 141–413. Paris: Seuil, 1980.

Eco, Umberto. *The Role of the Reader. Explorations in the Semiotics of Texts*. Bloomington and London: Indiana Univ. Press, 1979.

Genette, Gérard. *Narrative Discourse*. Translated by Jane E. Lewin. Ithaca, NY: Cornell Univ. Press, 1980.

———. *Narrative Discourse Revisited*. Translated by Jane E. Lewin. Ithaca, NY: Cornell Univ. Press, 1988.

Johansen, Jorgen Dines. *Literary Discourse: A Semiotic-Pragmatic Approach to Literature*. Toronto: Univ. of Toronto Press, 2002.

Labov, William, and Joshua Waletzky. "Narrative Analysis: Oral Versions of Personal Experience." In *Essays on the Verbal and Visual Arts, Proceedings of the 1966 Annual Spring Meeting of the American Ethnological Society*, edited by June Helm, 12–44. Seattle: Univ. of Washington Press, 1967.

Larivaille, Paul. "L'analyse (morpho)logique du récit." *Poétique* 5 (1974): 368–88.

Mink, Louis O. "History and Fiction as Modes of Comprehension." *New Literary History* 3 (1970): 541–58.

Peirce, Charles Sanders. *Collected Papers*. Edited by Charles Hartshorne, Paul Weiss (vols. 1–6), and Arthur W. Burks (vols. 7–8). Cambridge, MA: Harvard Univ. Press, 1931–58.

Pier, John. "After This, Therefore Because of This." In *Theorizing Narrativity*, edited by John Pier and José Ángel García Landa, 109–40. Berlin and New York: Walter de Gruyter, 2008.

———. "Is There a French Postclassical Narratology?" In *Current Trends in Narratology*, edited by Greta Olson, 336–67. Berlin and New York: De Gruyter, 2011.

———. "Narrative Configurations." In *The Dynamics of Narrative Form: Studies in Anglo-American Narratology*, edited by John Pier, 239–68. Berlin and New York: Walter de Gruyter, 2004.

———. "On the Semiotic Parameters of Narrative: A Critique of Story and Discourse." In *What is Narratology? Questions and Answers Concerning a Discipline*, edited by Tom Kindt and Hans-Harald Müller, 73–97. Berlin: Walter de Gruyter, 2003.

———. "Versions of the Iconic." In *Ré-inventer le réel. Actes du colloque GRAAT-CERCA, septembre 1997—Université de Tours*, edited by Thomas Dutoit and Trevor Harris. *GRAAT* 20 (1999): 209–19.

Prince, Gerald. *A Dictionary of Narratology*. Rev. ed. Lincoln and London: Univ. of Nebraska Press, 2003.

———. *A Grammar of Stories: An Introduction*. The Hague: Mouton, 1973.

———. "Narrativehood, Narrativeness, Narrativity, Narratibility." In *Theorizing Narrativity*, edited by John Pier and José Ángel García Landa, 19–27. Berlin and New York: Walter de Gruyter, 2008.

Ricœur, Paul. *Time and Narrative*. Vols. 1 and 2. Translated by Kathleen Blamey and David Pellauer. Chicago and London: Univ. of Chicago Press, 1984 (1983), 1985 (1984).

Sternberg, Meir. *Expositional Modes and Temporal Ordering in Fiction*. Bloomington and Indianapolis: Indiana Univ. Press, 1978.

———. "How Narrativity Makes a Difference." *Narrative* 9 (2001): 115–22.

———. "Narrativity: From Objectivist to Functional Paradigm." *Poetics Today* 31 (2010): 507–659.
———. "Telling in Time (II): Chronology, Teleology, Narrativity." *Poetics Today* 13 (1992): 463–541.
———. "Universals of Narrative and their Cognitive Fortunes (II)." *Poetics Today* 24 (2003): 517–638.
Todorov, Tzvetan. *Poétique*. Vol. 2 of *Qu'est-ce que le structuralisme?* Paris: Seuil, 1973.
Tomachevsky, Boris. "Thematics" (1925). In *Russian Formalist Criticism: Four Essays*, translated with an introduction by Lee T. Lemon and Marion J. Reis, 61–98. Lincoln: Univ. of Nebraska Press, 1965.

CHAPTER 3

The Eventfulness of Non-Events

PETER HÜHN

NARRATION AS A DISCOURSE TYPE is distinguished from other discourse types, such as argumentation or description, by the temporal organization of a sequence of happenings on the level of *histoire* constituted and mediated in a text—in other words, by a change of state or a succession of such changes within what is being told, in the "story." Although temporality (i.e., chronological sequentiality) is a necessary condition of narrating and an inherent feature of a narrated story, it is not sufficient. In order to be noteworthy or tellable, a proper story has to present some "point," some decisive, unexpected, and surprising turn within the sequence of elements, a significant departure from the normal or expected course. If it does not offer such a turn, it will not be considered a good story but instead elicit the disappointed reaction "so what?" from the reader. This decisive turn I will call an "event" in the emphatic sense of the term (see Hühn, "Forms and Functions").[1] Events are changes of state that fulfill the additional requirement of special significance. Eventfulness is a gradable quality, its degree depending on the extent of deviation from the expected or normal. Eventful narratives are found in a wide range of genres and media—from everyday storytelling, personal anecdotes, jokes, gossip, and

---

1. To be sure, tellability can also be created by, and consist in, other features (e.g., particular aspects of style, setting, characters), but in addition, at least one event is required.

news reports to fiction (novels, short stories, novellas), drama, and poetry, as well as film and still pictures, such as paintings and photographs.

The event as the prerequisite of a tellable story has been defined in a variety of ways. Labov (369), and similarly Pratt (46f., 63ff.), describes the "point," the *raison d'être* of a narrative, as deviation highlighted by "evaluation"; Lotman (233–39) circumscribes an event metaphorically as a transgression of a boundary within what he calls a semantic field; Bruner (11–13) speaks of "canonicity and breach"; Schmid defines an eventful change according to the five categories of relevance, unpredictability, irreversibility, effect, and noniterativity. It is more or less explicitly assumed—most clearly by Lotman in his notion of the semantic field—that the eventfulness of a change in this sense depends on the cultural and historical context: whether a change counts as eventful or not (and what degree of eventfulness is to be ascribed to it) will differ from one cultural context, and one period, to another. Two simple examples, one a novel, the other a poem are as follows: first, the marriage between a servant girl and a nobleman (Squire B.) in Samuel Richardson's *Pamela* of 1740 counts as highly eventful in the hierarchical class society of eighteenth century Britain but much less so today (if at all); second, in George Herbert's "The Collar" of 1633, the abrupt relinquishment of the speaker's desire for independence and self-realization in favor of total subordination to God's will at the end depends for its eventfulness on a Christian context and will be considered meaningless by a secular reader.

Not only does the eventfulness of a change depend on the historical and cultural context, but the very occurrence of events varies from one period or culture to another. Thus, one can observe that there are no unexpected events in traditional, premodern cultures,[2] since all or at least most changes are well regulated and foreseeable. Significant changes (like initiation, marriage, vocational career, death) occur along established scripts. The highly eventful plots of tragedies are a typical sign of the disruption of traditional social and cultural structures, as in ancient Greece, early modern England or in late-eighteenth- and early-nineteenth-century Germany. In English literary history, the early modern period (up to the eighteenth century) presents significant events in novels from Defoe's *Moll Flanders*, Fielding's *Tom Jones*, and Richardson's *Pamela* to Jane Austen's novels; but nineteenth-century fiction then features frequent examples of failing events (i.e., desired events that do not come about or are highly qualified), as in Thackeray's *Vanity Fair*, Dickens's *Hard Times*, or George Eliot's *Middlemarch*; the twentieth century exacerbates the difficulty

---

2. For example, in such small-scale, indigenous societies as described by van Gennep in *The Rites of Passage*.

of eventful changes and problematizes the very concept of eventfulness, as witnessed by the increasing number of non-events since the advent of modernism. To name a few examples: E. M. Forster's *Passage to India,* Joyce's *Portrait of the Artist as a Young Man,* Virginia Woolf's *Jacob's Room,* Malcolm Lowry's *Under the Volcano,* or D. H. Lawrence's *Women in Love.*

In the last analysis, the context-dependence of eventfulness always and unavoidably rests on the readers' knowledge and attitude, which can determine the interpretation in either of two ways. Their personal value system, meaning concepts and cultural horizon might directly, as it were, naively, be employed as the frame of reference for judging changes as eventful or not. But especially with texts from remote cultures or epochs, the appropriate values and concepts will differ considerably from what, say, present-day European or American readers spontaneously bring to their reading. In such constellations, it is necessary for the discriminating and conscientious reader to reconstruct the original context—that is, to scrutinize the text for signs indicative of the intended horizon of norms and concepts—which is a precarious and difficult process with possibly debatable results. In general, the reader possesses the power (and often also the inclination) to impose his or her own subjective notions on the text and, naively perhaps, determine what to regard as eventful, based directly on that criteria.

Two main types of event can be distinguished according to the dimension of the narrative setup in which they occur (cf. Hühn, *Eventfulness* 9–10): first, *events in the happenings* (i.e., decisive changes within the sequence of the narrated story) as in the example of Richardson's *Pamela;* second, *presentation events,* (i.e., decisive changes in the *narrator*'s position, attitude, or consciousness in the course of telling a story) as in Laurence Sterne's *Tristram Shandy,* where the narrator's opinions and his attitude to life take center stage and undergo an eventful reversal.

All the scholars mentioned above explicitly or implicitly take for granted that an event in a story is a *manifest* change of state, a decisive alteration or turn that actually takes place. Such events can be positive—that is, consist in changes desired by or advantageous to the protagonist—as in fairy tales, comedies, or in Richardson's *Pamela;* but they can also be negative, signifying failure, defeat, or disappointment, as in tragedies or in Richardson's *Clarissa.* However, although the occurrence of a decisive change of state is the normal or prototypical case of an event, there are also interesting cases where the nonoccurrence of an event—a *non-event*[3]—has to count as eventful,

---

3. A non-event can be considered a special instance of what Lotman calls "minus device" (*minus priyóm*): the meaningful absence, the nonfulfillment of what is expected, a failed action,

constituting the tellability of the story in its own right. The term non-event is meant to cover two cases: the failure of an (expected) event to occur and the non-eventfulness of a particular change.[4] Like events actually realized in the text, non-events are equally dependent on the historical, cultural, or literary context, and therefore, on readers' world knowledge, their system of norms and views, and thus on their expectations and perceptions.

I will now investigate under what circumstances and in what respects the nonoccurrence of a desired or expected change counts as significant, as eventful. Relatively simple and theoretically uncontroversial cases can be found in everyday life. If something that routinely happens or that normally takes place under specific conditions suddenly fails to occur, this nonoccurrence will be experienced as eventful—for instance, if the sun does not rise and daylight does not come in the morning, if one's child does not return from school at the usual hour, or if one's salary is not remitted at the customary date. The context in these cases is the routine of daily life, which provides the frame of reference for expectations. But events such as these can also occur in individual cases with specific expectations, as when a political candidate with top rankings in the polls does not win the election after all, when the computers do not crash on New Year's Day in 2000, or when the bride fails to turn up for the wedding ceremony.

As for literature, non-events usually refer to the sequence of happenings on the *histoire* level as represented by the text. But non-events can also occur in the mediation process of a story as negative equivalents to presentation events. If a narrator tells of horrifying deeds committed by formerly law-abiding friends without changing his or her approving attitude toward them, this would be experienced as a non-event. Other examples are nonmentioning in the narration of the outcome of a plan or course of action and the later nonreference to an important protagonist featuring in the text. The contextual frame of reference, and thus the "horizon of expectations," in literary texts is in part formed differently from comparable cases in the real-life world because of the intervening cultural and historical distance between text and reader. And eventful non-events are not just the absence of events but underlie partly

---

an omitted though expected technique as determined by social codes or literary conventions (see Lotman 51; cf. Iser).

4. Non-events must be distinguished from what Warhol calls the "unnarratable" and its four subcategories (the subnarratable, the supranarratable, the antinarratable, and the paranarratable). While the notion of the unnarratable covers cases where incidents are supposed to occur or exist in the storyworld but, for various reasons, are not or cannot be narrated and therefore cause some kind of absence in the text, the term non-event refers to the phenomenon that an incident, especially one that is expected, actually does *not* happen. Non-events are ultimately located on the *histoire* level whereas the unnarratable is a feature of discourse.

specific conditions. While manifest events may either be foreshadowed in some way or happen surprisingly and entirely outside the horizon of expectations, non-events occur only when there is a more or less clearly established expectation. And while events typically come about as abrupt changes or occur within a relatively short time span, eventful non-events are usually not located at one specific point in time but manifest themselves negatively as an absence over a longer phase of the temporal sequence of the story.

Expectation, on the part of readers, of an event may be established in three different ways. A first type consists of specific schemata, generic scripts for stories, especially within highly conventionalized genres in fiction, drama, and poetry, which genre-specifically guide readers' anticipation of what events are to come. Schemata of this type are defined, inter alia, by a particular structure of event: the elevation or transformation of the protagonist to an ideal state in fairy tales, the solution of the murder mystery in detective novels, the gratification of the lovers' longing for each other in their final union in romance stories and similarly in comedies, the hero's downfall in tragedies, and a sudden clarification and insight on the part of the speaker in the "greater romantic lyric," the ode. Examples where such events fail to occur are Anton Chekhov's tales,[5] James Joyce's short stories in *Dubliners* (e.g., "Eveline" and "Araby"), E. C. Bentley's detective novel *Trent's Last Case*, or John Keats's "Ode to a Nightingale."

A second type of expectation is based on expectations of a decisive change that a text *specifically* raises during the reading process, only to reject them in the end, as in the "jumping of the beast" in Henry James's "The Beast in the Jungle," the revelation and identification of the "figure in the carpet" in his tale of that title, the arrival of Godot in Samuel Beckett's *Waiting for Godot*, and the emergence of his poetic vocation during the speaker-poet's adolescence in Philip Larkin's poem "I Remember, I Remember."[6] What these two types have in common is that a non-event comes about when and where an event does not occur even though one is expected and where, as a consequence, the fact that something does not happen is foregrounded.

A third type of expectation includes cases where basically nothing significant happens (i.e., when a text presents a chain of episodes or incidents, none of which amounts to a significant and lasting change), as for instance in picaresque novels such as *Lazarillo de Tormes*. A specific subtype is made up of cases where an event seems to occur but is eventually revealed to have

---

5. Gerhardie specifically pinpoints this phenomenon by saying that Chekhov dispenses with the "event-plot" (83).

6. See Hühn, "Philip Larkin and Thomas Hood."

been none or is eroded subsequently, for instance Joyce's *Portrait of the Artist as a Young Man*, the first part of Charles Dickens's *Great Expectations*, or William M. Thackeray's *Vanity Fair*, but arguably also Thomas Mann's *Der Zauberberg* and Joyce's *Ulysses*, which, in the last analysis, present nothing but nonconclusive episodes and in the end just break off. That these novels ultimately do not contain events—that the changes which happen in the course of the plot only momentarily seem to be decisive but eventually turn out to lack substantial significance—is conditioned by the general expectation on the part of readers that texts should always present decisive and therefore noteworthy incidents or changes. And to name a different example in another medium, Pieter Bruegel's painting "Fall of Icarus" reduces and marginalizes the (negative) eventfulness of Icarus's crash by showing its total irrelevance (and complete nonperception) to others (ploughman, fisherman, people on the sailing boat). One has to know Ovid's narrative of Icarus's eventful accident (*Metamorphoses*, VIII, 183–235) in order to see that his fall (which actually features in the picture, seen with the legs in the water) is no event in the dominating context of the scene in the picture. In Ovid, shepherd, farmer, and fisherman see father and son flying in the sky and admire them as gods.

By way of illustration, I will now discuss two literary examples from the traditional genres of drama and fiction. Both are of the second type, which feature non-events as eventful but do so in different manners and with different functions and meanings. These narratives will also show how the eventful interpretation of non-events is guided by textual signals and implication of the appropriate context.

My first example is Samuel Beckett's *Waiting for Godot/En attendant Godot* (1953/1955), a particularly radical case of eventlessness. Although Beckett's text, a play intended for theatrical performance, presents a particular story mimetically rather than diegetically, the required features of a narrative apply here, as well—that is, spectators generally expect some decisive turn, an eventful change of attitude or recognition. In addition, irrespective of the controversial concrete meaning behind what is going on in the two acts, the characters' situation and dialogue specifically arouse and focus the readers' expectations that something decisive might and indeed should happen. The desirability of change is consistently suggested by the pervasive atmosphere of stagnation, monotony, repetitiveness, and sterility, as well as by the two protagonists' present desolate existence as characterized by vagrancy, poverty, and purposelessness. Their lack of initiative and their inability to act, marked by the assertion, "nothing to be done" (9), is subsequently repeated several times (e.g., 11, 21), and even more marked examples of blatant discrepancy between the decision to act and practical inaction can be found:

VLADIMIR: Shall we go?
ESTRAGON: Yes, let's go.
They do not move.
(54, 94; see also 12)

...

ESTRAGON: Let's go.
VLADIMIR: We can't.
ESTRAGON: Why not?
VLADIMIR: We're waiting for Godot.
(14, 48, 68, 84)

Equally frequent are expressions of suicidal despair and the inability to act on it, as when they contemplate hanging themselves on the tree only to admit its impracticality; the general atmosphere of inertia is also expressed explicitly: "Nothing happens, nobody comes, nobody goes, it's awful!" (41). This is further underscored by the protagonists' (especially Estragon's) forgetfulness and uncertainty about the correct place to meet Godot, for instance. The other two characters, Pozzo and Lucky, exemplify not only extreme human inequality and exploitation but also the sudden deterioration and decline of the powerful and wealthy when they return in the second act and Pozzo is blind and miserably helpless.

Against this pervasive background of hopeless stagnation and inaction, the behavior of Vladimir and Estragon and the happenings in the play repeatedly indicate the possibility and even the imminence of a decisive change or turn. This goes famously for the anticipated appearance of Godot: not only are the protagonists waiting for him to come, as is frequently and explicitly stressed, but he is twice announced by a boy for the following day, failing both times, however, to turn up (50, 91). Although Godot's personality, status, and intentions remain vague, his coming is obviously considered of great importance by the two characters, since it would break the monotony and stagnation of their lives and possibly introduce a fresh development. Vladimir encourages the more doubtful Estragon: "Ah Gogo, don't go on like that. Tomorrow everything will be better" (52), or expresses his hope more specifically:

VLADIMIR: We'll hang ourselves tomorrow. (*Pause.*) Unless Godot comes.
ESTRAGON: And if he comes?
VLADIMIR: We'll be saved.
(94)

And Pozzo likewise assumes that Godot "has your future in his hands ... at least your immediate future" (29).

This expectation of something new coming from the outside is intermittently corroborated, if only weakly and obliquely. This occurs with the new leaves on the tree at the beginning of the second act, Vladimir's reference to the salvation of one of the thieves crucified together with Christ, and Pozzo's blindness and need of help, which Vladimir sees as an opportunity for hope and action: "Let us not waste our time in idle discourse! . . . Let us do something, while we have the chance! It is not every day that we are needed. . . . What we are doing here *that* is the question. And we are blessed in this, that we happen to know the answer. Yes, in this immense confusion one thing alone is clear. We are waiting for Godot to come" (79 f.).

So in various, if only partly qualified ways, the happenings raise the anticipation of some new departure, only to disappoint it in the end. The conclusion of the play assembles several instances of non-events: the boy appears and announces that Godot won't come that evening, and the two protagonists again decide to leave but don't move. This stress on the absence of eventful change, without any indication that the future will be different, can only be taken as eventful in itself. Although the grotesque and partly fantastical nature of the figures and their behavior may seem to reduce the seriousness of the meaning of the play, the general drift of the play can be interpreted as a radical modernist critique of the very notion of eventfulness and of progressive change and thus projects a reductionist, pessimistic view of the world in general and even of the possibility of human orientation, purposeful action, and practical achievement.

In my second example, Henry James's tale "The Beast in the Jungle" (1903), the status of the expectation of an event—the precondition of an eventful non-event to occur—is structurally different from *Waiting for Godot*. While Beckett's play creates such an expectation through the interaction of various characters as performed before the spectators' eyes and ears "objectively," as it were (i.e., not restricted to any one person's consciousness), in James's story the anticipation of an event originates exclusively in one individual's purely subjective mind: early on, John Marcher has conceived the notion of being predestined to meet with some "rare and strange, possibly prodigious and terrible" incident during his life (71)—of being sprung upon, as he metaphorically puts it, by some "beast in the jungle" (cf. 76). A chance acquaintance, May Bartram, to whom he mentions this anticipation, is so taken by him and this concept that she decides to wait with him (or maybe she does this out of love for him). The entire story is told by a heterodiegetic narrator through John Marcher's internal focalization. During the subsequent years and decades, nothing manifestly happens to him. Then May Bartram dies. He mourns her loss (or so it seems).

James's tale is special in that the story itself explicitly thematizes and formulates the relevance of this non-event, suggesting that different ways of interpreting it is in fact highly eventful. The first character to do so is May Bartram. Toward the end of her life, she enigmatically tells Marcher that the event positively and definitively *has* already happened but that he will never know it (96). She refuses to clarify its nature before she dies, merely commenting that it has "marked him out" (96): "You were to suffer your fate. That was not necessarily to know it" (98). Significantly, at this point in time, he is unable to understand her.

As for Marcher himself, he goes through several attempts to interpret the nonarrival of the "beast" as meaningful. His first reaction, which is radical, is to see this as the "failure not to be anything" (87), since the prophesied attack of the beast had been his personal distinction and therefore part of his identity (cf. 100). Then he comes to interpret her dying and death, losing her, and his resultant solitude as his predestined doom, though a rather common one (95). And finally, witnessing the intense, unmitigated mourning of a stranger in contrast to his own mild feeling of loss, he suddenly understands what May had meant, realizing at last that his failure to recognize her love and to love her himself had been the leaping of the beast: "He had failed, with the last exactitude, of all he was to fail of" (106). In other words, the fact that he had done nothing, that he had not allowed something vital, their love, to happen was the significant and significantly negative event of his existence, ultimately caused by, and indeed indicative of, his particular personality and self-centered disposition.

The historical and cultural context of "The Beast in the Jungle" is implied by the belief in the notion that the life of an outstanding person is distinguished and guided by some supernatural power (e.g., "fate" or God), as expressed in the repeated reference to "the lap / secret of the gods" (77, 80, 87, 95). This is a premodern, archaic concept apt to provide the self with transcendent orientation and stability, which is lacking but painfully missed in the enlightened, secular modern society with the radical openness of the future in which James's tale is set. The presence and particular employment of this motif exemplifies the psychological problems an individual's existence is confronted with in the progressive modernization of life.[7]

---

7. In this connection, consider an interesting narrative which uses a non-eventful plot to highlight and intensify an eventful outcome: Bernard MacLaverty's short story "The Clinic." While waiting at the doctor's office for a diabetes checkup, the protagonist reads Chekhov's tale "The Beauties," a non-eventful story about the disappointing encounter of a boy with two enticingly beautiful girls who ignore him. When he later phones his wife to tell her he is ok, he suddenly thinks of his first encounter with her, a situation similar to that in Chekhov's tale

A FEW TENTATIVE CONCLUSIONS can be drawn from these considerations. (1) Although the nonoccurrence and the occurrence of significant changes may be equally eventful, they are not completely symmetrical in structure and appearance. While events can occur as complete surprises, totally unanticipated, for non-events to occur, a general or specific expectation on the part of the readers or characters is required,[8] which is then frustrated in the course of the narrative sequence. The disappointment of an expectation as the precondition of eventfulness thus applies to non-events with a vengeance. (2) Events can either occur at a particular point in time (the solution of the murder mystery in a detective novel, the fall of the hero in a tragedy) or develop in successive stages over an extended period (e.g., Joseph Conrad's "Shadow-Line" and "The Secret Sharer," V. S. Naipaul's "One Out of Many") whereas non-events often turn out to have "happened" after a lengthy stretch of time, as in James's "The Beast in the Jungle." (3) The expectation of an eventful turn or change as an essential feature of a proper story is so powerful and pervasive that even the nonoccurrence of an (expected) event can be, and typically is, interpreted as eventful. This is specifically exemplified by the characters in James's tale, who undertake several attempts to transform the fact that nothing has happened into an event in its own right. May, for example, could well have rejected the occurrence of any event whatsoever by accusing Marcher, in his obsession with the lurking beast, of selfishness; instead, she accedes to the idea that an event occurred. (4) Just as changes within the sequence of happenings acquire the status of an event only in relation to a particular context, so the failure of such a change to occur is also eventful only within the relevant contextual frame of reference. This context can be indicated more or less clearly in the narrative text. Henry James provides the pronounced clues for the intended reading of the nonappearance of the beast: that Marcher's final interpretation is meant to be taken as the appropriate one is signaled by its apparent congruence with May's earlier suggestions. Samuel Beckett, in contrast, is much less explicit about the concrete significance of the concluding instances of the protagonists' inaction and Godot's nonappearance, leaving its exact interpretation more or less open. (5) As to the meaning or significance of non-events, the failure of a decisive change to occur is typically

---

which, in his case, finally led to the happy event of their marriage. Here, two (positive) events are thematized and highlighted: the past development of his life and the present solution of a medical crisis or threat.

8. There are differences between expectations on the part of characters and those of readers. In the case of a character's expectations, the reader is found in the position of judging whether the expectations themselves or their (seeming) fulfillment are illusory or realistic. For more on this point, see Raphaël Baroni's contribution to this volume.

caused by some kind of interaction between the protagonist's personal deficits, shortcomings, mistakes, delusions, and so on, with the resistance, intractability, perversity, or complexity of the circumstances and the social conditions. (6) In all cases, the nonoccurrence of an event, analogous to a manifest event, ultimately functions as the point or decisive turn of the story and constitutes its tellability. (7) Finally, in one specific respect, the effect of non-eventfulness will differ from that of eventfulness: the eventful nonoccurrence of an event is apt to raise more questions than eventful closure—questions about reasons, causes, and significance. The fundamental openness and incompleteness of existence signaled by non-events can be seen as a result and symptom of the modern condition, and thus as specific to this historical period.

WORKS CITED

Beckett, Samuel. *Waiting for Godot*. London: Faber & Faber, 1956 (1955).
Bruner, Jerome. "The Narrative Construction of Reality." *Critical Inquiry* 18 (1991): 1–21.
Gerhardie, William. *Anton Chehov: A Critical Study*. London: McDonald, 1974 (1923).
Hühn, Peter. *Eventfulness in British Fiction*, with contributions by Markus Kempf, Katrin Kroll, and Jette K. Wulf. Berlin and New York: de Gruyter, 2010.
———. "Forms and Functions of Eventfulness in Narrative Fiction." In *Theorizing Narrativity*, edited by John Pier and José García Landa, 141–63. Berlin and New York: de Gruyter, 2008.
———. "Philip Larkin and Thomas Hood: 'I Remember, I Remember.'" In *The Narratological Analysis of Lyric Poetry: Studies in English Poetry from the 16th to the 20th Century*, edited by Peter Hühn and Jens Kiefer, translated by Alastair Matthews, 201–12. Berlin and New York: de Gruyter, 2005.
Iser, Wolfgang. *Prospecting: From Reader Response to Literary Anthropology*. Baltimore: Johns Hopkins Univ. Press, 1989.
James, Henry. "The Beast in the Jungle." In *The Jolly Corner and Other Tales*, edited by Roger Gard, 64–107. London: Penguin, 1990 (1903).
Labov, William. *Language in the Inner City*. Philadelphia: Univ. of Pennsylvania Press, 1971.
Lotman, Yuri. *The Structure of the Artistic Text*. Translated by Gail Lenhoff and Ronald Vroon. Ann Arbor: Univ. of Michigan Press, 1977.
McLaverty, Bernard. "The Clinic." In *Matters of Life & Death and Other Stories*, 49–61. London: Jonathan Cape, 2006.
Ovid. *Metamorphoses*. Translated by A. D. Melville. Oxford: Oxford University Press. 2008.
Pratt, Mary Louise. *Toward a Speech Act Theory of Literary Discourse*. Bloomington: Indiana Univ. Press, 1977.
Schmid, Wolf. "Narrativity and Eventfulness." In *What Is Narratology? Questions and Answers Regarding the Status of a Theory*, edited by Tom Kindt and Hans-Harald Müller, 17–33. Berlin and New York: de Gruyter, 2003.
van Gennep, Arnold. *The Rites of Passage*. Translated by Monika B. Vizedom. Chicago: Univ. of Chicago Press, 1972 (1909).
Warhol, Robyn R. "Neonarrative; or, How to Render the Unnarratable in Realist Fiction and Contemporary Film." In *A Companion to Narrative Theory*, edited by James Phelan and Peter J. Rabinowitz, 220–31. Oxford: Blackwell, 2005.

PART II

Rhetorical Perspectives on Narrative Progression

CHAPTER 4

Privileged Authorial Disclosure about Events

Wolff's "Bullet in the Brain" and O'Hara's "Appearances"

JAMES PHELAN

TOBIAS WOLFF'S "Bullet in the Brain" (1995), which recounts the last moments in the life of Anders, a fifty-year-old book critic who gets shot during a bank robbery, contains a highly unusual sequence in its second half. As the bank robber's bullet makes its way through Anders's brain, it triggers a memory from his youth. But rather than narrating that memory, Wolff pushes the pause button on the forward movement of the story and inserts three paragraphs of "disnarration" (Prince), during which the narrator recounts a variety of things that Anders did not remember. Wolff's move gives his audience access to events from Anders's past that Anders himself does not have. Consequently, we move from a position alongside Anders to one in which we have a much broader view: we share with Wolff a bird's-eye perspective on Anders that Anders himself never achieves. In addition, this passage of narration gives us a sense of the temporality of Anders's life that is not part of his own experience in the Narrative Now: for him, the temporality of the story consists only of the bank robbery and the youthful memory. For us, as a result of the disnarration, the temporality includes a much broader context within which to place both the bank robbery and the memory. Needless to say, our broader perspective significantly affects our understanding of and responses to those two events.[1]

John O'Hara's "Appearances" also gives its audience greater access to events than it gives any of its three main characters. Like Wolff's story, O'Hara's has a short duration in the Narrative Now, even as the audience's understanding of that Now depends on the revelation of events from the past. But "Appearances" also provides an instructive contrast with "Bullet in the Brain," as a description of its sequence indicates. "Appearances" consists of three conversations among the members of the Ambrie family—husband, Howard; wife, Lois; and their divorced daughter, Amy—with each conversation involving only two of the characters: first Howard-Lois, then Howard-Amy, and finally, Lois-Amy. As a result, O'Hara's disclosures to the audience are indirect rather than direct: they come about as byproducts of the dialogues. Furthermore, the sequence itself ensures the audience's greater access: we know what goes on in all three conversations, while each character knows only what goes on in two of them. Even more significantly, Lois and Amy share knowledge about the past that Howard does not have (or that they believe he does not have, a qualification I will return to) and then Lois refuses to share other knowledge when Amy asks her a leading question about the past. Thus, while each character is simply participating in two conversations that take place within about a half-hour period, the audience reconstructs a narrative that extends over a much longer timeframe. "Appearances" not only gives the audience more knowledge than it gives any one of the characters, it also suggests that those characters have different degrees of knowledge about the past: Lois knows the most, Amy the next most, and Howard the least. But the story is not called "Appearances" for nothing, because, as we shall see, it also gives the audience reason to question this apparent hierarchy. Both the questions and the more secure knowledge greatly influence our understanding of each character and of the Ambrie family as whole.

In this essay, I want to focus on the role of what I will call Wolff's and O'Hara's *privileged authorial disclosures about events* in the narrative progressions of their two stories, by which I mean the author's communication to the audience of actions involving their main characters that the characters themselves either do not have or cannot access in the Narrative Now.[2] In specifying that this authorial communication is about events, I distinguish it from other

---

1. My discussion of "Bullet in the Brain" in this chapter shares material with a longer treatment of it in an argument about the value of reading short fiction in *Life and Narrative: The Risks and Responsibilities of Storying Experience* (Schiff, Patron, and McKim, eds.).

2. This relationship is different from the one in standard cases of unreliable narration, because there the audience and the character narrator have the same access to the events but understand and evaluate them differently.

kinds of privileged authorial disclosures authors provide to audiences, such as those about the nature of characters (e.g., "Emma Woodhouse, handsome, clever, and rich, with a comfortable home and a happy disposition, seemed to unite some of the best blessings of existence") or about the conditions in which they act ("It was the best of times, it was the worst of times"). I shall argue that the disclosures in "Bullet in the Brain" and in "Appearances," and their locations in their respective narrative sequences, not only are crucial to the progressions of these two stories but also illustrate a previously undertheorized means by which authors can configure the relationships among characters, events, temporality, and audiences. More specifically, I shall argue that Wolff and O'Hara demonstrate two (of many) different ways in which privileged authorial disclosures about events can be deployed in the construction of hybrid forms: in the case of "Bullet in the Brain," Wolff constructs a lyrical portrait narrative, and in the case of "Appearances," O'Hara constructs a group portrait narrative. Finally, I offer these analyses to demonstrate the utility of a rhetorical approach to progression, one that attends not only to characters, events, and their interrelationships (whether causal, analogical, or something else) but also to the link between these interrelationships and the implied author's multilayered communications to his or her audience. Indeed, I submit that these analyses of privileged authorial disclosures about events support the broader claim that characters, events, and temporality, though crucial to a narrative's progression and effects, are themselves ultimately subordinated to the implied author's relationship with the audience.

THE *FABULA/SJUZHET* DISTINCTION, NARRATIVE PROGRESSION, AND PRIVILEGED AUTHORIAL DISCLOSURE OF EVENTS

Since Victor Shklovsky first introduced the *fabula/sjuzhet* distinction, it has demonstrated considerable explanatory power in narrative theory's efforts to analyze narrative sequence. Indeed, one could develop a useful (albeit not wholly adequate) understanding of the sometimes overlapping, sometimes contrasting models one finds in this book as well as in contemporary narrative theory more broadly by attending to each model's distinctive ways of working with, building on, or otherwise engaging with this distinction.[3] Attention to *fabula* highlights the chronological sequence of events and, thus, typically

---

3. In addition to the other essays here, see Baroni, Dannenberg, Kafalenos, Prince, Richardson, and Sternberg for a small sample.

(another qualification I'll return to), the sequence of the characters' experience of the events, while attention to *sjuzhet* hones in on the sequence in the narrative text and, thus, the sequence of the audience's experience of those same events. Consequently, examining the relation between the two sequences helps reveal the underlying logic of a narrative's progression. More generally, from my rhetorical perspective, which is concerned with an implied author's communications to an actual audience, this focus on *fabula* and *sjuzhet* works well for the countless narratives that recount the change in a character's situation between Time One and Time Two while also engaging their audiences in following the trajectory, causes, and significance of that change. Indeed, an author's departures from the order of events in the *fabula* are typically motivated by his or her interest in deepening the audience's engagement in the trajectory, causes, and significance of the change brought about by the *fabula*'s events.

So far, so good—and so standard. But this standard account depends on a well-grounded assumption about the default relationship between the experiences of the main characters and those of the audience that I would like to highlight: the characters act and the audience reacts; or more expansively, the audience follows the characters' progress through the events of the *fabula*, tracking them through their disparate experiences. The audience might reach different interpretive and ethical judgments from those of the protagonist(s), but the audience and protagonist(s) share access to the same events.

We can recognize both the power and the limitations of the usual assumption in Peter J. Rabinowitz's insightful work on the concept of path, by which he means the order of a character's experience. Working with the example of Raymond Chandler's *The Long Goodbye*, Rabinowitz persuasively argues that this concept is a necessary complement to the *fabula/sjuzhet* distinction whenever the path of a character's experience is different from both the order of events in the *fabula* and the order of events in the *sjuzhet*. Rabinowitz shows that attending to the differences between Philip Marlowe's path through a crucial sequence of events near the novel's ending and the order of those events in both the *fabula* and the *sjuzhet* enables us to recognize that Chandler builds into the ending an uncharacteristic gap between Marlowe's judgments and those of the novel's audience. More generally, Rabinowitz's concept of path is a valuable addition to the distinction between *fabula* and *sjuzhet* precisely because it expands our understanding of what might be involved in the audience's tracking the experiences of the characters.

Both "Bullet in the Brain" and "Appearances" alter the default relationship between characters and audiences by first establishing it and then deviating from it with the introduction of the privileged authorial disclosure about events. Furthermore, the audience's greater access to events involving the protagonist(s) gives the audience a different relation to the unfolding of time in the narrative: in "Bullet in the Brain," Anders remains suspended in the Narrative Now as Wolff takes the audience on a highly selective tour of Anders's past. In "Appearances," only the audience sees the three conversations as part of an overarching sequence of temporally related events that connect these conversations to the past. By contrast, each member of the Ambrie family regards his or her participation in each conversation as a discrete event.

A RHETORICAL APPROACH TO PROGRESSION

In previous work, I have defined narrative as a purposeful communicative act, somebody telling somebody else on some occasion and for some purpose(s) that something happened. This definition emphasizes the relation between the somebody who tells (the author—or if you prefer as I do, the implied author) and the somebody who listens (the actual audience), and, thus, it implies that the most important sequence is that of the communication between those two entities. At the same time, because the definition specifies that the communication is about characters and events ("something happened"), it suggests that another important sequence is that of those events. One consequence of this concern with both kinds of sequence is the distinction between textual dynamics and readerly dynamics as well as the definition of progression as the synthesis of these two kinds of dynamics.

Textual dynamics are the principles of movement underlying the *sjuzhet*, and these principles are themselves of two kinds: (1) the mechanisms governing the movement of events (plot dynamics) and (2) the mechanisms governing the movement of the disclosure of events (telling dynamics). I have identified three main patterns of movement: the first focused primarily on plot dynamics and the other two focused primarily on telling dynamics, though individual narratives will combine all three patterns. The first pattern is that of instabilities-complications-resolutions (often only partial). Instabilities exist within, between, or among characters, and they can either preexist the narrative or begin during it. The second pattern is that of tensions-complications-resolutions. Tensions arise from unequal knowledge or discrepant values, attitudes, or beliefs between and among authors, narrators, and audiences. The third pattern is that of interactions among authors, narrators, characters-as-tellers (in dialogue), and audiences, a pattern that begins with an initiation, continues through ongoing interactions, and ends with some kind of farewell, if only an implicit one.

Readerly dynamics are the trajectory of the audience's response to those textual dynamics. Readerly dynamics include (1) the activities of entering into the storyworld, configuring the events into a larger comprehensible shape, and (often) reconfiguring those events in light of new information; and (2) a multilayered set of responses—cognitive, affective, ethical, aesthetic—to the characters and events and to our configurations and reconfigurations of them. These responses are rooted in three kinds of judgments: interpretive (about the nature and significance of textual signals), ethical (about our moral evaluation of a character's actions), and aesthetic (about the overall quality of our reading experience).[4]

Progression is the synthesis of textual and readerly dynamics because the two kinds are mutually influential. An implied author who wants to produce a certain kind of response in the audience (say surprise) will adjust the textual dynamics accordingly. The precise nature of that audience response will be a function of just how the implied author adjusts the textual dynamics. The link between textual dynamics and readerly dynamics is provided by narrative judgments because implied authors encode them in texts and readers decode and activate them as they follow the progression.[5]

As this discussion indicates, the concept of progression subsumes the concept of plot, and, in so doing, provides a broader, more flexible approach to the phenomenon of narrative sequence. I favor the broader approach for two reasons: (1) as noted above, in order to explain the principles underlying the movement of narratives from beginning through middle to ending, we need to go beyond plot dynamics to include telling dynamics and readerly dynamics. (2) The principles underlying the textual dynamics of many works we call narratives are not adequately captured by tracing their patterns of instabilities-complications-resolutions. The principles underlying such works often have a hybrid form, fusing some parts of the logic of narrative progression with the logic of lyric progression (the gradual revelation of a situation, attitude, thought, or emotion) or the logic of a character portrait (the gradual revelation of a particular person in a particular situation). These different logics also often entail different kinds of readerly dynamics, with lyric progressions shifting readerly activity from observation and judgment to participation and sharing, and portrait progressions retaining judgment but focusing less on events than on the character(s) portrayed.[6]

---

4. My use of the first-person plural is shorthand way of referring to the audience that follows the signals of the textual dynamics, or what rhetorical theory calls the authorial audience. In other words, the "we" is a shorthand for actual readers who want to read rhetorically.

5. For more on this concept of progression, see my *Experiencing Fiction*.

6. For more on these hybrid forms, see Part Two of my *Experiencing Fiction*.

This approach to progression has several consequences for the way I think about privileged authorial disclosure of events. First, I define the concept in relation not to a specific technique but to a specific function: Wolff uses disnarration, O'Hara dialogue, but each gives his audience access to knowledge about events involving characters that the characters do not have. Second, while the disclosure will always be a part of the telling dynamics, it influences both the larger textual dynamics and the readerly dynamics. Third, as noted above, one possible (though not inevitable) influence of the disclosure, especially in a brief form like the short story, will be to contribute to a hybrid form of progression. Indeed, much of my analysis of the progressions of "Bullet in the Brain" and "Appearances" will focus on the relation between the privileged disclosure and the kind of hybrids Wolff and O'Hara construct.

"BULLET IN THE BRAIN"

Wolff divides the story of Anders's experiences at the bank into two parts, the first of which recounts the events leading to Anders getting shot, and the second of which gives the disnarration of what he does not remember before revealing what he does remember. In order to understand the overall progression of "Bullet in the Brain," we must come to terms with how the two parts of the story relate to each other, and especially with how the second part both contributes to and transforms the trajectory launched by the first.

As a first step, I note that Wolff develops a simultaneous pattern of events and of telling dynamics that cuts across these parts: Anders repeats someone else's words and in so doing expresses his own attitudes toward that person and his language—and these attitudes in turn capture something significant about Anders's character. In the first half, Anders thrice echoes the words of the pistol-toting bank robber, each time with mockery. When the robber says "One of you tellers hits the alarm, you're all dead meat," Anders comments, "Oh, bravo . . . *Dead meat*. . . . Great script, eh? The stern, brass-knuckled poetry of the dangerous classes" (264). When the robber calls him "bright boy," Anders remarks, "Did you hear that? 'Bright boy.' Right out of *The Killers*" (264). A little later the robber warns the still amused Anders, "Fuck with me again, you're history. *Capiche?*" Anders, snorting helplessly through his fingers, repeats "*Capiche*—oh, God, *capiche*," and the robber shoots him "right in the head" (266).

In the second half of the story, repetition of another's words is part of both what Anders does not remember and of what he does remember. He does not remember memorizing "hundreds of poems . . . so he could give himself the shivers at will," (267) and he does not remember "reciting Aeschylus himself" and how "his eyes had burned at those sounds" (267). But he does remember a summer day in his youth when a newcomer to the local ball field said that he wanted to play shortstop because "short's the best position they is." The story ends with Anders's memory of the elation he felt at hearing those words and of his own chanting repetition of them as he stood in right field smacking his glove: "*They is, they is, they is*" (268).

Tracing this pattern of repetitions is a good first step toward understanding the progression because it reveals one arc of the telling dynamics as Anders's attitudes move from disdain to reverence and because it leads us to thematize that movement. The pattern highlights the difference between Anders's ethically appealing younger self and his ethically deficient older self, between the Anders who can marvel at the world and language's way of interpreting it and the Anders who is cynical, jaded, and superior to everything he encounters. But we still need to relate the pattern of repetitions to the more fundamental principles underlying the story's overall movement.

The first half of "Bullet in the Brain" progresses according to the logic of instability-complication-resolution. The initial instability exists between Anders and the larger world: he is a man at odds with that world, viewing himself as superior to it, as his book-reviewing habits indicate: Anders is "known for the weary, elegant savagery with which he dispatched almost everything he reviewed" (263). Wolff economically establishes this instability and its consequences for Anders's interactions with others through the first lines of dialogue. After one of the bank tellers ignores the long line of waiting customers and leaves her station, the woman in front of Anders comments, "Oh, that's nice.... One of those little human touches that keep us coming back for more" (263). The narrator prefaces Anders's reply by reporting, in language colored by Anders's voice, that he "had conceived his own towering hatred of the teller, but he immediately turned it on the presumptuous crybaby in front of him. 'Damned unfair,' he said. 'Tragic, really. If they're not chopping off the wrong leg or bombing your ancestral village, they're closing their positions'" (263). The woman seeks to form a little community with Anders by inviting him to share in her ironically expressed judgment of the teller and the bank, but Anders not only rejects her invitation but also ridicules it with his far more hyperbolically ironic reply—even though his own judgment is in line with (albeit much more extreme than) hers.

Wolff then complicates this initial instability by using the pattern of repetitions to trace the way Anders's penchant for establishing his intellectual and aesthetic superiority to others leads to his eventually getting shot. Anders clearly hears the bank robber's warnings, but he proves totally unable to cease asserting his superiority.

With regard to readerly dynamics, what is most obvious are our strongly negative ethical judgments of Anders's attitude, and what is most surprising is the streak of sympathy we nevertheless feel for him. This sympathy stems in part from Wolff's handling of the telling dynamics so that we share Anders's interpretive and aesthetic judgments of the bank robber's cliché-ridden language (it's as if he got his patter from a chapter on "How to Talk Tough" in *Bank Robbing for Dummies*) and in part from our recognition that Anders's punishment far outweighs his crime. The byplay about the bank robber's language contributes to our feeling, before the robber shoots, that we're poised between comic amusement (we are inclined to laugh with Anders) and serious fear (we are apprehensive about the likely consequences of Anders's inability to stop expressing his disdain). This feeling is reinforced by Wolff's juxtaposition of the ominous sexual undertones of the bank robber's clichés ("You want to suck my dick?" "You think you can fuck with me?") with Anders's perception of the painting of Zeus and Europa on the bank's ceiling, which leads Anders to think that if there were "a caption bubbling out of [Zeus's] mouth, it would have said HUBBA HUBBA" (265). Once the robber pulls the trigger, our response tips wholly into the serious, but our negative ethical judgments of Anders and our interpretive judgment that he has brought the shooting on himself also mean that at this stage we do not feel a great sense of loss.

Once Anders gets shot, his fate is sealed, but Wolff exploits the potential of two elements of the first half to keep the story moving forward. First and most obviously, he opts to continue the narrative by describing what happens in the final moments of Anders's life as the bullet goes through his brain. Second, and more subtly, Wolff picks up on the initial instability of Anders's being at odds with the world, and, rather than complicating it, he uses the privileged authorial disclosure to elaborate on it, to give us some sense of its evolution and a clearer sense of how it has come to define who Anders is now.

Wolff marks the division between the two parts of the story with white space. In the first paragraph of the second half, Wolff's narrator reports that the bullet "set off a crackling chain of ion transports and neurotransmissions" that "flukishly call[ed] to life a summer afternoon some forty years past, and long since lost to memory" (266). But in the second paragraph, Wolff turns to the privileged authorial disclosure, as the narrator declares, "It is worth noting what Anders did not remember, given what he did recall" (266). The location of this disclosure in the overall sequence is crucial, because it brings about a major shift in the underlying plot dynamics and an even more significant shift in the overall mode of the progression from narrative to portraiture. Both shifts set up the final movement of the sequence, the report of what Anders actually remembers. In other words, the shift to the privileged authorial disclosure is the pivotal move in the narrative's overall sequence.

With the privileged disclosure, the plot dynamics shift from the pattern of instability-complication-resolution to a pattern of tension-delay-resolution. Wolff, his narrator, and Anders all know what he does remember, but we do not. The pause in the Narrative Now that accompanies the shift to the disnarration and its privileged authorial disclosure heightens the tension. Furthermore, within the disnarration itself, Wolff shifts from a movement governed by strictly narrative principles to one governed by those of a portrait narrative. That is, the various items Wolff has the narrator inform us about are all brushstrokes that contribute both to a larger gestalt of Anders-the-character and a fragmentary narrative of how he became this character.

The three paragraphs are also an instance of disnarration with a twist: whereas much disnarration is about events that are not themselves part of the fabula (wished-for events, events that might have happened but did not, and so on), Anders's nonmemories are about events that actually happened in the past. But disnarration is the appropriate term for these three paragraphs, because if the bullet had affected Anders's synapses differently, he could have remembered one, some, or even perhaps all of these events.

More significantly, the twist in the disnarration allows Wolff to take what may initially appear to be a random list of nonmemories and shape it into a coherent portrait. Anders is a man who had once regarded much of the world as fresh and wondrous but who now regards the whole world as predictable and inferior to himself. The emphasis falls on portraiture rather than narrative because the list of nonmemories is neither chronological nor causally linked. Their subjects range from Anders's first lover and his wife to his daughter, a former teacher, a former classmate, and a woman whom he watches commit suicide by jumping from a building. The conclusion of the disclosure succinctly conveys a sense of the resentful, unhappy, and jaded man Anders has become. "He did not remember when he began to regard the heap of books on his desk with boredom and dread, or when he grew angry at young writers for writing them. He did not remember when everything began to remind him of something else" (267).

The readerly dynamics accompanying the privileged disclosure complicate our earlier responses. By seeing Anders more fully and by learning that he was not always like the man in the Narrative Now, we soften our ethical judgments and increase our sympathy. While we continue to regard his way of interacting with the world as deficient, we are less inclined simply to condemn him and more inclined to find something deeply poignant in his situation.

The final paragraphs, in resolving the tension about what Anders did remember, further complicate both the textual and readerly dynamics. Even as Wolff guides us once again to track Anders's unfolding experience in the final moments of his life, Wolff shifts the dominant mode of progression from portraiture to lyric. His final paragraphs do include a mini-narrative—the story of choosing up sides in the baseball game, culminating in Coyle's cousin's simple tribute to the shortstop position—but Wolff clearly subordinates this mini-narrative to the lyric unfolding of the emotions the young Anders felt upon hearing the phrase "they is." He "is strangely roused, elated, by those . . . two words, their pure unexpectedness and their music. He takes the field in a trance, repeating them to himself" (268).

Just as significantly, Wolff emphasizes the agency of the older Anders in lingering over the memory of his younger self. After the narrator reminds us that the bullet in the end "will do its work," he turns back to Anders in the moment of memory: "But for now Anders can still make time. Time for the shadows to lengthen on the grass, time for the tethered dog to bark at the flying ball, time for the boy in right field to smack his sweat-blackened mitt and softly chant, *They is, they is, they is*" (268). Although Anders does not merge with his former self, his choosing to extend the memory indicates that he recaptures his pleasure in the surprise and wonder of language and, by extension, of life itself.

At the level of readerly dynamics, this section of lyric generates positive ethical judgments of the young Anders and activates our own pleasure in language as we perhaps chant along with him, "they is, they is, they is." The chant itself has a certain power, which arises, at the level of sound, from the repeating spondees and the pattern of long vowel-short vowel, and, at the level of sense, from the way the phrase exists between "there is" and "they are"—just as shortstop is the "best" position because it is in between second and third base. But the ultimate power of the chant depends on its role in completing the larger progression of the short story. As the chant marks the final resolution of the tensions and instabilities, it also provides a very effective farewell. It strongly contrasts with Anders's first biting irony ("Damned unfair") even as it rounds off the pattern of repetitions in the telling dynamics. Furthermore, at the level of readerly dynamics the chant contributes substantially to the affectively and ethically bittersweet quality of Anders's final moments. The sweetness resides in the fifty-year-old Anders's ability to reconnect with his love of language and his open attitude toward life, and the bitterness in his being able to do so only because his using language as a weapon of ridicule has brought him to the end of his life.

Thus, although "Bullet in the Brain" ultimately tells a story of change, the power of that story depends crucially on Wolff's integrating into that story both the portrait narrative of Anders and the lyric narrative of his final moments. And the portrait narrative, in turn, is crucially dependent on Wolff's strategic placement of the privileged authorial disclosure within the overall sequence.

"APPEARANCES"

With a dialogue story such as "Appearances," we can productively approach the telling dynamics by employing a distinction between *conversational disclosures,* the communications that occur between participants in the dialogue, and *authorial disclosures,* the communications between the implied author and his or her audience through that same dialogue—and across dialogues.[7] The art of dialogue narrative consists to a large degree in the implied author's using well-motivated conversational disclosures in the service of authorial disclosures that the participants in the conversation are not aware of. In one typical pattern of progression in a dialogue narrative, the two kinds of disclosure initially overlap almost completely and then increasingly diverge as the author and audience bring the knowledge of the previous disclosures to each new scene of dialogue. In "Appearances," O'Hara makes an especially ingenious use of that pattern.

"Appearances" begins with a brief passage of exposition that efficiently accomplishes several purposes: (1) it establishes Howard as the character whose experiences we initially track; (2) it locates the action on a clear, warm night; and (3) it identifies the Ambries as a well-to-do couple (they live in a house with a "porte-cochere") with an apparently careless daughter (she leaves the door of her MG open and the light on in the garage). In the first conversation, we continue tracking Howard and begin to track Lois, as the two of them discuss his plan to play golf in the morning rather than go to the funeral of his lifelong acquaintance, Jack Hill. In the second conversation, we continue to follow Howard and substitute Amy for Lois as our secondary interest, as father and daughter discuss why her marriage broke up and what her future holds. In the third conversation, we cease tracking Howard and shift over to

---

7. For more on this distinction and its application, see my "Authorial and Conversational Disclosure in the Dialogue Novel."

tracking both Lois and Amy as they discuss why Howard never liked Jack Hill. Although there is no compelling reason within the logic of the characters' actions for the conversation between mother and daughter to follow rather than precede the one before father and daughter, the logic of O'Hara's communication to his audience makes this sequence the most effective. With the shift away from Howard, O'Hara engages in his privileged disclosure about events that Howard seems to have no access to. That authorial disclosure in turn sheds retrospective light on both of the previous conversational disclosures: since this authorial disclosure reveals that Amy's marriage broke up because she had an affair with Hill and that Amy suspects Lois had her own affair with Hill shortly after she married Howard, O'Hara invites us to reinterpret aspects of the previous conversations.

To put this point another way, because the plot dynamics proceed more through tensions than instabilities, and because the third dialogue is the one that partially resolves the tensions and completes the privileged disclosure, our readerly activities of configuration and reconfiguration are especially important to the progression. More generally, the sequence of conversations does not trace a story of change but rather gradually discloses the relation between the present and the past in the service of painting a group portrait of the Ambrie family with Jack Hill as a shadowy presence in the background. And the most significant strokes in that portrait result from the privileged authorial disclosure about events in the third conversation. For that reason, I shall give more attention to that conversation, but first I want to highlight some salient features of the authorial and conversational disclosures in the first two scenes of dialogue.

The only instability of any significance in the Narrative Now is located in the initial conversation between Lois and Howard—she wants Howard to attend Hill's funeral and he does not want to—and it is decisively resolved by the end of that conversation, when Howard submits to Lois's repeated entreaties. But O'Hara uses the conversational disclosures to create tensions about why Howard is so set against going to Hill's funeral and why Lois is so insistent that he go. Although the conversational disclosures suggest that they speak frankly as they offer their reasons—Howard says that "I never liked Jack and he never liked me," and Lois says that "I don't want Celia [Hill's wife] knowing that you stayed away" (5–6)—O'Hara uses the initial strength of their respective positions in combination with his title to invite us to wonder whether they each have motives that they do not reveal to the other.

O'Hara complicates the tension with the movement to the dialogue between Howard and Amy, even as it "appears" to be about different subjects. When Amy comments that she is comfortable living home again, in part because she enjoys reading their many detective stories, and Howard responds that they have "early Mary Roberts Rinehart" (8), who is known as the American Agatha Christie and is credited with the phrase, "The butler did it," O'Hara's authorial disclosure is that his audience should be on the lookout for some mystery-solution structure in his own tale, which, after all, introduces the dead body of Jack Hill early on.

Again the conversational disclosures between father and daughter suggest that they are speaking candidly. When Howard advises the divorced Amy to have children right away if she remarries because children can help a couple stay together, Amy notes that he implies that the advice comes from his own experience. Howard agrees: "I know what I'm implying. And I know you're no fool. You know it's often been touch and go with your mother and I. You've seen that" (8). For her part, Amy explains that "nothing" would have kept her marriage intact because she had an affair with a married man, a man that she had been seeing even before her marriage. Amy also admits that she is no longer seeing that married man, that she now agrees with her father that he was a "son of a bitch" (10) and that she is currently sleeping with Joe, the doctor she has been dating and might soon marry. At the same time, for all its candor, the conversation calls attention to issues that Amy does not want to discuss. When Howard starts to ask for more details about Amy's history with that man, she says, "don't ask me any more questions, please" (9). From that point on, Howard offers judgments about the man ("He sounds like a real son of a bitch" [10]), but he does not seek any more information about his identity. Consequently, O'Hara uses the conversation to create the tension about his identity.

In the crucial final conversation, O'Hara gives us four exchanges where the relation between conversational disclosure and authorial disclosure, including authorial disclosure across conversations, is especially salient. The first comes right at the beginning of the conversation after Lois asks whether Howard said anything to Amy about Jack Hill:

"I'll be glad when Jack is buried and out of the way."
 "I know," said Amy.
 "Your father is getting closer to the truth, Amy."
 "I guess he is."
 "I had a very difficult time persuading him to go to the funeral tomorrow."
 "Why did you bother?"
 "Appearances. 'Why didn't Howard Ambrie go to Jack Hill's funeral?' They'd be talking about that for a month, and somebody'd be sure to say something to Celia. And then Celia'd start asking herself questions."

"I wonder. I think Mrs. Hill stopped asking questions a long time ago. She should have. I wasn't the only one he played around with." (11)

Here O'Hara uses this conversational disclosure to resolve tensions from the first two conversations—about Lois's motivation in persuading Howard and about the identity of Amy's lover. More than that, now that we are no longer tracking Howard, O'Hara uses this exchange to introduce the first significant privileged authorial disclosure with respect to him. O'Hara, Lois, and Amy now all share information that Howard (apparently) does not. In addition, the revelation begins the process of reconfiguration because it not only confirms the hypothesis that "Appearances" would follow the mystery-solution pattern of a detective story but does so in a way that ties the first two conversations together. Furthermore, the privileged authorial disclosure shows us that both conversations involving Howard were significantly less candid than they appeared and significantly less candid than this one: Lois and Amy share significant confidences with each other that neither shares with him.

Finally, certain moments in both of the previous conversations take on greater significance. In the first, Howard couples his consent to attend the funeral with the question of why Lois cares so much about whether Celia would know about his presence, but Lois responds only to his agreement: "But you will go?" (6). O'Hara uses this conversational disclosure to reveal why she was so selective. In the second conversation, when Howard asks whether the man with whom Amy had her affair has "gone out of [her] life," "she looked at him sharply" before answering yes. And it is when he follows up by asking whether she met him at Cornell that she tells him to stop asking more questions. O'Hara now allows us to see now what Howard apparently does not: that Amy suspects that he knows about her affair with Hill.

These reconfigurations rooted in the authorial disclosure across conversations also have consequences for our larger construction of the family portrait and for our affective and ethical responses to each member. Amy is not just a careless woman who will neglect to close the door of her expensive sports car and turn out the light in her garage but also someone who takes her marriage vows lightly. Lois is more concerned about keeping up appearances than about Amy's actual behavior. And both women conspire to keep Howard in the dark. Consequently, Howard emerges as the most sympathetic character, especially since he also has consented to Lois's request to attend the funeral. But the readerly dynamics continue to evolve as this conversation does.

The second especially salient exchange occurs right after Amy tells Lois that now that Jack is dead she feels that she can go ahead and marry Joe and settle down:

"He [Jack Hill] was no good," said Lois Ambrie. "Strange how your father knew that without knowing why."

"I know why," said Amy. "Jack was the kind of man that husbands are naturally suspicious of. Father was afraid that Jack would make a play for you. Instead he made a play for me, but Father never gave that a thought."

"I suppose so. And in your father's eyes it would have been just as bad for me to cover up for you as it would have been for me to have had an affair with Jack. I'll be glad when he's out of the way. Really glad when you can marry Joe." (12)

The conversational disclosures in this collaborative exchange not only add to the privileged authorial disclosure with respect to Howard but they also further reveal the two women's intimacy as they build on each other's thoughts and conclusions about the two men. It is especially striking that Lois is talking about her husband this way with her daughter, since O'Hara gives us no similar conversation between Lois and Howard about Amy's judgments. In addition, O'Hara discloses another layer to Lois's motives for keeping up appearances: she is as concerned about Howard's judgment of her as about his judgment of Amy. I will comment below on Lois's curious equation of covering up Amy's affair with Jack with having her own affair with him.

The third salient exchange switches from the focus on Jack, Howard, and the past to one on Amy, Joe and the future, as Lois asks Amy whether she will have to convert to Catholicism to marry Joe. This shift has three main effects: (1) it signals at least a temporary end to the configurations and reconfigurations about the past; (2) it introduces some significant differences between the previously intimate Lois and Amy, and (3) it influences our ethical judgments of both Lois and Amy. Where Lois is fixated on what a "feather in their cap" (13) it will be for Joe's Catholic family to make an alliance with the Ambries, Amy has no such concerns and, indeed, is able to imagine that Joe's family is likely not to regard his marrying a divorced woman so positively. "They may not see it that way. I understand they can be very tough about some things" (13). Indeed, she is willing to accommodate Joe's family: "When the time comes, whatever they say I'll do" (13). In order to underline Lois's unquestioned assumptions about the superiority of her WASP identity and the way her judgments of others are tied to those assumptions, O'Hara gives her the final word about Catholics with a topical reference to John Fitzgerald Kennedy: "I still can't get used to the idea of having one in the White House" (13). By marking this difference between Lois and Amy, O'Hara uses the conversational disclosures to shift our ethical judgments: the careless Amy is capable of seeing at least some of her own flaws, whereas Lois remains within the tunnel vision accompanying her class privilege.

The final exchange gives a further twist to our reconfigurations and to the readerly dynamics, as it turns back to past events. This exchange begins with Amy's apology and then itself takes a sudden turn, though one that the previous conversation, with its break in the intimacy between Lois and Amy, has prepared us for:

> "I'm sorry I caused you and Father so much trouble. You especially. All those lies you had to tell."
> "Oh, that's all right. It's over now. And it was really harder on your father. He never knew why he didn't like that man."
> "And *you* couldn't tell him, *could* you, Mother?"
> "What?"
> "Oh, Mother."
> Lois Ambrie looked at her daughter. "Is that another detective story you're reading? You mustn't get carried away, Amy." She smiled. "Goodnight, dear," she said, and closed the door. (13–14)

The conversational disclosures are simultaneously rich in authorial disclosures that make this exchange a brilliant end to the progression. Amy's move from sincere apology to sly insinuation about Lois's affair with Jack adds another significant element to the privileged authorial disclosure with respect to Howard. At the same time, Lois's nondenial denial introduces an element of differential knowledge between Lois and the audience on the one side and Amy on the other. Amy can have her suspicions, but she does not have confirmation of them. I will take up the audience's relation to those suspicions shortly, but first I want to note how O'Hara uses Amy's insinuation to round out Amy's character. Lois is right to note that Amy has been playing detective, but Amy's choice to reveal her suspicions shows that she is quite confident that they are well grounded and that she believes she has something to gain by expressing them. Either she and Lois will have something else to share—or she can learn something further by the manner of Lois's denial. Amy emerges from the story as a character who is by turns careless, immoral, aware of her faults, grateful, shrewd, and bold.

In order to assess what Lois's response reveals about her, we need to consider how O'Hara guides our own detective activities and how that guidance affects our reconfiguration. O'Hara gives us considerable evidence that Amy gets it right—and in so doing, introduces a privileged authorial disclosure with respect to Lois and Amy: Lois does not confirm Amy's suspicions, but O'Hara confirms ours. From the first and third conversations, we know that Jack did not start disliking Hill only recently but rather that he "never" liked

Hill. From the first conversation, we also know that Hill was as an usher at Howard and Lois's wedding. Consequently, they would have been in each other's orbit during the early years of Howard and Lois's marriage, the time when, according to Howard, they stayed together for Amy's sake. Moreover, we know that, if Amy is right, Lois has even more reason to keep up appearances so that Celia—and others—don't start asking why Howard would not go to Hill's funeral. In fact, we can see that, in light of Hill's age, this motive of keeping her own affair a secret from Howard and Celia becomes at least as compelling, since people would be more likely to suspect that Hill had been involved with Lois than with Amy. In addition, Lois's own curious judgment earlier in this conversation that covering up Amy's affair would have been as bad in Howard's eyes as her having an affair with Jack herself now seems less curious: she wants to minimize her own transgression and maximize Amy's. Furthermore, in terms of the overall sequence of the story, Amy's inference provides a nice final twist to the mystery-solution pattern: although that pattern seemed to be completed with the revelation about Amy and Jack Hill, we now discover, at the very end of the story, another, deeper layer to the pattern.

In light of these conclusions, we have further reason to interpret Lois's response as a nondenial denial, one in which she stops short of telling Amy that she did not have the affair even as she tries to discourage Amy's conclusion. With this nondenial denial, Lois refuses Amy's implicit invitation toward a greater intimacy based on their similar experience, a choice that reinforces what O'Hara has already disclosed about her character. Lois is committed to keeping up appearances, and to this point, she has appeared to be the concerned mother helping her daughter keep her daughter's affair from Howard. She is far more comfortable being Amy's older, wiser confidant than she is being Amy's equal.

At this point, the audience does not have any privileged access to events with respect to Lois, except for the exact details of Howard's conversation with Amy. But O'Hara's concluding with another reference to detective stories and to the mystery-solution pattern invites some further reflection. Might Howard, who after all is the original reader of the detective stories and the one who mentions Mary Roberts Rinehart to Amy, know more than Lois and Amy give him credit for knowing? If Lois and Amy are committed to keeping up certain appearances, isn't it plausible to wonder about the extent to which Howard is similarly committed, especially in light of his sudden capitulation to Lois's request that he go to Hill's funeral? Does Lois's suspicion that he is getting nearer the truth stop too soon—has he perhaps figured it out? Is Howard's question to Amy about the man having "gone out of [her] life" what she initially suspects it is, a covert reference to the recently deceased Hill?

George V. Higgins, himself a writer of very artful dialogue, believes that Howard knows about both affairs and "torment[s] his womenfolk by making veiled references designed to keep them constantly on the edge of fear of public humiliation, while lacking the guts to confront either of them or Jack Hill directly" (120–21). Higgins, I believe, is seriously overreading the story here as his leap from conversations in the privacy of their home to possible "public humiliation" indicates.[8] Neither Higgins nor O'Hara provides any evidence of Howard's knowledge equivalent to the pattern of hints O'Hara supplies to confirm Amy's insinuation about Lois's affair with Jack. And if O'Hara wanted us to have a degree of confidence about Howard's knowledge comparable to the one we have about Lois's affair, he could easily have planted such evidence—given Howard a reference to Hill whose veil was more transparent or introduced a revealing discussion between Howard and Amy about whether she was going to the funeral, or something else along those lines. Instead, O'Hara gives us enough evidence to suspect that Howard knows more than Lois and Amy give him credit for, but not enough evidence to confirm our suspicions with anything approaching the confidence we have about Lois's affair with Hill. In this way, he harnesses the power of a limited ambiguity in his deployment of privileged authorial disclosure with respect to Lois and Amy.

The result of O'Hara's rich authorial disclosures through the various conversational disclosures is a very complex and very intriguing family portrait, one which we can see more clearly than any of its subjects. To be sure, the figures of Lois and Amy emerge more clearly and sharply than the figure of Howard, but the overall portrait emphasizes each character's interest in keeping up appearances and the way that interest increases the distance among them. Lois clearly hides the most from the other two, even as she works hardest to manage how they all look to the outside world and retains a sense of her own superiority. Amy is both dependent on her parents and capable of seeing through them. Howard might be either the most put upon or the most devious of the three characters.

At the level of readerly dynamics, we partially sympathize with each family member even as we make some strong negative ethical judgments about each (though any final judgment of Howard must be tentative and provisional given the ambiguity about what he knows). The Ambries are not a family to admire but they are a family that demonstrates not only human frailty but humans' complicated ways of responding to their frailties. Above all, it is a brilliant indirect communication from O'Hara to us.

---

8. Higgins also overreads Lois's role in Amy's affair when he says that "she connived in her daughter's seduction" by Hill.

WORKS CITED

Baroni, Raphaël. *L'œuvre du temps: Poétique de la discordance narrative*. Paris: Seuil, 2009.
Dannenberg, Hilary. *Coincidence and Counterfactuality: Plotting Time and Space in Narrative Fiction*. Lincoln: Univ. of Nebraska Press, 2008.
Higgins, George V. *On Writing: Advice for Those Who Write to Publish (or Would Like To)*. New York: Henry Holt, 1990.
Kafalenos, Emma. *Narrative Causalities*. Columbus: The Ohio State Univ. Press, 2006.
O'Hara, John. "Appearances." In *The Cape Cod Lighter*, 3–14. New York: Random House, 1962.
Phelan, James. "Authorial and Conversational Disclosure in the Dialogue Novel: The Case of *The Friends of Eddie Coyle*." In *Narrative, Interrupted: The Plotless, the Disturbing, and the Trivial in Literature*, edited by Markku Lehtimäki, Laura Karttunen, and Maria Makelä, 3–23. Amsterdam: De Gruyter, 2012.
———. *Experiencing Fiction: Judgments, Progressions, and the Rhetorical Theory of Narrative*. Columbus: The Ohio State Univ. Press, 2007.
———. "Narrative Fiction, the Short Story, and Life: The Case of Tobias Wolff's 'Bullet in the Brain.'" In *Life and Narrative: The Risks and Responsibilities of Storying Experience*, edited by Brian Schiff, Sylvie Patron, and Elizabeth McKim. Oxford: Oxford Univ. Press (in production).
Prince, Gerald. "The Disnarrated." *Style* 21 (1988): 1–8.
Rabinowitz, Peter J. "They Shoot Tigers, Don't They?: Path and Counterpoint in *The Long Goodbye*." In *A Companion to Narrative Theory*, edited by James Phelan and Peter J. Rabinowitz, 181–91. Malden, MA: Blackwell, 2005.
Richardson, Brian. "Beyond the Poetics of Plot: Alternative Forms of Narrative Progression and the Multiple Trajectories of *Ulysses*." In *A Companion to Narrative Theory*, edited by James Phelan and Peter J. Rabinowitz, 167–80. Malden, MA: Blackwell, 2005.
Shklovsky, Victor. *Theory of Prose*. Translated by Benjamin Sher. Normal, IL: Dalkey Archive Press, 1990.
Sternberg, Meir. "Telling in Time (II): Chronology, Teleology, Narrativity." *Poetics Today* 13 (1992): 463–541.
Wolff, Tobias. "Bullet in the Brain." In *Our Story Begins: New and Collected Stories*, 263–68. New York: Knopf, 2008.

CHAPTER 5

Ending Twice Over (Or More)
Alternate Endings in Narrative

EYAL SEGAL

THE ENDING, as is well known, is an especially significant or privileged point (or section) of the narrative sequence, and of sequence in general. This article explores the phenomenon of alternate endings, which might shed some interesting light on the ending's special status. But, first, I would like to place my subject within the framework of a rhetorical (or communicative) and functional perspective.

The majority of narratological approaches—since Aristotle's *Poetics*, in fact—define narrative in mimetic terms, those of represented *action*. Such approaches present many variants, as shown in detail by Meir Sternberg in a recent article, "Narrativity: From Objectivist to Functional Paradigm." There, he surveys a wide spectrum of definitions of narrativity (that is, what constitutes the essence of narrative), starting from the minimalist demand of a single event and examining the addition of various kinds of extras. Such additions include, for example, the single event multiplied into a series, from two upward; causal enchainment of various kinds and degrees; the event chain reinforced by non-narrative patterning, such as thematic threads running through the events or patterns of equivalence; and features that apply to the entire represented world, such as fictionality. But notwithstanding all the variety, the common denominator that underlies all these definitions or approaches is that they are "objectivist," in the sense that they view narrative in terms of the represented object.

In contrast, Sternberg's own approach to narrative defines narrativity not in terms of represented or narrated action, but rather by the effect of the text on our mind, namely, in the rhetorical-communicative terms of *interest* and its processes.[1] This interest is aroused in the reader through the interplay between the two sequences that constitute a narrative text: that of represented events and that of their disclosure along the telling/reading sequence. This interplay creates informational gaps that can be related to any aspect of the represented storyworld; accordingly, Sternberg differentiates among three fundamental types of gap and three corresponding dynamics of narrative interest: those of suspense (or prospection), curiosity (or retrospection), and surprise (or recognition). This differentiation rests on the combination of two basic criteria: (1) To which temporal direction is the reader's interest channeled? That is, does the information withheld from the reader, via gaps, belong to the narrative past or future (always relative to what is perceived at any given point along the textual sequence as the narrative's "present")? (2) Is the reader aware that information is being withheld? In other words, do we know that we do not know? An awareness of not knowing would create an expectation for receiving the missing information. This would result either in *suspense*, if the expectation relates to the narrative future, or in *curiosity*, if it bears on the narrative past. However, if the reader is unaware that an informational gap exists, this gap will become perceptible and operative only when unexpectedly disclosed, thereby creating *surprise*.

It is important to emphasize both the rhetorical-communicative nature of this definition and the functional specificity of narrative that it reveals within this general framework. Let me clarify by way of disagreement with Gerald Prince's claim in the opening chapter of this volume:

> There is no doubt that pragmatic [Prince's use of this term is very close to my use of "rhetorical"] concerns play a role in shaping narrative sequences, that narratives are communicative acts, that evaluative passages emphasizing the pointedness of a narrative give the latter a particular form, or that narrative tension is an important narrative element. However, this does not mean that these concerns represent essential traits of all and only narrative sequences. After all, many communicative acts are not narrative and, unfortunately, too many narratives turn out to be pointless. (Prince 13)

---

1. In addition to the 2010 article mentioned above, see Sternberg "Telling in Time (I)," "Telling in Time (II)," and "How Narrativity Makes a Difference" (the latter presents the relevant ideas in the most succinct manner). See also Pier's contribution to this volume for a comparison between Sternberg's approach to the definition of narrative and Jean-Michel Adam's (objectivist) approach.

I would maintain that being a communicative act *is* an essential trait of narrative; and while it is true that many communicative acts are not narrative, the distinction of the narrative kind lies precisely in the play of suspense, curiosity, and surprise as effects/interests generated (separately or in combination) by the intersequential dynamics described above. Of course, this distinctive trio of master types of interest can further combine and interact with any number of other effects or communicative goals at which a specific narrative might aim.

Most narratological approaches that define narrative first and foremost by the level of represented events also tend to perceive this level as constituting "raw material" for various kinds of aesthetic manipulation on the level of narration. By contrast, relating narrativity to the interest produced by narrative's unique interaction of two sequences—the told and the telling/reading, as just outlined—does not conceptually privilege one of these sequences over the other. It allows us to analyze plots in terms of their structure of interest, in addition to the more common framework of the structure of events (or "action"). Any sequential ordering of events in a text might therefore receive a functional explanation, which makes basic narrative sense in terms of how that ordering is chosen and used to manipulate narrative interest. This is important, since functional explanations of sequential ordering tend to be ad hoc, as when they focus on thematic motivations specific to the text discussed.

Let me also note that the communicative-functional perspective I have outlined does not privilege or downgrade any specific type of narrative. Contrast this with how supposedly simple narratives, based on straight, or "natural," chronological ordering, are often opposed in value and interest to more complex narratives, whose order of telling deviates considerably from the order of represented events. For example, when Gérard Genette treats the issue of "order" in his highly influential *Narrative Discourse* (33–85), his discussion turns almost immediately to the phenomenon of "anachronies," and there it remains, sorting the latter out according to various criteria: he apparently thinks there is nothing interesting to say, from a theoretical viewpoint, about narratives without significant anachronies (at least, in their "main articulations," as he puts it) since they produce no tension, or "friction," between the narrational and the narrated sequences. On the other hand, from a perspective that emphasizes narrative interest and its possible manipulations, such a chronological narrative is, in principle, as legitimate and interesting an object of analysis as any other (e.g., anachronic) narrative type. Very generally, one might say that, among the major types of interest, straight chronological ordering tends to foreground the natural opacity of the future, and thus narrative suspense.

As already mentioned, I would like to focus on endings as an especially significant or perceptible part of the textual sequence and thus of strategic importance to the interplay between the two chronological sequences of narrative and to the structure of interest it produces. The ending constitutes a point to which every stage of the narrative "looks forward" (not for nothing does the word "end" mean also a goal, or a target), and once reached, it provides a crucial retrospective vantage point from which the narrative as a whole may be viewed, understood, and judged as a totality. As Marianna Torgovnick, speaking from the authorial viewpoint, puts it in her study *Closure in the Novel*: "An ending is the single place where an author most pressingly desires to make his points—whether those points are aesthetic, moral, social, political, epistemological, or even the determination not to make any point at all" (19).

I have dealt extensively with narrative endings in the context of the problem of closure—what creates the sense of stable conclusiveness or finality, or, alternatively, avoids or subverts such a sense. (In the latter case, we are talking about "openness"—a polar concept that belongs to the same metaphor or semantic field).[2] Ending and closure are distinct phenomena, but they are also strongly related since, as the text's termination point, the ending clearly plays a crucial role with regard to our ability to determine the nature and degree of the text's closure. The rhetorical-functional conception of interest-based narrativity allows us to define closure as a result of the termination, or resolution, of narrative interest. In other words, the ending of a narrative text as such produces an effect of closure when it brings to a halt the operation of all kinds of narrative interest by filling in all the significant informational gaps that have arisen along the textual sequence. Conversely, narrative "openness" results from significant gaps that remain open—or at least not definitely closed—even at the end of a text. In short, such openness results from permanent gaps. Note that, whereas such a definition of narrative closure (or the conditions for creating it) emerges directly from Sternberg's conception of narrativity, no such definition emerges from the objectivist perspective on narrative as a sequence of events. For the logic of a temporal sequence in itself, although providing an excellent principle of generation—A, then (or therefore) B, and so on—does not imply a termination point.

I would now like to discuss a somewhat related but different phenomenon—that of alternate endings. By this I mean the existence of several endings to the same work: it is a special case of what Genette (*Work of Art* 163–210)

---

2. See Segal "Closure in Detective Fiction," based on a chapter of my 2007 dissertation ("Problem of Narrative Closure").

terms a "plural immanence" of an artwork, namely, its having several versions or textual variants. In alternate versions that involve substantial differences in the narrated world itself—beyond the level of stylistic revisions—the ending is the part that is perhaps the most frequently revised, thus testifying again to its special status within the totality of the work. Among other things, this means that altering the ending can strongly influence the work as a whole even without taking the trouble of meticulously rethinking and rewriting that whole: an intense effect thus arises with relatively little effort. Further, alternative versions of endings are of course a matter of choice: this *or* that. Examining such alternativity in the framework of narrative interest might therefore provide an additional perspective on sequence in narrative, which is usually viewed in terms of the combinatory axis, by highlighting the axis of selection as well.

Whereas a basic definition of the alternate endings phenomenon, as offered above, may be quite clear-cut, drawing its borderlines with regard to specific cases is not always so simple—especially, when do we no longer perceive a single work with several versions, but rather several distinct works? The famous case of the two endings of Charles Dickens's *Great Expectations* might seem rather straightforward: it boils down to a rewriting of a relatively short concluding textual segment. But in some cases, the alteration of the ending is part of a more comprehensive rewriting. Think of Nahum Tate's version of *King Lear*, where the happy ending certainly constitutes one of the most significant revisions but is only a part of a long series of changes: the most notable ones, besides the ending, are the introduction of a love story between Edgar and Cordelia, and the elimination of the fool. Moreover, the revision was not done by the original author, Shakespeare; naturally, this factor would strengthen the tendency to consider Tate's alternate version as a separate work altogether.

Another factor leading to controversial cases might arise in adaptations from one medium to another. For example, Howard Hawks's film *The Big Sleep* features some very significant changes in the ending when compared with the Raymond Chandler novel on which it is based, and these changes are part of a thorough revision of the plot according to Hollywood conventions: can the film and the novel still be considered two versions of the same work?[3] And in the case of adaptations as well, it seems that an identity of the authorial source—for example, in Agatha Christie's own theatrical adaptations of some her detective novels (such as *Ten Little Indians*)—would strengthen the tendency to view the adaptation as an alternate version of the same work.

---

3. On the cinematic adaptation, and especially its ending, as a "re-conventionalized" version of Chandler's subversive novel, see Rabinowitz (235–37).

Therefore, the answer to the question of when we are dealing with versions of the same work and when with distinct works is gradable rather than categorical. A spectrum may be drawn, moving from relatively unproblematic cases of alternate endings of the same work to more problematic and unclear cases, and then to cases that would generally be perceived as something else. Take, for instance, what Lubomír Doležel (199–226) terms "rewrites" of classical works, which have become quite common in postmodernist literature. In the ending of Michel Tournier's *Vendredi ou les limbes du Pacifique*, a rewrite of Daniel Defoe's *Robinson Crusoe*, Robinson chooses to remain on the island, rejecting civilization, whereas Friday—after having converted Robinson to the wild life—departs with the visiting sailors on the English schooner. Here, the alteration of the ending compared with the "source" text is obviously perceived as significant—not, however, as an alternate version of the same text but rather as part of an intertextual dialogue between two distinct texts.[4]

In this context, we newly have to take into account the rhetorical or functional perspective. By defining what we consider to be the main rhetorical purpose or tendency of the ending, we have a useful reference point against which to measure the impact of the changes made; and this measurement goes beyond examining, from a formal viewpoint, the "amount" of changes made between endings which are perceived as variants. Accordingly, what may appear as only relatively small changes in the narrated world may produce in certain cases great changes in the rhetorical effect of the ending and of the text as a whole, and vice versa.

When examining the various circumstances leading to the creation of alternate endings, it turns out very often to be the result of what might be termed postcompletion pressures: the original ending (or the text as a whole) then meets some resistance or a negative response that leads to its modification, either by the author or by someone else. In *Great Expectations*, for example, the original ending was modified to the existing one, which strongly suggests that Pip and Estella will marry. This happened in response to the suggestion of Edward Bulwer-Lytton, whom Dickens apparently considered

---

4. Another interesting ontological issue concerns what Genette terms "partial manifestations" (*Work of Art* 211–29): when one or more of the endings are extant only indirectly, whether because they were never fully executed or because they were destroyed or are otherwise inaccessible. The degree of indirectness can highly vary. To illustrate, compare the case of an author telling only in very general terms of an idea that he or she had for an alternate ending with the original ending of Billy Wilder's film *Double Idemnity*—where the protagonist is put to death in a gas chamber—which survives in the form of a screenplay supplemented by production stills of the scene (according to Naremore).

a reliable representative of the reading public's preferences.[5] Sometimes the author complies with the publisher's demand for changes in order to get the book published, as with *The Floating Opera,* John Barth's first novel, in its first edition of 1956. Interestingly, such a dynamics of revision often results in chronology of publication that is reverse to that of the writing: the earlier, "original" ending is the later one to be published.

The two examples I have just mentioned draw attention to a further interesting variable: the relative status enjoyed by the alternate endings, once the suppressed one becomes known. In the case of the *The Floating Opera,* the (darker) original ending, which was restored in the freely revised 1967 edition,[6] seems to have acquired a canonical status, demoting the revised ending of 1956. On the other hand, the two endings of *Great Expectations* seem to have gained fairly equal status, usually appearing side-by-side in an uneasy coexistence, with the original, "unhappy" ending following the revised, "happy" one in a note or an appendix.

The theater and the cinema, with their different media and processes of production, might provide us with some additional perspectives. In the case of the theater, its nature as an art of performance might be said to operate as a factor that undermines textual stability, since each new performance might, in principle, involve a rewriting. An unfavorable reception of a play, or even the fear of such a reception, can be a strong incentive for such a rewriting, especially of the ending. This was the case, for example, with Henrik Ibsen's *A Doll's House,* when the play was produced in Germany.[7] Ibsen understood that there was reason to fear the publication of another translation or "adaptation" of the play with an altered ending that would probably be preferred by a considerable number of theaters. He then himself altered for the play's German premiere the memorable ending in which Nora slams the door on her husband and children. It was replaced by one in which she does not leave the house; instead, Helmer forces her into the doorway of the sleeping children's nursery, begging her to take pity on them. Nora says she cannot leave them and sinks to the floor, at which point the curtain falls.

Sometimes changes are made independently of the author. They often result from a different aesthetic or ideological outlook than the one behind

---

5. For a detailed and informed discussion of the circumstances in which the two endings of *Great Expectations* were written, as well as a comparison between them and a history of their publication and reception, see Rosenberg.

6. For a comparison between the novel's two versions, see Jordan "A Critical Study" (8–57), or "*The Floating Opera* Restored" (in summary).

7. See Törnqvist (41–42). On some other cases of theatrical endings that were altered by their authors following an unfavorable reception, see chapter 2 in Schmidt (35–61, 155–61).

the original work, and they might become significant in the history of the work's reception. Such is the case with Tate's version of *King Lear*. It systematically transformed the Shakespearean play according to the poetics of late-seventeenth-century Restoration drama and then dominated the stage for more than 150 years, creating a divide between the stage and the print versions of the play that lasted until well into the nineteenth century.[8]

In the cinema, the commercial factor—and thus, considerations pertaining to pleasing the audience—operates most strongly and directly. Therefore, a major role is played by test screenings (or previews), conducted before the film's general release in order to gauge audience reaction; these often lead, in the case of negative feedback, to alterations in the film, with endings being especially vulnerable, for reasons already mentioned. The DVD era has brought an important development regarding reception: alternate endings are usually included within the "special features" or "bonuses" of DVD releases and so become much more accessible to viewing and comparison. Also, because in recent films the DVD edition, with its bonuses, follows closely the distribution via movie theaters (known in the industry as the "theatrical release"), the "original" ending (sometimes along with other alternate endings) tends to resurface much sooner than it used to.[9]

To illustrate in greater detail some of the issues involved, let us now examine the complexities of a specific case, that of Ridley Scott's film *Blade Runner* and its alternate endings. This film has quite an intricate textual history. There are no less than three versions that may be said to feature distinct endings, specifically with regard to how they manipulate narrative interest: the work print, which was shown at test screenings in Dallas and Denver in March 1982; the theatrical release, which opened in the United States later the same year; and the director's cut of 1992.[10] The work print scored rather poorly with the test audiences. The two major criticisms were that the film was confusing and hard to follow, and that it was too grim; many of these critical comments focused

---

8. See, for example, Marsden (where Tate's *King Lear* is used as a major example of a Shakespeare adaptation) and Murray (153–66, 255–61) (which includes a detailed bibliographical survey).

9. For an example of such temporal proximity, see the case of *I Am Legend*, as reported in Billington 2008.

10. Overall, no less than seven versions of the film may be distinguished. In addition to the three mentioned above, there are also the San Diego sneak preview, shown on May 1982; the international cut, shown worldwide in 1982 and later released on video; the television broadcast version, first aired on 1986 (all of them very similar to the U.S. theatrical release); and the "final cut" of 2007, celebrating the film's twenty-fifth anniversary: it makes several changes in the director's cut, since Scott remained somewhat dissatisfied with the latter (but these changes do not go far enough to warrant a separate discussion here). For a meticulous documentation of the history of all these versions and the differences between them, see Sammon.

on the ending.[11] This led to several last-moment changes that were introduced in the theatrical release. Among them, two were the most important: the addition of a voice-over, first-person narration throughout the film (which, besides contributing stylistically to a film-noirish effect, performed a direct explanatory role, facilitating the understanding of the plot), and of a happy ending.

In order to explain the significance of the ending's alteration, let me first outline the film's overall plot dynamics. A major line of interest concerns the suspense generated by the mission forced on the protagonist, Rick Deckard, to track down and "retire" (kill) a group of rebellious replicants. These "replicants" (called "androids" in Philip K. Dick's novel *Do Androids Dream of Electric Sheep?* on which the film is loosely based) are the most advanced model of biologically engineered humanoids. They serve mostly as soldiers and slaves in off-world colonies; some of them have escaped and come to Earth illegally. Deckard's mission to hunt them down is complicated by his developing relations with Rachael, the assistant-secretary of Tyrell, the founder of the corporation that manufactures the replicants. In their first meeting, Rachael is identified by Deckard as an advanced replicant, even though she believes herself to be human. She then follows him to his home in order to dissuade him from believing that she is a replicant, and while mercilessly shattering her illusions about being human, he becomes emotionally attached to her. Later he finds out that Rachael has disappeared, and as an escaped replicant, she is added to his list of targets; at one point, while he is attacked by another replicant, she saves his life. The resolution comes after Deckard's encounter with Roy Batty, the last remaining replicant of those he was originally appointed to hunt down. Batty spares Deckard's life, and then dies himself. Deckard returns to his apartment to find Rachael alive, sleeping in his bed, and leaves with her.

At this point, the differences between the alternate endings come to the fore. The original conclusion of the work print shows the elevator doors closing on Deckard and Rachael, who are leaving Deckard's apartment and making their escape to an uncertain future. Whereas this image of the closing elevator doors "certifies the claustrophobic tone of the rest of the film" (Kerman 38), in the theatrical release, we next see Deckard and Rachael driving through an idyllic rural landscape, which stands in stark contrast to the barren, polluted urban wasteland that visually dominates the film. And while we watch this drive on the screen, Deckard's voice-over informs us that Tyrell has told

---

11. "A significant number of the negative comments also centered around the film's ending," which "climaxed with Ford stepping into his apartment building's elevator toward a waiting Sean Young as the elevator doors closed behind them. Specific objections found this culmination 'too abrupt,' 'unsatisfying,' or 'difficult to understand' (Gaff's tinfoil unicorn proved confusing as well)" (Sammon 289).

him Rachael is a special replicant, because she has no termination date. This information is crucial, since at the beginning of the film we learn that the replicants manufactured by the Tyrell Corporation have a built-in biological fail-safe mechanism—a four-year lifespan with a fixed termination date. This severely limited lifespan is supposed to prevent them from developing traits that are too human[12]; moreover, we learn that the replicants Deckard is hunting down throughout the film have come to Earth precisely in order to have their lifespans extended. Therefore, the information that we receive about Rachael constitutes a final surprise twist that, combined with the "idyllic" sequence as a whole, gives the ending of the film a stronger sense of closure compared with the original work print: it provides a more stable and less gap-ridden view of Deckard and Rachael's future, as well as making their future relations appear more conventionally gratifying. The 1982 theatrical release ends with the words, "I didn't know how long we had together. Who does?"—which, following the information about Rachael having no termination date, underline the similarity between her relationship with Deckard and a fully human relationship. These words also give a sort of upbeat answer to those spoken by Gaff, an employee of the blade runner unit who is following Deckard throughout the film. His words refer to Rachael and are echoed a bit earlier in Deckard's memory: "It's too bad she won't live. But then again, who does?"

The work print was rediscovered by accident in 1990 and shown a few times in theaters, this time eliciting a very enthusiastic response, which encouraged the release of the "director's cut" in 1992. Compared with the work print, the director's cut includes various elements that Scott considered technical improvements; but with regard to the two major changes noted above, which most clearly distinguish the theatrical release from the work print, the director's cut restores the decisions made in the earlier version, which Scott considered a better representation of his original intention. Accordingly, both the voice-over narration and the final, tacked-on pastoral sequence were deleted. But this is not all. The director's cut includes a further change that significantly affects the ending, even though it does not appear in the ending itself—to the extent of creating what might be seen as a third version, rather than merely a restoration of the "original." This change is based on new footage: Scott added a twelve-second scene in the middle of the film (part of footage that was filmed during postproduction in 1982), which shows a silvery white unicorn galloping in slow motion through a forest. This sequence is

---

12. This includes complex emotions, specifically empathy, which is supposedly the crucial mark that should allow one to distinguish humans from even the most advanced replicants; hence, empathy's major role in the "Voigt-Kampff test," which we see conducted for this purpose twice in the film.

inserted into a scene where Deckard is shown hanging drunkenly over his piano and plinking on it—after Rachael has fled his apartment—and thus tends to be perceived as subjective, reflecting Deckard's dream or reverie. Even though this inserted sequence is quite short,[13] it has a major impact on the understanding of the film because of the retrospective significance it acquires in the ending. When Deckard and Rachael leave Deckard's apartment for the last time, Rachael's shoe knocks over a very small, silver, tinfoil origami-folded unicorn, which Deckard then picks up to inspect. This unicorn indicates that Gaff had been there, because his trademark throughout the film is leaving origami paper-folding sculptures. In the earlier film versions, which did not include the inserted unicorn sequence, the key to the meaning of the origami unicorn seemed to reside only in the metaphoric or symbolic realm.[14] However, with the added unicorn-reverie sequence, the appearance of the origami unicorn takes on a directly plot-related significance[15]: it comes to signal that Gaff might be privy to Deckard's innermost thoughts, and therefore that Deckard himself might be a replicant, whose file has been inspected by Gaff. This is analogous to Deckard showing himself earlier in the film, just before the piano scene, to be privy to Rachael's innermost consciousness. He reveals his knowledge of two childhood memories of hers: playing doctor with her brother and watching a spider being eaten by the baby spiders it hatched. Deckard explains to Rachael that, like most of her "memories," these are not genuine but rather implants, based on the memories of Tyrell's niece.

The possibility that Gaff has access to Deckard's consciousness, just as Deckard has to Rachael's, and therefore that Deckard, the replicant hunter, is himself a replicant, clearly carries a major thematic significance in this film, which to a large extent revolves around the question of what constitutes the human.[16] Whereas the 1982 theatrical version ends by bringing the relation-

---

13. In the final cut of 2007, it becomes longer and more prominent—with Deckard clearly shown to be awake—and intercutting twice between his face and the image of the galloping unicorn.

14. Here is an example of such an interpretation, from an article written before the release of the director's cut: "The silver unicorn ... is the replicant woman with whom Deckard is in love. It is a *made* thing, a piece of human handiwork, beautiful and fragile and glittering, yet perceived as *waste*, thrown down and trodden upon, easily destroyed" (Warner 179; original emphases).

15. The origami, indicating Gaff's presence in Deckard's apartment, allows the important, plot-related inference that the former has decided to spare Rachael's life; but without the connection to the unicorn-reverie sequence, this still would not explain why Gaff chose to leave an origami in the shape of a *unicorn*.

16. For some interesting discussions of this theme, see the chapter "Replicants and Mental Life" in Bukatman (64–86); Barad; Knight and McKnight; and the chapter "Being Human" in Shanahan (22–42). They all bring up, in one way or another, the erosion of the difference

ship between Rachael (with no fixed termination date) and Deckard as close as possible to a human one, the director's cut does not give Rachael the said reprieve and introduces the possibility that Deckard himself is a replicant; it thus ends on a much more disturbing, as well as ambiguous, note. Here we can see a final surprise twist as well, comparable to the one produced by the information about Rachael given at the end of the 1982 version, but used for a very different purpose or effect. It operates to weaken closure rather than strengthen it, since the gap that suddenly emerges (or is, at least, highlighted), this time about Deckard's past, remains open (or at least not unambiguously closed), thereby producing unresolved curiosity, in turn.[17]

As already noted, the creation of alternate endings is very often meant to address an initial resistance or a negative response from the public. So it should come as no surprise that, in certain important respects, the direction in which the original ending is revised is quite consistent. Two tendencies stand out: (1) an unhappy ("downer") ending is replaced by a more upbeat variant; (2) a less conventional ending is replaced by a more conventional one—for example, by a revised ending that is less open or less ambiguous, or geared to more orthodox values. All of the examples I have mentioned thus far (*Great Expectations*, Tate's *King Lear*, *The Floating Opera*, *A Doll's House*, *Blade Runner*, the cinematic adaptation of *The Big Sleep*) seem to display both tendencies.[18] And since aesthetic criteria commonly prefer art to be gloomy and unconventional, no wonder that the original endings usually get more critical acclaim than the revised ones, especially since they are also commonly perceived as closer to the authors' intentions.

---

between humans and replicants throughout the film: the behavior of humans is "machine-like," while replicants gradually emerge as "more human than human" (in Tyrell's words).

17. Ridley Scott has stated on several occasions that Deckard is definitely a replicant, but the film's reception history indicates that the issue is highly contentious and cannot be easily resolved. The 2007 five-disc collector's edition of *Blade Runner* interestingly reflects this situation: "The documentary on Disc 4, discussing Deckard's possible replicant identity, offers Scott's interpretation but also invites many other readings, including those of Harrison Ford—who played Deckard as a human and maintains this interpretation—Joanna Cassidy; Rutger Hauer; Paul M. Sammon, author of *Future Noir;* the director Frank Darabont; and Jovanka Vuckovic, editor of *Rue Morgue* magazine. Scott may chuckle, 'If you don't get it, you're a moron,' but many other voices, of comparable cultural status, are placed in dialogue with his own" (Brooker 84). On the inconclusive nature of the evidence regarding Deckard's identity as a human or a replicant, see also Shanahan (15–18, 185–86n15). At any rate, even if Deckard's replicant identity is perceived in itself as clear and unambiguous, it raises retrospectively many disturbing questions about earlier parts of the film.

18. The director's cut of *Blade Runner* goes in the opposite direction, of course, but as I have noted, it is largely a reversion to the first ending, that of the work print. For further demonstrations of this dynamics of revision, see Christen on the alternate endings of Alfred Hitchcock's *Topaz* and Adrian Lyne's *Fatal Attraction*.

The two tendencies I have mentioned—toward happiness and conventionality in revision—are often related, but sometimes they diverge or even clash. An interesting case in point is Johann Wolfgang von Goethe's play *Stella* (written in 1775, his *Sturm und Drang* period, which also produced *The Sorrows of Young Werther*). Fernando has deserted both his wife Cäcilie and his mistress Stella. Several years later, by a series of coincidences, he meets them both at the same place and feels that he has to choose between them. The emotional claims of both women upon him, however, are so carefully balanced that choosing one feels like doing a great injustice to the other. This conflict is finally resolved by Cäcilie, who narrates the tale of a medieval Count who joined one of the Crusades, was captured, and returned to his wife with the Muslim woman who had freed him from her father's prison. The grateful wife accepts the other woman as her marital equal, and they all live happily ever after. The tale's moral is quickly accepted by the characters on stage, and the play ends with both women embracing Fernando, exclaiming, "We are yours!" As might be expected, the play generated some heated controversy,[19] and thirty years later when *Stella* was to be performed at Weimar, Goethe decided to defuse this controversy by revising the ending. While Cäcilie narrates her parable, Stella takes poison, whereupon Fernando shoots himself. So in this case, greater conventionality goes together with a "downer" ending: although tragic in character, this ending is much more in line with monogamous morality, whereas the original ending, which culminated in a celebration of love, did so in a surprising—even shocking—manner that might be said to reflect an unabashed male wish fulfillment, subverting prevailing social codes and ethical standards.

In general, when we consider the replacement of less conventional by more conventional endings, the type of (un)conventionality involved can vary. The comparison between the different endings can therefore illuminate the range of conventions (aesthetic, ethical, or otherwise) that operate in the relevant context by identifying the conventions whose undermining is perceived as disturbing in the original ending. Note that within the rhetorical-functional perspective on narrative that I have outlined, following Sternberg, any operative convention (or system of conventions) may be viewed—just like an event or any other narrative world-element—as a means of achieving the fundamental rhetorical end of manipulating and controlling narrative interest. (For

---

19. Part of the controversy was manifested in alternate endings produced by the critics. Several sequels to the play were written at the time, ranging from a single ("sixth") act to a whole play, in which Goethe's ending was adjusted to conform to more socially acceptable behavior (as documented by Schmidt 49, 158).

example, observance of a convention could then be explained as regulating suspense, or a breach of a convention as producing surprise.)

Finally, there is an interesting relation between the phenomenon of alternate endings and that of multiple endings *within* the same text, which is typical of postmodernist aesthetics.[20] Of course, given a linear text, it cannot really feature multiple endings if "ending" is understood in the strict sense of a final textual segment. The narrator of John Fowles's *The French Lieutenant's Woman* (one of the best-known examples of a multiple ending) admits it when he declares his intention to provide Charles and Sarah's story with two endings, so as to avoid "fixing the fight" (409) in favor of a modern or a Victorian poetics. He acknowledges that he cannot give both versions at once—only one will necessarily acquire the status of the "truly final" version. But which one? As a solution, the narrator decides to toss a coin in order to determine the order of the two endings, but of course, this only underlines the conscious and nonrandom nature of the choice that we tend to assume Fowles, the author, makes. (He chooses to end in the "modern," rather than the Victorian-like, way.) Besides the possible thematic significance of such a choice, the very fact that the author has to make it—whichever way, random or nonrandom— is crucial. Unlike the alternate endings I have been discussing, when multiple (and alternative) endings constitute part of the same text, they do not replace each other: their effect stems precisely from their coexistence within the same sequence, and from the manner in which the later ending(s) in the sequence reopen and/or reclose the development of narrative interest that was reached in the earlier ending(s).

But I believe that the similarity between the two phenomena should not be completely downplayed either. Both create multiplicity at a point that is one of the most salient at any text's structure, providing a significant metanarrative dimension to the work by making us reflect on the nature of the ending and its influence on the narrative as a whole; and the unintentional, or unplanned, nature of the process by which alternate endings usually come to exist, with its suggestion of randomness, might even intensify this effect. The image of a work with alternate endings comes to reside, at least to a certain extent, in the totality of these endings and the different options or perspectives they provide. On a higher level yet, this problematizes the sometimes too-facile notion of the artwork as an "organic whole," in which every detail is necessary and irreplaceable.

---

20. On multiple endings within the same text, see Richardson ("Endings in Drama and Performance" 190–91; "Unusual and Unnatural Narrative Sequences" in this volume (173–74).

WORKS CITED

Barad, Judith. "*Blade Runner* and Sartre: The Boundaries of Humanity." In *The Philosophy of Neo-Noir*, edited by Mark T. Conrad, 21–34. Lexington: Univ. Press of Kentucky, 2007.
Billington, Alex. "Must Watch: *I Am Legend*'s Original Ending—This Is Amazing." Last modified March 5, 2008. URL: http://www.firstshowing.net/2008/must-watch-i-am-legends-original-ending-this-is-amazing.
Brooker, Will. "All Our Variant Futures: The Many Narratives of *Blade Runner: The Final Cut*." *Popular Communication* 7 (2009): 79–91.
Bukatman, Scott. *Blade Runner*. London: British Film Institute, 1997.
Christen, Thomas. "Mehr als ein Ende: Wie Filme zu verschiedenen Schlüssen kommen." *Montage/Av* 12, no. 2 (2003): 155–68.
Doležel, Lubomír. *Heterocosmica: Fiction and Possible Worlds*. Baltimore: Johns Hopkins Univ. Press, 1998.
Fowles, John. *The French Lieutenant's Woman*. London: Vintage, 2004 (1969).
Genette, Gérard. *Narrative Discourse*. Translated by Jane E. Lewin. Ithaca, NY: Cornell Univ. Press, 1980.
———. *The Work of Art: Immanence and Transcendence*. Translated by G. M. Goshgarian. Ithaca, NY: Cornell Univ. Press, 1997.
Jordan, Enoch P. "A Critical Study of the Textual Variants in John Barth's Novels: *The Floating Opera, The End of the Road,* and *The Sot-Weed Factor*." PhD diss., Univ. of Oklahoma, 1974.
———. "*The Floating Opera* Restored." *Critique* 18, no. 2 (1976): 5–16.
Kerman, Judith B. "Post-Millenium *Blade Runner*." In *The Blade Runner Experience: The Legacy of a Science Fiction Classic*, edited by Will Brooker, 31–39. London: Wallflower Press, 2005.
Knight, Deborah, and George McKnight. "What Is It to Be Human? *Blade Runner* and *Dark City*." In *The Philosophy of Science Fiction Film*, edited by Steven M. Sanders, 21–37. Lexington: Univ. Press of Kentucky, 2008.
Marsden, Jean I. *The Re-Imagined Text: Shakespeare, Adaptation, and Eighteenth-Century Literary Theory*. Lexington: Univ. Press of Kentucky, 1995.
Murray, Barbara A. *Restoration Shakespeare: Viewing the Voice*. Madison, NJ: Fairleigh Dickinson Univ. Press, 2001.
Naremore, James. "Making and Remaking of *Double Indemnity*." *Film Comment* 32, no. 1 (1996): 22–31.
Rabinowitz, Peter J. "Rats behind the Wainscoting: Politics, Convention, and Chandler's *The Big Sleep*." *Texas Studies in Literature and Language* 22 (1980): 224–45.
Richardson, Brian. "Endings in Drama and Performance: A Theoretical Model." In *Current Trends in Narratology*, edited by Greta Olson, 181–99. Berlin: de Gruyter, 2011.
Rosenberg, Edgar. "Putting an End to *Great Expectations*." In *Great Expectations (A Critical Edition)*, edited by Edgar Rosenberg, 491–527. New York: W. W. Norton, 1999.
Sammon, Paul M. *Future Noir: The Making of Blade Runner*. 2nd ed. London: Gollancz, 2007.
Schmidt, Henry J. *How Dramas End: Essays on the German "Sturm und Drang," Büchner, Hauptmann, and Fleisser*. Ann Arbor: Univ. of Michigan Press, 1992.
Segal, Eyal. "Closure in Detective Fiction." *Poetics Today* 31 (2010): 153–215.
———. "The Problem of Narrative Closure: How Stories Are (Not) Finished" [in Hebrew]. PhD diss., Tel Aviv Univ., 2007.
Shanahan, Timothy. *Philosophy and Blade Runner*. Basingstoke: Palgrave Macmillan, 2014.
Sternberg, Meir. "How Narrativity Makes a Difference." *Narrative* 9 (2001): 115–22.
———. "Narrativity: From Objectivist to Functional Paradigm." *Poetics Today* 31 (2010): 507–659.
———. "Telling in Time (I): Chronology and Narrative Theory." *Poetics Today* 11 (1990): 901–48.

———. "Telling in Time (II): Chronology, Teleology, Narrativity." *Poetics Today* 13 (1992): 463–541.
Torgovnick, Marianna. *Closure in the Novel*. Princeton, NJ: Princeton Univ. Press, 1981.
Törnqvist, Egil. *Ibsen: A Doll's House*. Cambridge: Cambridge Univ. Press, 1995.
Warner, Rebecca. "A Silver-Paper Unicorn." In *Retrofitting Blade Runner: Issues in Ridley Scott's Blade Runner and Philip K. Dick's Do Androids Dream of Electric Sheep?* Edited by Judith B. Kerman, 178–84. Bowling Green, OH: Bowling Green State Univ. Popular Press, 1991.

CHAPTER 6

Virtualities of Plot and the Dynamics of Rereading

RAPHAËL BARONI

> Concerning the reality of the novel, it is only one of the possible realities. It is not essential, it is fortuitous, and contains other possibilities.
>
> —Bakhtin 470–71, m.t.[1]

AS ILLUSTRATED in the two previous chapters, by linking the dynamics of plot with the "inferential walks" (Eco 31) of a reader progressing gropingly through an unknown text, new conceptualizations of narrative sequence have helped to highlight a rhetorical dimension that was previously left out of account in formalist and structuralist paradigms. However, these new perspectives seem to imply that there is a limitation to the "textual force" of the plot: considered not as a textual structure but rather as a dynamic representation of the storyworld, the interest of the plot might be altered when the reading is reiterated, a situation that will be called here *repetition*.[2] Basing my reflections on an analysis of the Passion according to Mark, a narrative whose outcome is well known by most readers, my aim is to show that it is possible to describe the existence of a lasting *narrative tension* based on explicit virtualities associated with value-laden hypotheses formulated by characters, such as unfulfilled promises or impossible hopes.

---

1. "m.t." means "my translation."
2. In this chapter, unlike James Phelan but like Hilary Dannenberg, I always consider plot in its dynamic aspect, and therefore, synonymous with "narrative progression."

FROM FORMAL TO DYNAMIC CONCEPTIONS OF PLOT

The links between the virtualities of the *fabula* and the dynamics of reading were generally neglected in formalist and structuralist theories. In these models, the objective description of the *fabula*'s immanent features overlooked the alternative possible worlds that readers project as they progress through the narrative. As early as 1973, Claude Bremond criticized Propp's *Morphology*, drawing attention to the risk of missing the true interest of stories when focusing exclusively on the actual course of events:

> Even if the hero always wins, and even if the listener knows this outcome in advance and demands it, this victory has dramatic interest only to the degree that the chances of failure, in competition with the strong finality of the story, manage to keep the listener holding his breath until the end of the fight. (21, m.t.)

However, instead of exploring the many ways narratives articulate virtualities in the actual course of the *fabula*, structuralists and formalists mostly retained from his model the idea that every well-formed story is supposed to follow a three-step development: a complication, followed by a development, and leading toward a resolution. Nevertheless, since the mid-seventies, the virtualities of the *fabula* came under scrutiny again, along with the rise of reception theories and the introduction of "possible worlds theory," imported from modal logic.[3] In 1979, Eco distinguished between three kinds of "possible worlds" that can be related to narratives: (1) the possible world(s) asserted by the fiction; (2) the possible worlds shaped in the mind of the characters belonging to the *fabula*; (3) the possible worlds inferred by readers while they progress through the text. While Eco was mainly concerned with the cognitive dimension of the reader's "inferential walks," Peter Brooks, adopting a psychoanalytic framework inspired by Freud's theory, explored the "desire that carries us forward, onward, through the text" (37), thus incorporating the emotional dimension of narrative experience that was previously occulted in formalist paradigms:

> I think we do well to recognize the existence of textual force, and that we can use such a concept to move beyond the static models of much formalism, toward a dynamics of reading and writing. (47)

The dynamics of reading is also a central issue in rhetorical models, especially in the works of Meir Sternberg and James Phelan. The latter made a decisive move by exploring the links between "progression" and "narrative interest":

---

3. For precursors of this evolution in 1975 and 1977, see Pavel and also Vaina.

> Progression, as I use the term, refers to a narrative as a dynamic event, one that must move, in both its telling and its reception, through time. In examining progression, then, we are concerned with how authors generate, sustain, develop, and resolve reader's interests in narrative. (15)

More recently, with the rise of narratological models influenced by the cognitive sciences, David Herman stressed the fact that "the interest and complexity of narrative depends on the merely probabilistic, not deterministic, links between some actions and events" (94). In the same line of reasoning, Hilary Dannenberg comes to the conclusion that

> the spice of the tale lies in the emergence of one actual story version which in the course of the narrative has to vie for supremacy over other alternatives.... An analysis of a narrative's story tells us very little about the true dynamics of plot and about the fascination of fictional worlds for the reader; this stems from the fact that narrative does not simply tell one story, but weaves a rich, ontologically multidimensional fabric of alternate possible worlds. ("Ontological Plotting" 160)

Thus, while underlining the polysemy of the notion, Hilary Dannenberg insists on the interaction between an "ontologically unstable matrix of possibilities" that represents "plot in its still unresolved aspect" and the progression of a reader driven by the "*cognitive desire* to be in possession of the second aspect of plot—the final configuration achieved at narrative closure when (the reader hopes) a coherent and definitive constellation of events will have been achieved" (*Coincidence and Counterfactuality* 13).

In my own model (see *La tension narrative*), I have built on rhetorical and cognitive models to define "narrative tension" as the dynamic aspect of plot, encompassing the effects of *curiosity* and *suspense* as distinguished by Todorov[4] and Sternberg. More precisely, I consider narrative tension to be the uncertain anticipation of a possible resolution in the form either of a *prognosis* or a *diagnosis*, both of which are based on cotextual information and intertextual and/or actional scenarios stored in the memory of the reader. The engagement of the reader in this process of anticipation is elicited by "textual reluctance," that is, the deferring of narrative information concerning the nature of the action

---

4. "We realize here that two kinds of interest exist. The first can be called *curiosity*, it works from effects to causes: starting from a certain effect (a corpse and some clues), we must find its cause (the culprit and what drove him to the crime). The second form is *suspense* and it works from causes to effects: first we are introduced to the causes, initial data (some gangsters who prepare mischief), and our interest is elicited by the expectation of what will happen, in other words, the effects (corpses, crimes, clashes)" (Todorov 60, m.t.).

told or its future development. In addition, I associate the cataphoric function of the *nœud* with the elicitation of narrative tension, and the anaphoric function of the denouement with its resolution. Thus, like Dannenberg, I consider plot to be an "ontologically unstable matrix of possibilities" in relation to the progression of the reader in the text, and the final configuration of the *fabula* is only one possible final stage of this dynamic process.

In this rapid overview, we see that the notions of *fabula, sequence,* and *plot* have evolved considerably since the formalist period: in some models, plot is no longer considered a fixed attribute of representation[5] but rather a constantly evolving configuration of events that determines the interest of the story and that, in return, is determined by the progression of the reader through the narrative representation. Emma Kafalenos, in her reinterpretation of the Proppian sequence, insists on this important shift:

> By assigning the construction of *fabula* to perceivers (including readers), I open the possibility not only of comparing individual perceivers' *fabulas* but of directly addressing the instability of a *fabula* as it grows and changes during individual perceivers' process of perception. (37)

The different models I have mentioned also suggest that the "textual force" of a plot—its narrative tension—is influenced by the number of virtualities, their predictability, and/or their relative importance, which can be sketched at different stages of the story, turning the narrative highway into a labyrinth or, to use the Borgesian metaphor, a "garden of forking paths."[6] The importance of virtualities and contingencies led Johanne Villeneuve to renew the repertoire of metaphors that can be used to refer to the notion of plot:

> To address the paradigm of plot, we should turn not to the metaphor of the room, but to that of the forest as it appears to those who get lost into it: a labyrinth with paths intertwined, a prison open on an infinite sky, streaked with branches and multiple paths. In the middle of the forest, the story is no longer an object the researcher contemplates from a distance or the celebrated triumph of Aristotelian concordance over Augustinian discordance. In the midst of plots, the story leaves something still going: breath, wind, rumor. The meaning of plot determines these circuits on which narrative imagination runs. (53, m.t.)

---

5. This conception, based on the dichotomy content/form, can be associated with what Passalacqua and Pianzola consider an "objectivist paradigm" (see the last chapter of this volume).

6. I have discussed this metaphor in "The Garden of Forking Paths."

THE PARADOX OF SUSPENSE AND THE ENDURING VIRTUALITIES OF THE PLOT

In theories that distance themselves from formalism, the dynamics of plot requires the temporal immersion of a reader who infers possible developments of the story through a process of trial and error. Thus, we must focus on "plot in its still unresolved aspect," linked to an ideally virginal progression in the narrative representation. Of course, this progression is informed by intertextual knowledge and by co-text, which configure a horizon of expectations and sets milestones in a forest of countless possibilities.[7] But it is also a reading process that hesitates at the crossroads because each story is unique and because we suspect that some attractive pathways are deceptive, while unlikely alternatives might become actual. Consequently, ignorance about "what is to come" is short lived: narrative tension—the power of stories to *intrigue* us—is condemned to wane over time while the narrative path is not explored by an adventurer anymore but paced up and down by a Sunday walker or a professional topographer.

Yet while narrative tension seems fundamentally linked to uncertainty, many critics acknowledge a seemingly paradoxical phenomenon: readers may experience suspense even after multiple readings of a narrative. This phenomenon can be observed not only in children who are moved over and again by the fate of the Valiant Little Tailor, even after hearing his adventures for the hundredth time, but also in adults who compulsively reread (or view again) their favorite stories with unabated passion. Robert Yanal summarizes the paradox of suspense as follows:

(i) repeaters experience suspense regarding a certain narrative's outcome;
(ii) repeaters are certain of what that outcome is;
(iii) suspense requires uncertainty. (148)

Several conflicting proposals have been put forth to explain this paradox.[8] For Walton, resistance to suspense is due primarily to the immersion process that causes us to forget on a fictional plane what we know on a factual plane. Gerrig ("Suspense in the Absence of Uncertainty") claims that, when immersed in

---

7. As stated by Michael Toolan, "There are, one must recognize, broad extratextual forms of textual guidance beside the guidance 'in' the text" (109). On the importance of intertextual configurations related to abductive reasoning by the reader, see Pier ("Narrative Configurations").

8. See, for example, the discussion between Robert Yanal and Richard Gerrig ("Is There a Paradox of Suspense?"). For a more complete overview on this paradox, see also Ryan (*Narrative as Virtual Reality* 140–63) and Baroni (*La tension narrative* 253–56 and 279–95).

the story, the repeater expects that the fictional world will operate according to the same laws as the real world in which no event is repeated twice. Yanal, in contrast, thinks that true repeaters are very rare and that suspense in repetition is primarily due to some details being forgotten or to a confusion between real suspense and another kind of narrative interest.

I think we can deepen our understanding of this paradox by exploring two hypotheses: (1) *pathos* will be more enduring when it is associated with specific value-laden virtualities, leading, for example, to a contradiction between the reader's knowledge concerning the storyline and a better alternative he desires for the hero; (2) unactualized virtualities remain in force, especially when they are explicitly mentioned by the characters of the *fabula*, thus becoming what Gerald Prince coined as "disnarrated" events.

EMOTIONAL IMMERSION AND VALUE-LADEN HYPOTHESIS

I think that we can agree with Yanal on at least one point: even though some suspenseful situations prove to be surprisingly enduring, narrative tension can change over time in intensity and even in nature. For example, many narratologists agree on the fact that *curiosity* (or what Marie-Laure Ryan describes as a "who" suspense[9]) is less resilient than *suspense*. For example, in a *whodunit* story we might not suspect an innocent, since we know who the culprit is. Other virtualities, however, remain readable and continue to produce their effects: for example, we can always hope for an alternative when an innocent character dies after being unjustly suspected.

On the other hand, Gerrig and Walton are probably right when they insist on the importance of immersion. For Ryan,[10] "Temporal immersion is the reader's involvement in the process by which the progression of narrative time distills the field of the potential, selecting one branch as the actual, confining the others to the realm of the forever virtual, or counterfactual, and as a result of this selection, continually generates new ranges of virtualities" (*Narrative as Virtual Reality* 141). While experience in temporal immersion must be affected by repetition,[11] Ryan argues that "emotional immersion" makes situations present in the mind; therefore, "it does not matter whether the envisioned state of

---

9. *Narrative as Virtual Reality* 144.
10. See also Noël Carroll.
11. By "repetition" I mean the reiterated experience of the same narrative, or, more generally, a narrative experience related to a predictable story.

affairs is true or false, and its development known or unknown, because simulation makes it temporarily true and present, and from the point of view of the present, the future has not happened" (*Narrative as Virtual Reality* 156). Emotional immersion, associated with feelings of empathy or sympathy for the fate the characters, therefore becomes an essential ingredient in order for suspense to endure. Based on this hypothesis, William Brewer, who conducted empirical studies on this phenomenon, comes to the conclusion that if suspense "is assumed to be based on reader uncertainty, then it should be eliminated on a second reading because the reader will no longer be uncertain about the underlying event sequence. However, if suspense is based on the reader's concern for the plight of the character, then it should show little or no reduction during a rereading" (123). Along the same line, José Prieto-Pablos explains that a spectator plunged into the course of a tragedy continues to articulate desired alternatives despite the predictability of the events:

> So, for example, in our response to the suspense situation prior to a tragic dénouement (e.g., in Hamlet's fight with Laertes), we know that the protagonist will die, also that he *must* die, in application of the principles both of tragic resolution and poetic justice, as he has committed at least one crime for which he must pay with his life. We are probably familiar with these principles, and yet *we do not want him to die*. Suspense is held as long as we can build up hypotheses which feature him succeeding against the final obstacles—as long, therefore, as the author keeps placing obstacles for him to overcome and postponing the fatal moment. (106)

Nevertheless, in connection with the irreversible nature of temporal immersion, we can make the assumption that the number and nature of virtualities can change over time. For example, we might not consider all the possible ways the protagonist could have won his fight, since we know *how* he lost, but we can still dream of a happier ending: In addition, while the nature of our engagement might change over time, when hope or fear of several possibilities is replaced by the exploration of a single counterfactual alternative, this doesn't necessarily result in a decrease in the intensity of the plot, since, as Ryan argues, the *climax* of many stories is reached when we are confronted with the "imminent resolution of a binary alternative" (*Narrative as Virtual Reality* 143). In conclusion, suspense could be maintained in repetition because even if the virtualities are reduced in number and transformed in nature, our emotional engagement in the fate of the character still pushes us to articulate desired alternatives that come into contradiction with the known resolution of the story.

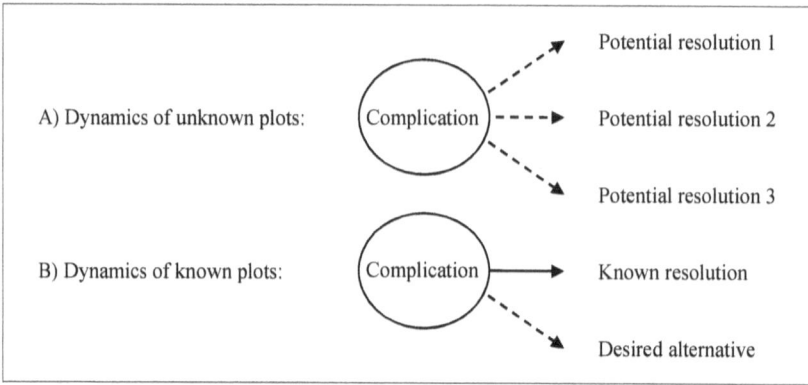

FIGURE 6.1. Dynamics of known and unknown plot

Does this mean that suspense is more enduring in tragedies than in adventure stories with happy endings? The passion manifested by children who listen to the same fairy tale frequently seems to contradict this view, although it must be admitted that this audience is quite particular. While children live in a new and ever-changing world whose routines are still to be learned, they tend to seek in fictions a comforting alternative to the constant challenge of daily experience, as though a story were the actualization of a script.[12] Adults, on the contrary, mostly find pleasure in suspense or in tragic stories, because fictions represent a way of escaping daily routines and/or a simulation designed to cope with dramatic events they might encounter in real life.[13]

In any case, the opposition between *knowledge* and *desired alternative* highlights an important aspect of enduring suspense that must be linked to a modal analysis of value-laden virtualities. This question has emerged in reflections on possible worlds semantics, especially in the works of Lubomír Doležel (*Heterocosmica*) and Ryan ("From Parallel Universes to Possible Worlds"), and it has been discussed lately by Daniel Candel Bormann, who advocates a "model that allows us to move from neutrality to value" (180). Candel Bormann identifies three main modalities: *alethic, deontic,* and *axiological*:

> It is certainly possible to subject the world of a text to a full modal analysis in which every operator is taken into account. In the case of the alethic

---

12. For a contextual definition of eventfulness, see Hühn in this volume.

13. For a more complete description of the distinction between "*suspense by contradiction*" and "recall" ("*rappel*"), see my *La tension narrative* 254–55 and 279–95. According to Eco, some adults might also enjoy the pleasure of repetition in popular culture, as discussed in the following article.

modality, this would include the operators "necessity," "possibility," and "impossibility"; in that of the deontic modality, there will figure "obligation," "permission," and "prohibition"; and in applying the axiological modality, the terms "positive," "indifferent," and "negative" will play their roles. (187)

In our case, the alethic modality of a desired alternative highlights the *impossible* nature of our projection, since we know that what happens in the story (what has already been read) cannot be changed; however, deontic and axiological modalities remain fundamental sources for fueling the "cognitive desire" of this *impossible world*, because our desire is grounded in social norms and in the feeling that some virtualities represent better or worse versions of reality. For example, transgressions necessarily entail the deontic exploration of what would have happened if the character had respected his obligations. Similarly, we can refer to the axiological modality in order to determine whether an alternative subworld might represent a better or worse version of the storyworld asserted by the fiction, and therefore, perhaps a more desirable alternative for the character.

EXPLICIT ALTERNATIVES SKETCHED BY CHARACTERS

If we admit that suspense that endures involves value-laden alternatives opposed to the known course of events, and if we admit that readers don't make the same "inferential walks" when they are dealing with known or unknown narratives, then there is a new problem to be solved: what are those *always-readable alternatives* whose effect remains over time? Among these alternatives, we can note that it is not uncommon for some of them to be presented explicitly by narrative discourse. Prince has proposed to extend the existing terminology for describing the temporal structures of narratives in order to include alternatives:[14]

> Some textual factors ... relate to different *moods* that the text brings into play and, especially, to the *alternarrated* or *disnarrated* (as well as its questioning or its denial), in other words to the virtualities explicitly designated by the text, to the opportunities that have remained or will probably remain unfulfilled and whose ordinary model is: "This could have happened, but in the end it never did"; or "This might (or might not) happen instead of that";

---

14. In his first essay on the subject (in 1988), Prince distinguishes three categories of negation in narrative. In two of them (the "unnarratable" and the "unnarrated"), elements of the fictional world are not included in the narration. The "disnarrated," by contrast, includes narrated elements that are not actualized in the fictional world.

or even "If only x could happen instead of y." . . . In the words of Claude Bremond, criticizing the teleological orientation of the Proppian system, it is difficult to tell the story of Hercules at the crossroads without letting him explore, in his imagination, one or the other direction. (Prince, "Périchronismes et temporalité narrative" 15, m.t.)

For Prince, the "disnarrated" can be either (1) an unrealized possibility imagined or evoked by a character; (2) a forking path in the realm of the possible outlined by the narrator; or (3) a narrative possibility that was not chosen by the creator of the textual universe but which is mentioned by some kind of authorial voice. Ryan has proposed a different way of dealing with virtualities. She is not concerned with the problem of describing all kinds of virtualities expressed by narrative discourse but rather with showing that the "tellability" of a story "is rooted in conceptual and logical complexity" and consequently that it "depends on an underlying system of purely virtual embedded narratives" (*Possible Worlds* 156). These "embedded narratives" are described as "story-like constructs contained in the private worlds of characters":

> These constructs include not only the dreams, fictions, and fantasies conceived or told by characters, but any kind of representation concerning past or future states or events: plans, passive projections, desires, beliefs. . . . Among these embedded narratives, some reflect the events of the factual domain, while others delineate unactualized possibilities. (Possible Worlds 156)

In contrast to Prince's theory, virtualities like dreams, plans, or desires can be actualized later or not, and they can be explicit as well as remain implicit. Also, Ryan "admits counterfactual worlds into this category only if they are a product of the speculative activity of a character" (Dannenberg, "Ontological Plotting" 172). Thus "embedded narratives," as understood by Ryan, fully belong to the *storyworld* and can be more or less objectively reconstructed by readers based on their knowledge about the semantic properties of actions in real and in fictional worlds. Even when the reader does not understand what the intention of a character is, he knows that the character *must* have a plan when he is acting and that this plan will be realized or fail.

Disnarrations and *embedded narratives* represent two useful heuristic tools, especially when they are combined, because they can be considered as always readable manifestations of meaningful tensions between the actual storyline and the multiple alternatives in the *fabula*. Indeed, being explicit, disnarrations remain readable, while in a well-known story, some implicit virtualities can be ignored and even progressively forgotten by the reader.

In addition, alternatives associated with the inner self of the characters (what Ryan defines as "virtual embedded narratives") play an essential role in the reader's emotional immersion in the storyworld; conversely, disanarrations by a narrator or by an "authorial voice" might increase the distance between the character and the reader, and therefore it might alter suspense in repetition.

In summary, narrative tension is an enduring effect of plot because in order to reach the resolution, we are forced to walk the path along its entire length, passing by the same crossings. The first walk will never be the same as later walks, but even if one knows how to get oriented in the maze, the same disnarrated events are still readable and the same projections are made by characters, who continue to dream, hope, and plan their actions the same way. All those objective virtualities, even though it is recognized that they lead to dead ends, will not cease to intrigue readers.

ALTERNATIVES IN THE PASSION ACCORDING TO MARK

We have now reached the threshold of what could be an analysis of narrative dynamics that is resistant to reiteration and for which biblical stories seem to provide exemplary forms. Among them, there are few stories whose outcome is as familiar as the episode of the Passion of Christ. The periodic return of Easter celebrations leads Christians to a collective reiteration of the story, inscribing the linear time of the narrative (extending from the betrayal of Christ to his death and resurrection) into the circular temporality of the liturgical calendar. One might conclude that we no longer need to read, listen to, or watch the story for the quality of its plot, for interest has necessarily shifted toward other nonemotional values such as the symbolic meaning of the event. Nevertheless, studies on the historical reception of this narrative confirm that the story manages to do more than simply evoke the suffering of a character. As stated by Claire Clivaz:

> An ancient account of the fourth century, written by a woman traveler named Egeria, underscores the strength of this narrative immersion collectively reiterated each year. She tells the Easter celebrations in Jerusalem in the year 380. Reading, listening, participating in the reenactment of the Passion narrative arouses a catharsis of emotions in listeners. On Holy Wednesday, Egeria recounts that "[a priest] takes the Gospel and reads the passage where Judas Isacriote went to the Jews and fixed the price they would give for handing over the Lord. When we read this passage, there were so many

cries and shouts that no one could resist being moved to tears."[15] (Baroni and Clivaz 154–55, m.t.)

Thus, the "passion" suffered by the protagonist is such that it can arouse strong emotions in at least some readers. Moreover, Jesus himself appears as a character who, although aware of the fate awaiting him (his martyrdom but also his resurrection and glory), is not fatalistic and resigned. He is both prescient and suffering, he passively accepts his fate but continues to desire an alternative. In this episode a number of elements of disnarration and embedded narratives can be found, all of them coinciding with the most pathetic moments of the story.

It is notable that Jesus manifests his knowledge of the outcome of the story and thus shows a form of epistemic homology with the reader, while the chief priests and the scribes are still "seeking how to arrest him by stealth and kill him" (Mark 14:1). For example, at the anointment at Bethany, after a woman has broken a flask of expensive ointment, Jesus declares: "She has anointed my body beforehand for burial" (Mark 14:8). Later, while Judas is still seeking "an opportunity to betray him" (Mark 14:11), Jesus announces to his disciples: "Truly, I say to you, one of you will betray me, one who is eating with me" (Mark 14:8). On this occasion, Jesus' omniscience contrasts with the ignorance of the disciples, who are "sorrowful" and ask, "Is it I?" (Mark 14:19). During his last meal, Jesus formulates a morbid prediction: "Truly, I say to you, I will not drink again of the fruit of the vine until that day when I drink it new in the kingdom of God" (Mark 14:25). Despite the threats against him, Jesus doesn't try to escape his enemies, nor does he fight adversity. Rather, he submits to the foreordained: "For the Son of Man goes as it is written of him" (Mark 14:21).

At this point, plot seems to depart from the usual dynamic of conflict and suspense, structured by aggressive and defensive actions influencing an unknown and unforeseeable resolution.[16] Despite the lack of conflict, several alternatives continue to unfold through hypothetical or impossible predictions formulated by the characters, contrasting with the prophetic discourse and the

---

15. I am grateful to Claire Clivaz for having found this quotation and for allowing me to reproduce it here. For an extensive analysis of the episode of Gethsemane and its reception, see Clivaz, L'ange et la sueur de sang.

16. We can imagine a naive reader who, reading this story for the first time, might wonder whether, at this crucial moment in the story, the disciples will try to stop Judas. It is surprising—and can be considered as a "plot hole" (Ryan "Cheap Plot Tricks")—that none of them reacts when Jesus explicitly designates the disciple who will betray him. Still, I think it is unlikely that this virtuality of a counteraction may survive after frequent reiteration of the narrative, since it is a counterfactual event that remains completely implicit.

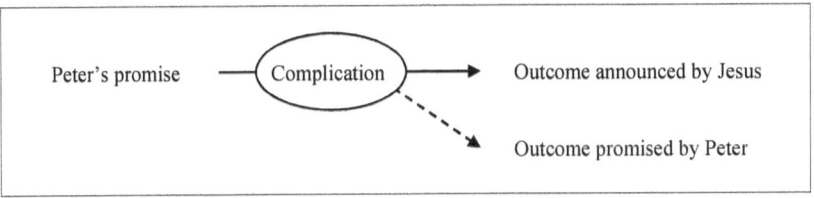

FIGURE 6.2. Virtualities of Peter's Promise

actual course of the story. The first of these explicit alternatives is expressed by the disciples, including Peter, in the form of a promise that will not be kept:

> "You will all fall away, for it is written, 'I will strike the shepherd, and the sheep will be scattered.' But after I am raised up, I will go before you to Galilee." Peter said to him, "Even though they all fall away, I will not." And Jesus said to him, "Truly, I tell you, this very night, before the rooster crows twice, you will deny me three times." But he said emphatically, "If I must die with you, I will not deny you." And they all said the same. (Mark 14:27–31)

Peter's denial appears to be symptomatic of a tension between a deontic virtuality (a promise that creates the *obligation* to undertake a future action: "If I must die with you, I will not deny you") and an alternative ("you will deny me three times") expected by Jesus and by the reader. The end of the chapter, by telling the events announced by Jesus, emphasizes the *pathos* ("he broke down and wept") of the situation when Peter becomes aware of the discrepancy between his conduct and his initial promise:

> And as Peter was below in the courtyard, one of the servant girls of the high priest came, and seeing Peter warming himself, she looked at him and said, "You also were with the Nazarene, Jesus." But he denied it, saying, "I neither know nor understand what you mean." And he went out into the gateway and the rooster crowed. And the servant girl saw him and began again to say to the bystanders, "This man is one of them." But again he denied it. And after a little while the bystanders again said to Peter, "Certainly you are one of them, for you are a Galilean." But he began to invoke a curse on himself and to swear, "I do not know this man of whom you speak." And immediately the rooster crowed a second time. And Peter remembered how Jesus had said to him, "Before the rooster crows twice, you will deny me three times." And he broke down and wept. (Mark 14:66–72)

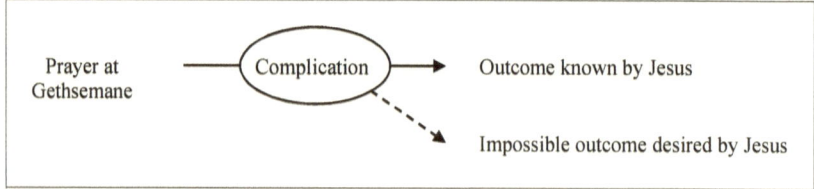

FIGURE 6.3. Virtualities of Prayer at Gethsemane

Here, the actual world asserted by the fiction leads to a situation that is both prohibited and negative for the character. And while this necessary situation cannot be changed, it contrasts with the alternative that was explicitly promised. Through emotional immersion, the succession of the three denials appears as three missed opportunities to act differently, thus intensifying the dramatic tension between the actual and the more desirable alternative.

Another well-known explicit virtuality in the Passion, and probably the one most commented on, is set in the garden of Gethsemane. There, even knowing perfectly how the story will end, Jesus falls on the ground and prays that "if possible, the hour might pass from him" (Mark 14:35), continuing: "Abba, Father, all things are possible for you. Remove this cup from me. Yet not what I will, but what you will" (Mark 14:35–36). This moment of the story is particularly revealing because, here again, the alternative is clearly linked to *pathos:* the hope of an alternative coincides with the evocation of the pain endured by Jesus, of whom it is said that he "began to be greatly distressed and troubled," adding that his "soul is very sorrowful, even to death" (Mark 14:33–34). Even if it is impossible to change one line of a book written by somebody else, Jesus asks desperately for a different ending to the one for whom "all things are possible." But as he fully respects his commitment to go "as it is written of him," Jesus does not really consider a possible action that could change his fate but rather expresses his sadness that relies on the desire for a better version of the story where the alethic, the deontic, and the axiological modalities would not enter into conflict. This being the case, Jesus' prayer is not exactly the "disnarration" of an alternative course of events but the explicit wish for it, and thus, it entails an implicit "embedded narrative" that highlights the difficulty experienced by the character in meeting his destiny.

In value-laden terms, this episode shares with Peter's broken promise the axiological desire for a better alternative. However, from a deontic perspective, the two episodes can be opposed: while Jesus respects his commitment to go "as it is written of him," Peter transgresses his word. Also, in connection with the alethic modality, we can observe that the pathetic moments don't share the same temporal orientation: hope expressed by Jesus is oriented toward a still possible future, while Peter, in his regrets, expresses his desire for an impossible alternative situated in an unchangeable past. On the moral side, the retrospective comparison between the two developments highlights the importance of keeping one's word, even if it is followed by death, because transgression and survival do not seem to constitute a better alternative[17]. Even so, the path followed by Jesus does not appear to be easier than the one chosen by Peter, and the story, even if we know how it ends, retains the power to inspire, at least for some readers, the desire for a different alternative.

Even after the prophecy is accomplished and the story is over, there are some complications that remain unsolved. This is not because it is unknown how they have been resolved but rather because different pathways of reading are still possible and open for imaginative exploration, such as Peter in his eternal regrets and Jesus in his impossible desires. It should be added that the apocryphal tradition, as well as literary works inspired by the biblical narrative, did not fail to exploit the potentialities left open by the Gospel. Nor does *The Last Temptation of Christ* by Nikos Kazantzakis, which explores the possibility that Jesus had the final choice to escape his fate, at least in a dream world, or *Ponce Pilate* by Roger Caillois, in which the Roman administrator saves Jesus' life,[18] allowing him to live to an old age while condemning Christianity to remain a mere virtuality of history. Thus, the theory of "possible texts," developed in a collection of essays edited by Marc Escola, represents an interesting extension to the investigation of the enduring virtual worlds of fiction. It illustrates that the ending of a narration never corresponds to a complete reduction of contingency: even though, retrospectively, the story seems to mold itself into some poetic, moral, or causal necessity, its aesthetic interest, its lasting emotional impact, and its ethical value depend more directly on the many other ways the story could or should have unfolded. Thus, every story is a matrix for an infinite range of alternative stories that might be explored in the reader's mind and remain silent, or later written by the reader, thus forming a specific kind of *extradiegetic disnarration*.

---

17. In my reading of Mark, I focused on the emotional impact of the alternatives the text generates, but I did not address the purpose of the story as it was designed for its implied reader, namely to arouse a desire to follow the apostolic life with greater fidelity and courage than the Apostles did. In my perspective, the emotional impact of the story on an empirical reader, with its enduring suspense that has survived throughout history, goes far beyond the original communication involving "events that are told by someone to someone for some purpose," to quote the famous transactional definition of narrative by Phelan.

18. Here again, the episode with Ponce Pilate involves a disnarration with clear deontic and axiological implications.

In my commentary on the Passion, I don't claim that suspense is impossible when it is mostly based on a process of immersion that brackets our knowledge concerning the unfolding of an already known *fabula*. In line with the conceptions advocated by Walton, Gerrig, Carroll, and Ryan, I subscribe to the enduring *pathos* of implicit virtualities concerning the risks that threaten the protagonist, even when we know (at least in some parts of our mind) that they will remain mere virtualities. But I think that those implicit virtualities are not necessarily permanent, and I have sought to highlight additional ingredients that have the power to increase narrative tension without ever being altered by repetition. Some alternatives belong explicitly (through disnarrations) to the world of the characters, and unfortunate stories will generally inspire in the reader the desire for a better fate. This may be one way to explain why tragic stories seem to have a more enduring narrative tension than adventures with a happy ending.[19]

WORKS CITED

Bakhtin, Mikhaïl. *Esthétique et théorie du roman*. Paris: Gallimard, 1978 (1975).
Baroni, Raphaël. "The Garden of Forking Paths: Virtualities and Challenge for Contemporary Narratology." In *Emerging Vectors of Narratology*, edited by John Pier, Philippe Roussin, and Wolf Schmid. Berlin and New York: de Gruyter, forthcoming.
———. *La tension narrative. Suspense, curiosité et suspense*. Paris: Seuil, 2007.
Bremond, Claude. *Logique du récit*. Paris: Seuil, 1973.
Brewer, William. "The Nature of Narrative Suspense and the Problem of Rereading." In *Suspense, Conceptualizations, Theoretical Analyses, and Empirical Explorations*, edited by Peter Vorderer, Hans J. Wulffand and Mike Friedrichsen, 107–27. Mahwah, NJ: Lawrence Erlbaum Associates, 1996.
Brooks, Peter. *Reading for the Plot: Design and Intention in Narrative*. Cambridge and London: Harvard Univ. Press, 1992 (1984).
Candel Borman, Daniel. "Moving Possible World Theory from Logic to Value." *Poetics Today* 34, no. 1–2 (2013): 177–231.
Carroll, Noël. "The Paradox of Suspense." In *Suspense, Conceptualizations, Theoretical Analyses, and Empirical Explorations*, edited by Peter Vorderer, Hans J. Wulffand, and Mike Friedrichsen, 71–92. Mahwah, NJ: Lawrence Erlbaum Associates, 1996.
Clivaz, Claire. *L'Ange et la sueur de sang (Lc 22, 43–44) ou comment on pourrait bien encore écrire l'histoire*, Leuven: Peeters, 2010.
Clivaz, Claire, and Raphaël Baroni. "Résistance du *pathos* dans les récits de la Passion." In *La surprise en exégèse*, edited by Geert van Oyen and André Wénin, 137–56. Leuven: Peeters, 2012.

---

19. Some elements of this chapter, especially the analysis of the gospel of Mark, were developed in an article written with Claire Clivaz (Baroni and Clivaz, "Résistance du *pathos* dans les récits de la Passion"). I am also thankful to Emma Kafalenos, Gerald Prince, Peter J. Rabinowitz, and John Pier for their useful comments.

Dannenberg, Hilary P. *Coincidence and Counterfactuality: Plotting Time and Space in Narrative Fiction*. Lincoln: Univ. of Nebraska Press, 2008.
———. "Ontological Plotting: Narrative as a Multiplicity of Temporal Dimensions." In *The Dynamics of Narrative Form: Studies in Anglo-American Narratology*, edited by John Pier, 159–89. Berlin and New York: de Gruyter, 2004.
Doležel, Lubomír. *Heterocosmica: Fiction and Possible Worlds*. Baltimore: Johns Hopkins Univ. Press, 1998.
Eco, Umberto. *The Role of the Reader*. Bloomington: Indiana Univ. Press, 1979.
Escola, Marc, ed. *Théorie des textes possibles*. Amsterdam and New York: Rodopi, 2012.
Gerrig, Richard. "Is There a Paradox of Suspense? A Reply to Yanal." *British Journal of Aesthetics* 37, no. 2 (1997): 168–74.
———. "Suspense in the Absence of Uncertainty." *Journal of Memory and Language* 28 (1989): 633–48.
Herman, David. *Story Logic: Problems and Possibilities of Narrative*. Lincoln: Univ. of Nebraska Press, 2002.
Kafalenos, Emma. "Not (Yet) Knowing: Epistemological Effects of Deferred and Suppressed Information in Narrative." In *Narratologies: New Perspectives on Narrative Analysis*, edited by David Herman, 33–65. Columbus: The Ohio State Univ. Press, 1999.
Pavel, Thomas. "Possible Worlds in Literary Semantics." *Journal of Aesthetics and Art Criticism* 34, no. 6 (1975): 165–76.
Phelan, James. *Reading People, Reading Plots: Character, Progression, and the Interpretation of Narrative*. Chicago: Univ. of Chicago Press, 1989.
Pier, John. "Narrative Configurations." In *The Dynamics of Narrative Form: Studies in Anglo-American Narratology*, edited by John Pier, 239–65. Berlin and New York: de Gruyter, 2005.
Prieto-Pablos, José. "The Paradox of Suspense." *Poetics* 26 (1998): 99–113.
Prince, Gerald. "The Disnarrated." *Style* 22 (1988): 1–8.
———. "Périchronismes et temporalité narrative." *A Contrario* 13 (2010): 9–18.
Ryan, Marie-Laure. "Cheap Plot Tricks, Plot Holes, and Narrative Design." *Narrative* 17, no.1 (2009): 56–75.
———. "From Parallel Universes to Possible Worlds: Ontological Pluralism in Physics, Narratology, and Narrative." *Poetics Today* 27, no. 4 (2006): 633–74.
———. *Narrative as Virtual Reality*. Baltimore and London: Johns Hopkins Univ. Press, 2001.
———. *Possible Worlds, Artificial Intelligence, and Narrative Theory*. Bloomington: Indiana Univ. Press, 1991.
Sternberg, Meir. "How Narrativity Makes a Difference." *Narrative* 9 (2001): 115–22.
Todorov, Tzvetan. *Poétique de la prose*. Paris: Seuil, 1971.
Toolan, Michael. "Narrative Progression in the Short Story: First Steps in a Corpus Stylistic Approach." *Narrative* 16, no. 2 (2008): 105–20.
Vaina, Lucia. "Les mondes possibles du texte." *Versus* 17 (1977): 3–13.
Villeneuve, Johanne. *Le sens de l'intrigue, ou la narrativité, le jeu et l'invention du diable*. Laval: Presses de l'Université Laval, 2003.
Walton, Kendal. *Mimesis as Make-Believe*. Cambridge, MA: Harvard Univ. Press, 1990.
Yanal, Robert. "The Paradox of Suspense." *British Journal of Aesthetics* 36, no. 2 (1996): 146–58.

PART III

Sequences in Nonliterary Narratives

CHAPTER 7

Intrigue, Suspense, and Sequentiality in Comic Strips

Reading Little Sammy Sneeze

ALAIN BOILLAT and FRANÇOISE REVAZ

THE RICH DEBATE that took place during the First International Conference of the Narratology Network of French-Speaking Switzerland [*Réseau Romand de Narratologie*] demonstrated that there is no such thing as a unified narratology, be it classical or postclassical, but rather a diversity of methods and approaches in the study of narrativity. This is also the case of sequence, the central theme of the conference, which we shall be examining in a medium and field of study that are somewhat apart from the mainstream of the usual objects of narratology: American serial comic strips. This means of expression unquestionably represents a fruitful object of study, as indicated by the term "sequential art," which is often used to designate narrative.[1] We will consider the narrative sequences found in our corpus of comics not only in their textual structure but also in the dynamic dimension resulting from the seriality of their production. We will also look at the position of the reader who discovers a new adventure each week, from the point of view of content, but one that is unchanged in its outcome and formatting. The question that arises, then, is the following: what can intrigue the reader even though he knows the resolution of the story in advance?

---

1. For instance, the well-known theorist and author of comics, Will Eisner, chose *Comics and Sequential Art* as the title of one of his textbooks.

Our corpus is made up of pages from the *Little Sammy Sneeze* series by Winsor McCay, one of the pioneers of the American comic strip and, later, of the animated cartoon. The series centers on a recurring character, the "Little Sammy" of the title, and appeared weekly in the popular press in the United States between 1904 and 1906, mainly in the Sunday pages of the *New York Herald*. Since one of the present authors has already outlined a number of premises for a narratological and intermedial analysis of this series that is grounded in action theories (Boillat), we thought it opportune to reexamine this extremely rich corpus from the more specific perspective of sequentialization, despite an apparent "poverty" due to the minimalism and repetitive nature of the situations. Indeed, this type of comic strip bears in its very structure the stamp of its mode of distribution, for every week the cartoonist needs to come up with a new episode, one complete in itself, which, without presenting the characteristics of a serial, nevertheless belongs to a series by virtue of the repetition of certain features. This type of systematization reaches its paroxysm in *Little Sammy Sneeze*—a "textbook case" if ever there was one—as each episode invariably tells the same tale in four or six panels, each framed in a strictly identical way, a story whose contents essentially boil down to the physiological action of Little Sammy: in the strip, the little boy can be seen progressively building up to a sneeze that, when it finally erupts and all the breath in his airways has been expelled, destroys everything around him,

FIGURE 7.1. Winsor McCay, *Little Sammy Sneeze*, September 25, 1904

with the result that the mischief-maker is generally punished by being forcibly ejected from the previously defined setting (figure 7.1^2). The juxtaposition of identically formatted panels in which the representation is characterized by an invariant point of view, and constant image scale creates a recurrence exemplifying the principle of compartmentalization that, according to the hypothesis advanced by Harry Morgan, "possesses three structural characteristics, which are indexical of sequentiality . . . contiguity, regularity and vectorization" (129). Our goal in this chapter, then, is to examine the specificities of how sequentialization functions in *Little Sammy Sneeze,* for the radical options underlying this series seem to favor a more general reflection on the medium of the comic strip.

SAMMY VS. POLLY

Apart from his sneezing, which is completely beyond his control (as indicated at the outset by the subtitle of the series, *"He just simply couldn't stop it"*), Sammy Sneeze totally fails to engage in any interaction with his environment, and his position, in the foreground of the image, is that of a spectator. Several of the pages are devoted to the representation of a scene in which Sammy is only present as part of the scenery. This is suggested, in the overwhelming majority of the episodes, by the strictly identical position that he occupies in each of the panels. Sammy, moreover, whose sole, overriding function is to sneeze, seems totally indifferent to anything going on around him. An examination of one of the episodes of *The Naps of Polly Sleepyhead* by the cartoonist Peter Newell (figure 7.2),[3] a series that appeared in the same newspaper and at the same time as *Little Sammy Sneeze,* allows us to highlight through comparison the particularities of McCay's character: as in *Little Nemo in Slumberland* (the best known of McCay's titles), we are transported (from the second to the penultimate panel) into a dream world, and in this case, each episode in the series recounts one of little Polly's nightmares. In the particular dream in question, Polly sneezes: Newell makes use, in this instance, of the central motif of McCay's *Sammy,* exploiting its surrealizing potential by depicting the unexpected effects of physiological activity. As a result of Polly's sneezing, the

---

2. In this chapter's illustrations, the dates given passim are those of the strip's first publication as found in Maresca.

3. Peter Newell, *The Naps of Polly Sleepyhead,* "Polly and the Screen," *New York Herald* (European Edition), Paris, 1906. Patrimonial collection of comic strips, Bibliothèque Municipale de Lausanne (Switzerland). Our thanks to the curator of this collection, Cuno Affolter, for making this image available to us.

FIGURE 7.2. Peter Newell, *The Naps of Polly Sleepyhead*, 1906

stork embroidered on the screen becomes real, emerging from the representation gazed at by the girl, who, like Sammy, is in the position of a spectator (the strip bears the telling title, "*Polly and the Screen*"). It will be observed that, in this episode—which is symptomatic of the influence of Japanese graphic arts upon the pioneering authors of comics, who readily included areas of flat color into their drawings—there comes into play a veritable interaction between the girl and the animal, which towers over her in a threatening way: indeed, the captions of panels 4 and 5 explain that Polly takes fright until a second sneeze releases her from the clutches of the bird by transforming the polka dots sneezed off her dress into projectiles. Through the text and the facial expressions of the two opposing protagonists, Newell gives the reader access to the feelings of Polly, whose subjectivity, projected by her imagination upon a "screen," pervades the entire narrative, whereas in McCay, little Sammy remains a totally dehumanized source of disturbance, a mere cog in the mechanism of the gag.

THE SNEEZE AS AN "ATTRACTION"

Whereas there are numerous comics and early films with narratives based upon child practical-jokers—directly inspired, in particular, by the German caricaturist Wilhelm Busch[4]—Sammy is devoid of intentionality. It is our contention that the penultimate panel, which in all the episodes of the series is dedicated to the illustration of the spectacular effects of his sneezing, belongs to what historians of early cinema have called a *logic of attractions*: as with the numerous types of explosions to be found in the early cinema (e.g., Gunning 1986), we have here a clear demonstration of the purely visual potential of the medium. Tom Gunning, who was the first author to reappropriate, with reference to the early cinema, the expression the *cinema of attractions*—taken from the Soviet filmmaker and theorist S. M. Eisenstein—has examined the workings of just this type of gag, which is omnipresent in comic films of the period 1895–1910[5] and in which, according to this author, the unfolding of events is based upon the contriving of actions with a predictable outcome. We refer here to what he terms the *mischief gag*, frequently involving the figure of a young rascal:

---

4. See Chemartin and Dulac.
5. For a recent discussion of comic processes in the early cinema, see Guido and Le Forestier.

FIGURE 7.3. The Lumière brothers, *L'Arroseur arrosé*, 1895

The first pattern found in these early gag films delineates an action, precisely laying it out in two clearly defined phases. First, a preparatory action is undertaken with a precise aim in view. The audience usually anticipates what the result of this preparatory action will be (which is sometimes obvious, sometimes surprising).... The second phase of the action is the result and effect of this preparatory phase; in our example [the Lumière brothers' *L'Arroseur arrosé*—literally, "the waterer watered"], the gardener getting sprayed in the face. ("Crazy Machines" 90)

While the context of the explosion is developed over a certain length of time, the effect produced by the anticipated action is of an eruptive, instantaneous nature. From this perspective, this motif can be compared with the seminal, emblematic example of the Lumière brothers' *L'Arroseur arrosé* (1895) (figure 7.3),[6] which Gunning does not fail to mention and whose central theme

---

6. The Lumière brothers made two other versions of this reel in 1896–97 (see Aubert and Seguin 106–7) and reused this motif in other films such as *Joueurs de cartes arrosés*—literally, "card-players watered"—(1896) (this type of game is also present in McCay's series). The popularity of this gag in cinema was considerable, as evidenced by the versions described in the catalogues of other filmmakers, Méliès in particular (*L'Arroseur*, 1986, and *Les Mésaventures d'un*

belongs, as several historians have pointed out,[7] to the tradition of the Épinal print. Similarly, the organization of each episode in the *Little Sammy Sneeze* series is centered upon the buildup to the sneeze, which, in one of the strips, is accompanied by an instance of "spraying" (a frequent motif in McCay's work),[8] when the child splashes water from a bathtub or a bowl onto the face of a servant (figures 7.4–5).[9] Gunning points out that the outcome of the gag can easily be anticipated by the spectator—*Little Sammy Sneeze* is interpreted by the reader through reference to a generic framework, that of the gag, to which a bipartite structure is attached (preparation/payoff)—and that it is "sometimes obvious, sometimes surprising." This detail concerning the dual modalities of closure is important for an understanding of the implications of the sequentialization found in *Little Sammy Sneeze* which, despite the inevitable arrival of his sneeze, creates a certain form of *suspense* (even though the reader knows perfectly well what is going to happen, he has no idea of the size of the explosion, nor what feats of virtuosity the artist will enlist to represent it) and *surprise* when he discovers the mind-blowing panel showing the catastrophic disruption of the initial situation. As Meir Sternberg has demonstrated ("Telling in Time [II]"), such surprise might also be accompanied by *curiosity*, as the reader backtracks over the panels leading up to the explosion to see what has paved the way for this denouement (this is equally true at the level of the verbal elements, as will be shown below). The effects of Sammy's ever-unchanging action, then, are of the same order as those examined by Gunning with reference to the "explosion film," which he considers emblematic of the comic mechanism of early slapstick: "The shock of a disastrous disruption becomes extremely literal in the explosion film, in which little happens other than something blowing up and inflicting injury on the characters" ("Crazy Machines" 96). Gunning's observations on early films are applicable in every particular to the *Little Sammy Sneeze* strips: both film and

---

photographe, 1908; see Frazer 201 and 241), Edison (*Bad Boy and the Gardener*, 1896; see Musser 221), and Pathé (*L'Arroseur n'a pas de chance*, 1913, according to Bousquet 651).

7. It should be noted that the cinema historian Georges Sadoul wrote of the reel entitled *Fred Ott's Sneeze*—made in 1894 by Dickson for the Edison company and which simply shows the eponymous character sneezing—that this subject presents a "scenario which is not entirely unrelated to that of *L'Arroseur arrosé*" (258). In the same work, Sadoul points out that he asked Louis Lumière if the inspiration for this film was the Épinal image published by the Quantin company ("L'Arroseur," Hermann Vogel, 1887), but the filmmaker refuted this hypothesis (298). On the tradition of the *arroseur* in the cinema and sequentialized drawn images, see Rickman.

8. McCay was, moreover, to propose a new version of the *arroseur arrosé* motif in an episode of his *Dream of the Rarebit Fiend* series, published in the *New York Herald* on July 6, 1913.

9. Details taken from McCay 153 and 171. For figure 7.5, the precise date of the publication is not indicated.

FIGURE 7.4. Winsor McCay, *Little Sammy Sneeze*, April 2, 1905

strips are similarly literal in their presentation of the comic process. The often disproportionate destruction brought about by Sammy's sneezing serves as the disruptive element enabling the narrativity of the episode as whole.

THE QUESTION OF THE INTERVAL

To pursue the comparison of *Little Sammy Sneeze* with the emergence of the cinema, it should be noted that the temporal progression toward the sneeze is achieved through reference to the chronophotographic model of the representation of movement. In fact, not only do the four phases of the opening of Sammy's mouth echo certain experiments in the decomposition and recomposition of motion by means of photography, but they also highlight, by virtue of the brevity induced by the character's single action, the importance of the

FIGURE 7.5. Winsor McCay, *Little Sammy Sneeze*, 1904–6

interval occurring between two images. In this connection, the phases of Sammy's sneeze set the pace for the division of the page into panels, which contributes to the establishment of the sequence's diegetic duration. The sequentiality thus set in motion is a carbon copy of the mechanical model of successive film frames. However, the situation is quite different as far as the actions taking place in the background are concerned: while they are unquestionably governed, from a temporal point of view, by the unfolding stages of Sammy's sneezing and vectorized by this irrepressible, irreversible act, such peripheral actions nevertheless seem to imply a temporality all of their own—at times, with a total disregard for verisimilitude. If we examine the background actions from the perspective of the supposed diegetic duration of the interval between two panels, we see that this duration is elastic and does not necessarily correspond to the length of time implied by the transition from one phase of Sammy's sneeze to the next.

Indeed, in the upper tier of the episode at the village blacksmith's shop (figure 7.1)—in which the gaze of the two horses has not yet been directed toward the center of the images in order to concentrate attention upon Sammy, who is placed between them—the implied time gap between panels 2 and 3 is considerably greater than that between panels 1 and 2: in the second panel, one of the farriers has merely put his toolbox on the ground and turned around, while the other is still standing in the same place; in the third, these two background figures have started working, while the old gentleman with a pipe, partially visible at the right edge of panel 2, has moved and is now standing opposite us, occupying the third plane of the image. Moreover, the dialogue placed within the speech balloons implies a diegetic duration that we can legitimately assume to be longer than that between the first signs of Sammy's sneezing. This speech is however fragmentary in nature, and its role is more that of "background noise." It is nevertheless clearly apparent that the internal duration of the panels varies to quite an extent, whereas the sneeze suggests an instant. In fact, if it is possible to fill in the ellipsis corresponding to the gutters between panels, this is because the background action is grounded in scripts that the reader can easily identify and whose different stages are predictable for him or her (in this case, the sign "The Village Blacksmith" pointing to the "shoeing a horse" script). In a recent book on early comic strips, Thierry Smolderen describes in the following terms the interaction between the two levels of sequentiality operating in *Little Sammy Sneeze*: "Windsor McCay amuses himself, in Sammy, by reproducing in an identical manner, from one episode to the next, the five stages of the principal character's sneeze, while other characters absorbed in an everyday activity, i.e., one or other social scripts, carry on with their occupations" (131).[10] The notion of "script" mentioned by Smolderen (following numerous narratologists)[11] seems to us particularly pertinent for the study of *Little Sammy Sneeze:* here, the surrounding actions are indeed governed by one or more types of stereotypical organization, which might easily be induced by the reader as long as he or she is at least slightly familiar with the universe represented. It is true that all the actions shown in the panels are dependent upon the temporal scansion imposed by the phases of the supposedly rapid movement of Sammy's mouth; however, the phases associated with a given script provide important cues for establishing and understanding sequentiality.

SCRIPTS IN GAME SITUATIONS

In order to examine how scripts work in McCay, we have identified a subcorpus made up of pages in which the protagonists accompanying Sammy in the images are playing a game. This is a frequent motif in *Little Sammy Sneeze:* not only does it foreground the playful component of the strips themselves and the faintly dramatic nature of the situations represented (principally involving pastimes), but it also presents the interest of referring to a preestablished system, since the reader is familiar with the *rules of the game* (both those of the game that is represented and those of the *Sammy* series) and can place the unfolding events within a succession of stages.

We offer below a comparative analysis of three episodes in order to demonstrate the variability in the importance of any given script depending upon the nature of the game and modalities of its representation.

Indeed, the *Little Sammy Sneeze* series originates in this sort of representation, since the very first episode published[12] shows Sammy sitting at the same table as chess players concentrating in silence upon their game (figure 7.6, McCay 111). As the pieces are in an identical position in each panel, we can

---

10. It should be pointed out that Smolderen sees in this practice a baroque, parodic dimension that is hardly in tune with the mass culture of the period. McCay, in fact, makes the fullest possible use of the principal of repetition/variation specific to his particular vehicle of publication, without eschewing the logic of this type of production.

11. The notion of "script" (or "frame") was developed in the 1970s by cognitive psychologists (Bower, Black, and Turner; Schank and Abelson; van Dijk) and is used to refer to a predetermined, stereotypical sequence of actions. Within the framework of narrative, the notion of script enables us to understand how the reader identifies a routine, actional sequence and, if need be, fills in the stages that have not been mentioned.

12. According to Canemaker.

FIGURE 7.6. Winsor McCay, *Little Sammy Sneeze*, 1904–6

FIGURE 7.7. Winsor McCay, *Little Sammy Sneeze*, March 12, 1905

assume that neither player plays during this time interval, both waiting in anticipation of a crucial move. The situation is then one of suspense that is on the verge of reaching its resolution (in checkmate) just as the character on the right prepares to move a pawn, but it is precisely after the panel in which this gesture is depicted that Sammy sneezes and blows all the pieces off the board. In this case, the reader's knowledge of chess is irrelevant for perceiving the events unfolding. All that is required is recognition of the situation itself: that of a game demanding concentration on the part of the players and whose

INTRIGUE, SUSPENSE, AND SEQUENTIALITY IN COMIC STRIPS • 119

FIGURE 7.8. Winsor McCay, *Little Sammy Sneeze*, January 29, 1905

outcome depends on the position of the pieces on the board in addition to awareness of the fact that the game has already reached an advanced stage in the first panel.

In the second episode, devoted to a game of bowling (figure 7.7), the importance of the throw is made clear right from the first image, as one of the players tells the participant who is about to play that he needs to get a strike (i.e., knock down all the pins) in order to win the game. A knowledge of the game is obviously important, but the perspectival construction clearly points to the character's objective. The decisive factor for understanding the action is to break down the different stages in the swing of the bowler, who stands out clearly from the background thanks to the flat area of black representing his trousers. In cases such as this, the model of the chronophotographic decomposition of motion underlies the two actional pathways that are synchronous at the moment of the payoff: that of throwing the bowling ball down the lane and that of Sammy's mouth movements. We can also see that the competitor making fun of the player in the second panel ("don't break the pins or tear out the end of the building") foreshadows the devastating outcome of the game without completely giving away its modalities.

Our last example is that of a game of billiards (figure 7.8). In this case, the precise point in the game is clearly indicated in the dialogue, as are the various stages illustrated: the player puts a first ball in the end pocket and then gets ready to try to hit the last ball, a red one, into the pocket near Sammy. As it is customary for the player to announce what he intends to do before each shot, this makes it possible to verbally specify the intentions of the acting subject. Moreover, the chronological unfolding of events is suggested by the position of the balls on the table and the cupboard in the background, to which can be added the ball previously pocketed by the player in the third panel. The dialogue dramatizes the progress of the game and, as a result, increases the disappointment when the sneeze spoils the decisive shot as the white ball, rather than the red, goes into the pocket, as predicted by the player's opponent. In the exchanges between the players, several allusions are made to the rules of the game, which serve, here, as the indispensable script for placing the actions within a narrative sequence.

WHAT SUSPENSE?

The structure of the pages of *Little Sammy Sneeze,* underpinned by the progressive unfolding of Sammy's sneeze, presents a mode of sequentiality borrowed from the chronophotographic model. Its chronological structure, which mimes the supposed temporal and causal order of events, can be considered to constitute a narrative sequence:

> To be sure, nobody who has thought about narrative structure and interpretation is likely to deny that for narrative to make sense *as* narrative, it must make chronological sense. For if the events composing it do not fall into some line of world-time, however problematic their alignment and however appealing their alternative arrangement, then narrativity itself disappears. From early to late is, moreover, not only the order of nature but also the order of causality, hence of plot coherence. (Sternberg, "Telling in Time (I)" 903)

If, from the perspective of the temporal criterion, the "narrative" character of Sammy's adventures seems undeniable, what of suspense? Indeed, if it is always the same story that is being told (each episode being "preformatted" through Sammy's sneezing), why would a follower of the series want to read a new episode? In other terms, what is there for him to find intriguing, and in particular, is it acceptable to speak of suspense when the ultimate chaos is predictable and expected? Before answering this question, let us briefly examine an episode (figure 7.9) from a different comic series, taken from the "*bande dessinée*" entitled *Aventures de Boule et Bill* [Adventures of Boule and Bill],

FIGURE 7.9. Roba, *Aventures de Boule et Bill*, 1999. Boule & Bill 27 - Bwoufallo Bill. © DARGAUD BENELUX (DARGAUD-LOMBARD S.A.) 1991, by Jean Roba. © Studio Boule & Bill - 1999. www.dargaud.com. All rights reserved.

which is well known in French-speaking Europe. In this particular episode, just as in *Little Sammy Sneeze,* it is the occurrence of a violent sneeze that interrupts the normal flow of a game—with the signal difference that this time it is absolutely unexpected. The sneeze occurs in the last panel, after the suspense has been building up for quite a long time, during which the reader has been wondering why Boule appears unwilling to play pick-up-sticks with his friend Pouf. As early as the second panel, Boule's facial appearance has been changing: his smile has vanished and he seems increasingly irritated. Also, his answers are saturated with the conjunction *but,* signaling a problem:

Panel 2: "It's great, BUT perhaps today isn't the day for it";
Panel 4: "No, that's true (implying, "I've never refused to play pick-up-sticks before") BUT . . .";
Panel 6: "BUT despite everything . . . ," which is logically linked to the "all right" of the previous panel in answer to Pouf's remark: "No BUTS, let's start playing the game."

The effect of the dog's sneeze is to resolve the tension, bring the plot to its denouement, and put an end to the suspense with a noisy illustration of Boule's last line: "Bill has a cold." In this connection, his remark represents the argument in the logical channel, which leads to the conclusion, "We will not play the game"—one that is never expressed in words, but merely through facial expressions. What is remarkable about this episode is the fact that the origin of the problem only appears in the last panel, leaving the reader enough time to imagine other possible causes. The point of this short excursion by way of another sneeze narrative is to show that, for the reader to be fully able to appreciate the payoff, he or she is obliged to comply with the sequential order of the comic strip and read it adopting a step-by-step approach. While the reader is unquestionably free to glance over the entire page, or even to start by looking at the last panel, he or she cannot get away from the linear order of the panels.[13] What, then, is the position of the reader of *Little Sammy Sneeze?* Does certainty of the outcome of Sammy's sneezing modify the reading path? In order to answer this question, we will examine a subcorpus of pages in which the vectorization of reading is induced not only from the predictable unfolding of Sammy's sneeze, on the one hand, and routine activities, on the other, but also from other chronological threads. We will thus observe three

---

13. This is where the whole problem of suspense (or, according to some authors, lack of suspense) in comic strip narratives lies: when suspense emerges in single-register or single-plate format. The risk, then, is that a synoptic glance will destroy the effect of surprise or totally preclude suspense.

INTRIGUE, SUSPENSE, AND SEQUENTIALITY IN COMIC STRIPS • 123

FIGURE 7.10. Winsor McCay, *Little Sammy Sneeze*, October 23, 1904

levels of vectorization, namely: (1) the decomposition of the different stages of the sneeze into a series of iconic representations; (2) the unfolding of the activities of the secondary characters; (3) the successive stages of a narrative told by one of the protagonists (the narrative appearing in the balloons).

VERBAL NARRATIVES IN COMIC STRIP NARRATIVE

In the first page (figure 7.10), a "secondary" character, the black cook, states her intention to tell Sammy a story while preparing biscuit dough. The three lines of vectorization mentioned above can be observed: the temporal development of the sneeze, the progressive unfolding of the "making pastry" script, and the cook's story. All three are set out in parallel in the foreground.

In the first panel, the servant offers Sammy a story in return for his good behavior ("you set still . . . an' I'm gwine tell you . . .").[14] She presents its theme: a ghost story at night in a cemetery. This is somewhat out of the ordinary, and it might be expected to arouse a certain degree of interest. But Sammy,

---

14. We shall not go into the way McCay represents the speech of the black servant, whose pronunciation and grammar are clearly underpinned by social and racial prejudice.

FIGURE 7.11. Winsor McCay, *Little Sammy Sneeze,* January 15, 1905

as usual, remains unresponsive. The cook's story, then, is destined to remain strictly monologal. It is borne by the continuity of her words from panel to panel and has a canonical narrative structure:[15] an initial situation ("I was walkin' ah long tendin' to ma own business") and a development of the narrative complication ("wen all at once, a great big ghost all white cum up to me"). At the point where, in panel 4, the narrator gives it to be understood that she has thought of a possible resolution for her adventure ("jes den I thinks to my sef dez only one—"), her tale is interrupted by Sammy's sneeze, the effect of which is to undermine both her narrative performance and the biscuit-making script. Paradoxically, it is the interruption of the verbal narrative that provides the sneezing episode with its payoff. Furthermore, the ultimate chaos, in which black is transformed into white, is prefigured as early as the first panel, where "heah ghosts [in the] dahk night" echoes the activity of the black servant mixing the white flour.

In the second page (figure 7.11), several lines of vectorization can be found: in the foreground, the temporal development of the sneeze and the activity of the black worker; in the background, the strolling couple recounting a worldly narrative. To this can be added the insertion of a minimal, banal narrative into the foreground, a story told by the black employee to Sammy in panels 1 and 2:

---

15. On narrative structure, see Revaz, *Introduction à la narratologie.*

"I slid down heah one day mysef an I done seen—stahrs fo a week." The verbal background narrative progresses through snatches of conversation: it is not continuous from panel to panel, as was the story told by the black cook. It begins, moreover, *in medias res* and "off frame," since the narrator cannot be seen in the first panel, and only the answer spoken by the man wearing a top hat enables the reader to understand that someone else has started speaking. Unlike the previous page, the narrative here is dialogal in nature. Indeed, it prompts reactions from the interlocutor (evaluations and questions) and is interrupted just as we come to the tying of the narrative knot (in the fourth panel: "reconciled ourselves when a terrible storm arose"). Once again, the narrative performance is disqualified and undermined. We are never told how the voyage ended. Moreover, the interlocutor's reactions to the story are ridiculed. This parodic tone is particularly noticeable in panel 4, in which the close succession of exclamations ("Go on. Go on. How interesting, yes. Oh! You did? Yes, go ahead! Oh yes. Yes. Oh, dear!") appears, at the very least, excessive. It should be noted that the type of disturbance causes Sammy to sneeze (the cloud of ash) is "prefigured" in the woman's line: "Our ship plunged into a dense fog, we could not see—." Once again, the contrast will be noted between the white of the snow (and the skin color of the people out walking) and the black of the ashes (and the skin color of the laborer) together with the transformation, this time, of white into black.

In the last page we have selected to illustrate this type of situation (figure 7.12), several lines of vectorization progress in parallel: the sneeze, a conversation, a song recital. While Sammy (in the foreground) is working up to a sneeze, an elderly gentleman, somewhat further back, tells a lady sitting close to him of his thwarted ambition to become an opera singer, a subject that is not unconnected to the recital situation. His story comprises the canonical stages of narrative: an initial situation ("Yes, when I was little, I was very musical"), a complication ("one day my voice changed"), the evaluation and resolution projected by the father ("and father said he will be an auctioneer instead of an opera star"). The narrative is interrupted just as it reaches the final evaluation ("so I just—"). The scene in the background, for its part, might go relatively unnoticed at a first reading. What is portrayed is a song whose words are completely "flat" and unintriguing and that merely serves as background noise in the first four panels. It recounts a chronological series of events, each more boring than the previous one. But in panel 3, the words sung by the singer, "I think it's going to snow," prefigure the type of disturbance that Sammy's sneeze is soon to bring about, for it is the conversing couple's wigs that will appear to come down from the sky. The fact that the singer alone is mobile (his posture changes between panels 1 and 4) might encourage the reader to take a closer look at the content of the speech balloons. In this

FIGURE 7.12. Winsor McCay, *Little Sammy Sneeze*, October 16, 1904

page, the narrative performance is once again ridiculed. The old gentleman's tedious story is punctuated with excessive evaluations on the part of the lady sitting near him ("Oh so cute!"; "Oh mercy"; "Oh so cruel"), despite the fact that it is of absolutely no interest. Furthermore, we are confronted with a sort of cacophony produced by the superposition of the different voices (Sammy's onomatopoeias and the voices of the old gentleman, the lady, and the singer). In the latter's vocal performance, there is a mention of the blowing of a dinner horn, adding a virtual voice to the ambient din.

From this brief overview of the three pages, we draw the following observations on the mechanisms at work in the *Little Sammy Sneeze* series:

- The reader of the series recognizes the same basic sequential unfolding of events: Sammy's sneeze, which creates a disturbance in the surrounding world;
- The reader anticipates the possible paths by progressively gathering clues; he or she waits almost sadistically to see the thwarting of the activities in which the secondary characters are engaged;
- The reader backtracks in order to verify or reinterpret a clue or to discover one that might have been overlooked in the first reading.

CONCLUSION

The detailed analysis of several strips in the *Little Sammy Sneeze* series shows that the repetition of the same basic scenario in no way diminishes the pleasure experienced in reading further adventures, nor does it at all undermine their intriguing character. Indeed, the strength of this series lies in arousing the interest of the reader despite the invariable occurrence of Sammy's sneezing and the banal nature of the activities of the characters who gravitate around him (games, "script"-type activities, social chit-chat, and polite conversation). Even if we already know the outcome of the story—Sammy's familiar world inevitably ends up being turned upside down or even destroyed by his devastating sneeze—several uncertainties remain: how far will the activities of the various protagonists be able to proceed? What will the consequences of the sneeze be? How much disturbance will it cause to Sammy's familiar environment? and so on. From this point of view, we suggest suspense[16] is indeed present in *Little Sammy Sneeze* strips. But what is involved is a particular form of suspense, grounded not in the "What?" but the "How?" of the episodes. Even if the reader knows what is going to happen (the immutable sneeze), he or she still wonders how it will occur and what effects it will have.[17] The fact that he or she is aware of the threat hanging over the heads of the various protagonists, and therefore possesses information that the characters in the narrative do not, allows the reader of the series to anticipate and savor the impending chaos. It is conceivable that this pleasure is largely due to actually knowing what is going to happen. Indeed, we must not forget that the pleasure of the reader is not only related to narrative "tension" but also to the relaxation caused by the return of the same and the expected, as convincingly explained by Umberto Eco in his analysis of the James Bond series by Ian Fleming:

> The story itself remains unchanged and, curiously, the suspense is created by a sequence of totally predictable events. . . . The pleasure of the reader is to be immersed in a game of which he knows the pieces and the rules—and the outcome—taking pleasure in following the smallest variations through which the winner will make his next move. (217, our translation)

---

16. See Baroni.

17. Sometimes the devastating effects of Sammy's sneezing are highly localized (as, for instance, in page 11, in which only the black servant is affected by the sneeze when she is covered in flour), while at other times the whole surrounding environment is destroyed (as for instance in page 1, where the building is completely blown apart).

There is one final element that should be pointed out: the interest aroused in the reader as he or she searches for clues prefiguring the final catastrophe among the various protagonists' activities. If, on first reading, certain clues sometimes go unnoticed, upon rereading, it is possible to find links between the different plot threads, which are developed in parallel with the sneeze (scripts, conversations, or verbal narratives) and to detect in them hints as to the nature of the denouement.

To conclude, we wish to insist upon the need for an approach to the narrative sequence that takes into account its dual nature: both structured, coherent, and organized into a whole and, at the same time, dynamic, emergent, and unpredictable. Indeed, each strip in the series offers a narrative sequence that can be considered, on the one hand, a finished product (the tabular dimension of the page) and, on the other, a succession of panels progressively apprehended by the reader-interpreter. Through our examination of the sequential structure of strips from the *Little Sammy Sneeze* series, in conjunction with reading, which involves the progressive yet hesitant gathering of information through anticipation, backtracking and rearrangement, we hope to have demonstrated the pertinence of the inclusion of comic strip productions in the field of narrative studies.

WORKS CITED

Aubert, Michelle, and Jean-Claude Seguin. *La production cinématographique des frères Lumière.* Paris: BIFI/Mémoire du cinéma, 1996.

Baroni, Raphaël. *La tension narrative: Suspense, curiosité, surprise.* Paris: Seuil, 2007.

Boillat, Alain. "Le récit minimal en bande dessinée: L'histoire constamment réitérée d'un éternuement dans la série *Little Sammy Sneeze* de Winsor McCay." In *Le récit minimal*, edited by Sabrinelle Bedrane, Françoise Revaz, and Michel Viegnes, 103–17. Paris: Presses de la Sorbonne Nouvelle, 2012.

Bousquet, Henri. *Catalogue Pathé des années 1896 à 1914.* Vol. 4. Bures-sur-Yvette: H. Bousquet, 1995.

Bower, Gordon H., John B. Black, and Terrence J. Turner. "Scripts in Memory for Text." *Cognitive Psychology* 11 (1979): 177–220.

Canemaker, John. Introduction to *Little Sammy Sneeze by Winsor McCay*, edited by Peter Maresca. Palo Alto, CA: Sunday Press, 2007.

Chemartin, Pierre, and Nicolas Dulac. "La figure du garnement aux premiers temps du *comic strip* et de la cinématographie." In *Les cases à l'écran*, edited by Alain Boillat, 125–48. Geneva: Georg, 2010.

Eco, Umberto. *De Superman au Surhomme.* Paris: Grasset, 1993 (1978).

Eisner, Will. *Comics and Sequential Art.* Tamarac, FL: Poorhouse Press, 2005 (1985).

Frazer, John. *Artificially Arranged Scenes. The Films of Georges Méliès.* Boston, MA: Hall, 1979.

Guido, Laurent, and Laurent Le Forestier. "Un cas d'école. Renouveler l'histoire du cinéma comique français des premiers temps." *1895* 61 (2011): 9–76.

Gunning, Tom. "The Cinema of Attractions: Early Film, Its Spectator and the Avant-Garde." *Wide Angle* 8, no. 3/4 (1986): 63–70.

———. "Crazy Machines in the Garden of Forking Paths: Mischief Gags and the Origins of American Film Comedy." In *Classical Hollywood Comedy*, edited by K. Karnick and H. Jenkins, 87–105. London and New York: Routledge, 1995.

Maresca, Peter. *Little Sammy Sneeze by Winsor McCay: The Complete Sunday Comics 1904–1905*. Palo Alto, CA: Sunday Press Book, 2007.

McCay, Winsor. *Early Works*. Vol. 1. Miamisburg, OH: Checker Book Publishing, 2003.

Morgan, Harry. *Principes des littératures dessinées*. Angoulême: Editions de l'An 2, 2003.

Musser, Charles. *Edison Motion Pictures, 1890–1900: An Annotated Filmography*. Washington, DC, and Pordenone, IT: Smithsonian Institution Press and Le Giornate del Cinema Muto, 1997.

Revaz, Françoise. *Introduction à la narratologie: Action et narration*. Brussels: De Boeck-Duculot, 2009.

Rickman, Lance. "*Bande dessinée* and the Cinematograph: Visual Narrative in 1895." *European Comic Art* 1, no. 1 (September 2008): 1–19.

Roba, Jean. *Billets de Bill*. Marcinelle, BE: Dupuis, 1987.

Sadoul, Georges. *Histoire générale du cinéma. 1. L'invention du cinéma 1832–1897*. Paris: Denoël, 1946.

Schank, Roger C., and Robert P. Abelson. *Scripts, Plans, Goals and Understanding: An Inquiry into Human Knowledge Structure*. Hillsdale, NJ: Lawrence Erlbaum Associates, 1977.

Smolderen, Thierry. *Naissances de la bande dessinée*. Brussels: Les Impressions Nouvelles, 2009.

Sternberg, Meir. "Telling in Time (I): Chronology and Narrative Theory." *Poetics Today* 11 (1990): 901–48.

———. "Telling in Time (II): Chronology, Teleology, Narrativity." *Poetics Today* 13 (1992): 463–541.

van Dijk, Teun A. "Macrostructures sémantiques et cadres de connaissances dans la compréhension du discours." In *Il était une fois . . . compréhension et souvenir de récits*, edited by G. Denhière, 49–84. Lille: Presses Univ. de Lille, 1984.

CHAPTER 8

Musical Narrativity

MICHAEL TOOLAN

> Which tale is told here? It seems less entertaining to know this for sure than it is to imagine.
>
> —Daniel Crozier, program notes to his musical composition *Fairy Tale*

AT A CONCERT PERFORMANCE of a purely instrumental composition, many in the audience will experience the work as a kind of story; this helps them enter into the music's world and be cognitively and emotionally engaged or immersed. It is banal but uncontroversial to say that music stimulates our imagination; taking this a step further, I suggest that what many listeners do is imagine a story both in and through the music—though admittedly, one that is vague in all particulars (who? what? when? where? why?) and thus barely reportable and immune to verification. They are almost private stories (in the sense of Wittgensteinian private language).

The above suggestion constitutes part of an answer to the question: what actually happens to or in members of the audience during the course of a purely instrumental music performance, for example, Beethoven's string quartet op. 18, no. 1. If the piece is brief, a matter of a few minutes, we might concede that nothing more complex than a mood or "snapshot" is created—a glimpse of a world (one so quickly reaches for metaphors despite their potential to mislead: these two are visual). But for anything of greater duration, amateurs and musicologists routinely allude to structure, texture, and the creation of something with extension. More abstractly, we are sometimes told that the listener witnesses a problem or challenge "masterfully worked out," solved, or transcended.

Alongside all these familiar descriptions, I want to argue that many listeners hear and experience instrumental music as narratives, and that the narrativizing of music is a default strategy listeners draw upon to help them engage with what they are hearing (immersion) and to make sense of it. A simple sonata form falls into three recognizably distinct movements, comprising an initial melody, a second tune or theme that in some way "answers" or derives from the first, and a final movement, in which the initial melody returns or is restored or repeated but with some noticeable differences from the initial statement. Thus in the sonata as in the narrative, there is a beginning, middle, and end, and the end largely repeats the conditions of the beginning but with significant variation (narrative coherence). And crucially, in neither the sonata nor the narrative, as we move from initial to the middle phase, can the recipient fully predict what will happen next. In both cases, the auditor/reader comes to see that the middle reasonably or coherently follows whatever has constituted the beginning and that the ending equally makes for sense and coherence as a completion of the preceding phases; but the natures of those middles and ends are emphatically not foreseeable from the beginnings, however intensively we analyze them. In all the foregoing, what defines the sequence as narrative or narrative-like is its coherence, not its "logicality": in my view, the predicate "logical" has been mistakenly and misleadingly applied to narratives.

Significant numbers of listeners, significantly often, find narratives in sonatas, quartets, and symphonies, imagining characters in a situation and events and outcomes, just as they find them in modern dance and ballet, only the characters and events come without names attached or easy ostension or discursive revisiting once the performance is over. Some of these claims run counter to the received wisdom that instrumental music has sequence but is blessedly free of narrativity since it flourishes beyond the reach of the collectivist symbolizing systems of language (systems that do indeed label and describe the world and also use negation to specify what is not the case—tasks that no violin or saxophone can fulfill). In his contribution to *Narrative across Media*, Peter Rabinowitz makes the foundational point that "reading (and I'm using that term broadly to include listening and viewing) is always 'reading as'" (313). My starting point has been that *many* people who listen to classical instrumental music choose to read such pieces as, however vaguely, a storytelling.

Music is no less intrinsically sequential than literature. But there seems to be no scope for anachrony (analeptic or proleptic) in purely instrument-based musical forms (sonata, symphony, etc.) and very little resort to it in opera. Does music then lack *narrative* sequence? Anachrony itself—the possibility of telling or representing events in a different order than their presumed actual or inferable chronological occurrence—presupposes a notion of *events*: without a sense that within the artwork under scrutiny events are identifiable and might be witnessed in sequence, there can be no anachrony of telling or presentation, nor an inferring of anachrony by the recipient. The validity of the idea of events as applied to the art form or object of study is a necessary condition for the development of temporal reorderings in the narrative presentation—but it is not a sufficient condition.

Do musical compositions contain events? That all depends on how you understand or define the term *event*. Here we should not be deterred by our philosophical difficulties in devising an agreed and irreproachable definition of an event—any more than linguistics and rhetoric are rendered null by the difficulties in defining what a word is. I couldn't tell you how many events I have participated in since breakfast, but it remains enormously convenient for the coordination of my activities with other peoples to be able to refer to certain changes of state, deemed by an interpreter to be contextually significant, as events (see Huhn, and the discussion by Passalaqua and Pianzola, in this volume). And the same principle applies in our summarizing a particular film or novel as involving such and such main events, along with a lot of minor ones. Similarly in the case of music: many listeners, critics, and performers will refer to a number of moments in a piece as events, moments, or passages, in which something distinct happens that is noticeably distinct from most of what precedes and most of what follows. (I say distinct from "most of" the environing material to allow for iterative happenings, which are common in written narrative, and even more common in musical compositions.)

Events are necessary but not sufficient for anachronic presentation. But more importantly for the present discussion, anachronic presentation is not a necessary feature of all narratives (even if I am inclined to treat it as one of the most decisive proofs of *full narrativity*). If one looks at everyday personal narratives of the kind Labov analyzed, anachrony seems to be the exception rather than the norm. But it is always a *potential* within spoken and written narratives, even if particular subgenres do not exploit it; whereas it seems not to be even potentially available in instrumental music. Is that a key ground for excluding music from the narrative family? It may also be worth noting that some of the multimodal forms that use music are clearly narratives, such as opera and the musical, and infrequently use anachronic or temporally reordered diegesis—although they have the potential to do so. There's nothing in principle to prevent a story such as that of Floria Tosca from being told with, for example, the scene of attempted rape by Scarpia and Tosca's killing of him being presented at the opera's opening, followed by a "jump back" in time to the church-based exchanges between Cavaradossi and the sacristan. But it is almost unthinkable, aesthetically: why? What violation of our assumptions about "natural" opera plot development, and the intertwining of this with a broadly unidirectional emotional "journey," would be entailed? Is it that nineteenth-century opera needs to maintain all the suspense it can muster? Such proleptic anachronies, experienced as anticipatory, seem particularly to be eschewed; an analeptic one, delaying the expectable progression by dramatizing some antecedent background, seems more acceptable. Consider Bernstein's *A Quiet Place,* which in its revised form embeds in Act 2 his short opera *Trouble in Tahiti* as a flashback to thirty years earlier; and recent productions from Stefan Herheim, who has controversially used flashback in his productions of *Madame Butterfly* and *Eugene Onegin.* It is possible that the eschewing of proleptic anachrony in opera in part reflects the primacy of mimesis over diegesis in this particular art form, the relative *proximity* of the representation, by the performer on stage, to a real human being, who experiences life (regardless of the effects of "psychological time") in an inexorable unidirectional sequence. When Anna Netrebko sings the part of Lady Macbeth in the Verdi opera she *is* Lady Macbeth for those three hours. It is as if there are constraints on temporal manipulations—sequential "unnaturalness"—within opera, to counterbalance the deep unnaturalness of a drama in which characters mostly, if not exclusively, sing to each other, rather than speak. Only in an art form where diegesis, at least intermittently, overrides mimesis (thus, not opera) can the power and immediacy of this natural experiential sequencing be more regularly contested.

It is also worth recognizing that there are varying degrees (down to zero) of narrative-evocation in different instances of instrumental music. In terms of breadth of category, music can be treated as on a par with language, or glottic writing (most classical music is most reliably "archived" in nonglottic writing—that is, in scores; the obvious literary counterpart of this is the playscript that serves as a blueprint for a performed drama). If music is (roughly) categorically equivalent to glottic writing, then we should no more require all music to have narrative qualities than we require all writing to.

QUESTIONING THE SKEPTICS

In her contribution to the *Handbook of Narratology,* entitled "Narration in Various Media," Marie-Laure Ryan states:

> Language is the only semiotic system (besides formal notation systems) in which it is possible to formulate propositions. Stories are about characters

placed in a changing world, and narration is crucially dependent on the ability of a medium to single out existents and attribute properties to them. Neither images nor pure sound possesses this intrinsic ability: sound has no meaning, and pictures can show, but they cannot refer. (475)

How many of these claims bear close scrutiny? I would agree that in a language we have the potential to single out individuals and communicate evaluations of them far more routinely, straightforwardly, and thoroughly (in depth) than often seems possible with images. Can images never do this, to any degree? If we consider how a wordless cartoon strip works, it is hard to see how the partly repeated images do not single out existents with properties, undergoing events, communicating all this to the viewer. And I am often amazed at the depth of commentary and interpretation people can derive from a murky black and white photograph, taken eighty years ago or more: on occasion, we seem remarkably confident in the ascribing of propositional meaning to pictures. But again, the commentary standardly comes in the form of verbal discourse—that is, in language (it does not *have* to: one can comment in sighs, laughter, gestures, or music). A form that appears capable only of showing (the photographic image) becomes the basis for a remarkable amount of description, in which existents are singled out and properties are attributed to them. In a similar way, we have program notes at concerts, informing us of the meanings and references—the existents and attributes—that we will encounter in the sounds of a particular composition, such as Mahler's second symphony. One such text, a translation of Mahler's own program notes, declares that the second movement "*represents* long-forgotten pleasure, is a gentle, old-fashioned dance of lilting grace, yet challenged by creeping shadows," while the third movement "is a grotesque and wickedly sarcastic waltz, *shot through* with anguished outcries" (my emphasis). These are nicely judged, mutedly personificatory: mentions of a dance and a waltz hint, but do not assert, that *people* are dancing and waltzing in the "represented" scenes, and by extension, other tellable circumstances also involving the same or different people warrant the mentions of creeping shadows that challenge the dance and anguished outcries that punctuate the waltz. Let us admire, too, the creativity of the propositional meanings assigned here to Mahler's sounds—"sarcastic waltz" especially impressed me. Googling the phrase reveals that it has quite frequently been used, probably involving borrowings from the Mahler translation. A recent rerelease of a 1956 F. Charles Adler recording of the symphony prompts one Internet review (Lemco, n.d.) to say of the third movement: "Mahler's penchant for grotesquerie enters in the *Scherzo* with tympani strokes that invite [a] wicked and sarcastic waltz punctuated by percussive, anguished outcries."

Where, then, should we stand in regard to the claim that sound, or "pure sound"—a phrase intended to exclude speech, the sounds of a spoken language—has no meaning? The first difficulty with the claim is that it treats sound, or sounds, as if we can encounter them divorced from all context; whereas, in fact, I believe that upon noticing any sound, we are inclined to relate it first to a source and then, if we deem this appropriate, to an extensive embedding situation—just as we do with any visual stimulus. (This is an integrational linguistic principle: that any things treated as signs are always so treated in the context of what has gone before, what is cotemporal, and what follows. Strictly speaking, integrationally, things do not *become* signs until they are so treated, in situations of communicational interaction.) So if we are walking along a British city street and hear a particular repeated minor third mechanically produced, blared out from a source that seems to move nearer us and then further away again, with slight drop in pitch, we may be quite inclined to attribute this to an ambulance, whose driver is telling everyone to clear out of the way, that an emergency call is being answered, even that an accident has happened somewhere. Such a nonspeech sound has abundant meaning. That example involves a human agent as sound-source, which for me is definitional of music, but what about human-agent-free sounds? As I am composing these sentences, I can hear a rustling and squeaking outside my office window: it is the sound made by the wind among the branches of a flowering cherry tree, one of whose overgrown branches is rubbing against my window (hence, the squeaking sound). Inter alia, the sounds tell me that it is pleasantly breezy today—and that the tree should have been pruned earlier in the spring. Is my deriving of such meanings from the sounds irrelevant to Ryan's claim, since the meanings are not formulated, propositionally, "in" the sounds? The tree's swishing sounds are not saying, "It is breezy today," in tree-language. Or is this propositional standard of meaningfulness, this *linguistic* standard of meaningfulness, inappropriate for modes such as music and paintings, which have different standards of meaningfulness?

As Linda and Michael Hutcheon recognize in their essay on opera as narrative, opera lacks prose fiction's descriptions but offers action instead; like much drama, opera depicts and acts out ("In short, it depicts as it narrates," [442]). I am tempted to see this as paralleling the descriptive/performative distinction in speech act theory (where "He promised to be there" is a descriptive report, while "I promise to be there" is a performative act), although it could also be assimilated to the diegesis/mimesis distinction, and in particular to mimesis in the narrower sense of what Halliwell calls "dramatic enactment" (132). Relative to the witnessing audience, everything that is said and done within the storyworld of an opera such as *Tosca* is performative:

we understand the things that the characters do and say to be genuine acts of promising, torturing, ordering, denying, seducing, bargaining, and killing, all with story-world consequences. And when Tosca tells us that she has lived for art and for love, noone *reports* to us that Tosca says she has lived for art and love. If *Tosca* were a novel, especially a third-person novel (and how could it be otherwise, short of postmodern trickery, since the opera ends with Floria throwing herself to her death?), things would be different, and we would have a strong, unshakeable sense that, even if her testament was recorded as a direct speech avowal, someone else was reporting this direct speech avowal. We would have description or telling, rather than a witnessed action. There is a chorus in *Tosca,* but it does not function outside of the ongoing action to provide the audience with an explanatory commentary; like Scarpia and Tosca, it is as it were unaware that we are present.

In her contribution to the *Handbook of Narratology,* Ryan makes a number of persuasive foundational points: that "as a semiotic substance, sound possesses neither the conventional meaning nor the iconic value that allow words and images to create a concrete world and bring to mind individuated characters" (481). But this is very much what the semiotic substance known as speech does, so Ryan must be referring only to nonspeech sounds. She adds that music "cannot imitate speech, represent thought, narrate actions, or express causal relations. Its mimetic abilities are limited to the imitation of aural phenomena: the gurgling of a brook, the song of birds, or the rumbling of thunder" (481). Again, it seems to me that it depends what you mean by "imitate" and "represent." Ryan sets the bar very high by saying, in effect, artistic sounds can only imitate natural sounds. By that standard, what can artistic writing imitate? No sounds obviously, no smells or tastes, and pictures only with much contrivance (as when a poem about a river is set out on the page to look a bit like a mapmaker's representation of a river); artistic writing by this standard can only fully imitate other forms of writing. Or you have to abandon this narrow idea of mimesis and representation in favor of a broader one, which allows that artistic writing can represent (i.e., depict, evoke, "visualize") ideas and emotions, often by embedding their evocation in a highly particularized human situation. But I don't see how representation in this broader sense can be denied application to language-free activities like dance and mime, and many forms of wordless music, too, where many performers and listeners attest to the powerful emotions and mental absorption (the cognitive activity) that the performances generate in them. Those emotions and ideas might not be easily put into words, or if they are, then the result can look feebly vague or banal, but so what? Why blame music for our linguistic failings? And putting the ball back in language's court, although we tend to assume that our verbal resources are unparalleled in their enabling us to represent thoughts, there are some rather large gaps in this story, beginning with the fact that we have no very clear understanding of what thought or "a thought" is. The streams of consciousness and represented thoughts in our modern novels are only by convention and illusion a simulation of those things we believe to be thoughts and consciousness. As for actual thought, actual cognition, it is impossible to show there is more (or less) thought embedded within a short story than in a symphony or in a statue: since we have no secure understanding as to what thought actually is, we are only discussing, somewhat awkwardly, the *representing* of things we have no secure knowledge of, thoughts. The orthodox view is that language can represent thought but that music cannot, but this orthodox view rests on a question-begging conflation of thought/idea with propositional statement. By virtue of being the latter, "Caesar conquered Gaul" is uncritically assumed to be one of the former also; whereas the three notes of a C-major triad played in sequence are not a proposition and are therefore assumed not to be an idea either.

In light of the overwhelming superiority of language for purposes of storytelling, Ryan remarks (possibly with quiet irony) that "one may wonder why mankind ever bothered to develop other narrative media" (483). She might have added that, given the seeming superiority of language in all kinds of representational tasks, one might wonder why humans bothered to develop other media of representation and expression. The answer is immediately clear: language is tops at only certain kinds of representation, not others, and that for these others, we look to music, art, dance, film, sculpture, and so on. So it is not enough, I think, to say that in multichannel media, things like pictures and sounds can enrich what is foundationally given by the narrating language and acknowledge that "music [narrates] through its atmosphere-creating, tension building and emotional power" (483). Music does these things and has these qualities, but it does a lot more besides, particularly when it is the predominant mode (in the concert hall) or the sole mode (in the audio-only recording), rather than ancillary to other channels such as the visual or speech.

If narratives are, to begin with at least, "natural" and even defining of humankind, where by contrast does music sit? Is it just a useful secondary resource, something pleasing and decorative but lacking the richness and survival advantages and cognitive hard-wiring that we can ascribe to narrativity? That characterization does not fit well with my own experience of music, nor with how millions of people around the world seem to value and experience instrumental music in their cultural and intellectual lives, in ways that suggest that *some* degree of narrativity is being ascribed to it even though it appears to lack the kinds of character and situation found in narrative literature.

So I am a little uncomfortable with what I see as an *over*privileging of language itself in some models of narrativity that exclude music. One reason for such privileging is that language is the superior, perhaps exclusive, medium of representation *for the explicit expression of causality*:

> Only words can say "the king died and then the queen died of grief" because only language is able to make relations of causality explicit. (Ryan, "Narration in Various Media" 476)

Passing over the oddity of the first part of this claim (compare "only musical notes can reproduce the *Vissi d'arte* tune"), is it true that only language can make causal relations explicit? Suppose that the queen's faithful maidservant observes her mistress every waking hour after the king's death, but never actually hears her, or anyone else, remark on her growing morbidity or on how this was brought on by her beloved husband's death. And suppose, after her mistress's death, the maid becomes quite sure in her own mind that her queen has died from grief. Add to all this the fact that the maid is severely learning disabled, has never developed language beyond a basic vocabulary, and has certainly never learned the concept and word "grief." Would we say that the maid had a less clear understanding of the causal relation between the queen's death and the king's death, despite the absence of language's explicit terms? I would not. Causal relations can be quite clear without language (again, the causes and effects we identify in the sequence of panels in a wordless cartoon strip is a second counterexample); at the same time, *true* causal relations can remain unclear despite the assistance of the fullest most unambiguous language. In its seeming explicitness language can make causal relations overdetermined, simplified, and reduced; we can be misled by it into thinking we have learned true causes. But the problem of never being quite sure haunts our attributions of causation in verbal narratives just as much as in filmic ones—it is just that the loquacity of verbal-text narrators enables them (of course!) to verbalize causes (real or spurious) with dangerous facility. We can never be absolutely sure about causes, as anyone who has served on a jury in a criminal trial will agree.

People come away from a Mahler symphony or a jazz session feeling they have been hugely mentally stimulated, that they have witnessed a kind of performed sequence of musical events, beautifully paced, beautifully played, with many difficult passages requiring both technical accomplishment and a sense of "taste" (in the playing) that they themselves mostly could not begin to match—not, at least, without much rehearsal. In the course of attending that

Mahler concert, the listener routinely attests, they have witnessed something happen—or quite a lot of things happen. More than witnessing, they have *experienced* quite a lot of things happen, and they have recognized and felt that sequence of happenings come to a close with the final notes or chords and the arms of the conductor descending to a position of rest. What very many music lovers at this point do *not* want to do is to tell you what has happened, produce a paraphrase, or check for intersubjective agreement about the events just experienced. On the contrary, and for the very good reason that to a much greater degree than in written narratives or even narrative paintings, paraphrase is inappropriate, irrelevant, and a kind of category mistake. The narrative sequence or sequences that concert-goers experience cannot satisfactorily be reduced to words (program notes notwithstanding), and music lovers take pleasure and comfort from knowing this. They know they have shared in a narrative, performed by others but experienced in the whole by them, the listeners; and they know that each person's experience will in some respects be quite unique, colored by their own thoughts and reactions. And yet, with allowance for distracting coughs and poor seats and recalcitrant hearing aids, everyone in the audience has heard the *same* performance containing the *same* musical events. There is much comfort in shared participation in a collective developing sonic drama, by turns exciting, calming, somber, awesome, delicate, inspiring, all of which prompts a flood of thoughts and evaluations, memories and imaginings; the power is in the logical ineffability and variability of response, alongside the far-greater-than-chance degree of convergence among reactions where listeners *do* risk expressing their experiences (in words or other means).

What else, specifically, does viewing a musical performance in these terms, not merely as a single temporally extended event but as an event-sequence, a narrative, suggest? I believe it most centrally confirms our narrativizing cognitive predisposition: we are predisposed, in the course of apprehending a temporally extended art form such as the piano quintet (or the dance, for that matter), to help ourselves feel our way into the piece by efforts of creativity and imagination of our own—imagining that these performers are characters in that situation; that the situation is perceptibly changing, gradually or otherwise (the music *tells* us this); and that the characters are changing with it. By "entering into" the spirit of the music in this way we enable at the same time a cognitive projection *out* from the *materia specifica* of the composition, ascribing to it a beginning and middle and end, a counternarrative, perhaps a crisis point, and other narrative desiderata that might not otherwise be at all agreed upon as intrinsic elements of the piece.

QUESTIONING THE BELIEVERS

Let us turn again to opera. It has three core elements, I suggest, that enable it to be deemed a narrative-carrying form: it is an integration of singing, language, and instrumental music. Two of these are easily imaginable in a particular kind of orchestral work scored for instruments and voices singing wordlessly. Would narrativehood then be absent, in virtue of the fact that those voices were not carrying "meaningful content" in the way that they could if—as it were—they were singing utterances rather than notes? It's not that voices carrying words *guarantee* narrativehood—or even comprehensible sense—but only that this condition makes narrativehood a possibility. In fact the differences, in terms of semiological modes, between a musical work involving instruments alone and one also involving wordless voices are quite minor: a wordless soprano line can be produced equivalently by a woman or a clarinet. So the thought-experiment reduces to the question of whether the "voices" of, for example, a chamber orchestra, can convey or perform a narrative. Is a composition for such players (we use the same term to denote both musicians and actors) incontrovertibly eventless?

A good place to begin an answer is with Meelberg, who argues that the narrative study of music "can teach us about the way the listener makes sense of music" ("Sounds Like a Story" 244; see also *New Sounds*). Someone listening to music relates the sounds to each other *as music,* doing so by relating sounds and phrases to each other and to other sound phenomena, musical and nonmusical (kinds of intra-, inter-, and extra-textuality), outside the piece. "The listener tries to structure the music" during this "unifying activity," Meelberg argues ("Sounds Like a Story" 245). Thus he attends closely to the listener's activity, where in the course of listening they "structure the music as if it were a musical narrative" (246) and use this to enhance their comprehension of the music. This argument has the virtue of chiming with widespread reported experiences with instrumental music: that we often, to a degree, "structure" or interpret it in narrative terms. We do this, Meelberg suggests, in the interest of certainty:

> Turning music into a story means establishing some kind of control over, or comprehension of the music, creating a sense of certainty in an uncertain situation, which listening to an ephemeral object such as music might sometimes be. ("Sounds Like a Story" 251)

A separate motivation might be our concern for stable memorability. Still, the narrativity of music is incomplete at best: the "themes" in music are quite unlike the themes in *Macbeth*: "It is not an easy task to explain what this narrative is exactly about ... since music has no clear referential qualities" (252). Or, as Stravinsky once famously declared, "Music, by its very nature, is essentially powerless to *express* anything at all," surely realizing he was obscuring matters as much as illuminating them.[1] Again the nonpropositionality of music imposes a limit, and this prompts Nattiez to reject the analysis of music in narrative terms as a "superfluous metaphor" (257). We can never know "the content of the discourse," if indeed music has one. Wolf is as skeptical as Nattiez: he requires a truly narrative medium to be able to achieve "precise heteroreference" ("Das Problem der Narrativität" 77), which would seem to approximate what some linguists call exophoric reference, which is, for example, referring within a narrative to *the sun*, or to *London*, and having some confidence that readers will recognize the "external" referents that these phrases denote. Firm though this criterion at first seems, "precise heteroreference" tends to buckle under pressure: *must* we agree that there are incontestable (external) heteroreferences in *Emma*, for example, and that the "Surrey" and "Box Hill" of *Emma* denote (precisely) the remote ancestors of the areas bearing those names today? While the visual arts can do this to some extent, "at least as concerns spatial objects" (77), Wolf qualifies, music cannot. Thus, while more inclusive than the skeptics, Wolf, too, draws a line to separate the robustly propositional and referential art forms from those that are not and reserves narrativity for the former. Against this, we might consider whether Meelberg's claims about the content in musical compositions—and listeners' construal of that content and its development over the course of the performance—justifies the idea that music is representational after all, albeit nonpropositionally:

> The temporal development that can be heard in music is the result of a representation. It is this temporal development that is the content of the musical narrative, however abstract that content might be. (254–55)

Here we reach a crux, perhaps. Just as formalists and contextualists battled over the ontological status of characters in the novel (are there characters—a Miss Bates, a Mr. Knightley, etc.—in Jane Austen's *Emma*, or only words?), here perhaps is a parallel radical difference of perspectives: is there content in music (in Mendelssohn's "Italian" Symphony, for example), or merely notes?

As for instrument and melody, I believe we are entitled to say of them what James said of character and incident, and Yeats of the dancer and the dance.

---

1. There are many other scholars one might address at this point, including Langer, Vickers, and the recent interesting contribution of Murray.

What is a musical instrument but a means of expressing melody? What is melody but the expression of one or another instrument (where these include the human voice, the wind among the reeds, and so on)? Those instruments, as quasicharacters, often function like focalizers. At least, the instruments that take the lead are the focalizer at any point in the performance, and this focalizing role will tend to shift repeatedly during a work of music and even involve all the instruments focalizing at certain points in the piece, such as climaxes; this group focalizing is arguably analogous to an episode in a film narrative in which something is viewed as seen by all the leading characters, collectively. A switch from one "leading" instrument (or section of instruments) to another often does feel akin to a point of view shift in film or written narration or film documentary.

The use of instruments as voices, carrying a melody, or answering it, brought forward or moved into the background, taking the lead or following others, is music's solution to the problem of narrative dramatization. Our narrative preference is for one or more human or quasihuman agonists: the counterpart in music is the human (singing) voice, or by a further remove, the musical instrument. The wordless song of a performer is akin to the speaking and acting of a character on stage, in a narrative drama. The wordless melody of a lyre, flute, or violin is akin to the human song line. Each is a voice, and the voice is metonymic of a character. Things are further complicated in an orchestra, for example, where a group of violins might play in unison and comprise one voice, and in that sense constitute one character (but compare the chorus in some plays, the collective voice of a crowd). Still, the general suggestion remains: the different instruments in a symphony are tantamount to human voices, and since voices imply individuals, in the coordinated interplay of the instruments we might detect the interacting and changing "characters" of the story that musical work tells.

An interesting alternative source of "characterhood" in wordless music is proposed by the American composer Daniel Crozier, whose views are reported in Stedman. As here, Crozier believes "abstract orchestral music" has the capacity to carry on a narrative of sorts—perhaps virtual rather than concrete. But for him the "characters" are not the interacting voice-like instruments, but the musical ideas themselves:

> I sort of feel like the musical ideas can become like characters in a sense, in the way that they interact, what happens to them, the way they change by the end, by virtue of what they've been through, just like characters in written drama or theatrical drama. I think—that's how our mind perceives them, I think, if they have enough profile to resonate with us, and we remember

them. But that's what I'm trying to do here, is send my musical ideas on a journey that hopefully is gripping for the listener. You want to have some suspense about what happens here. (qtd. in Stedman 127)

If (for some listeners, perhaps, not all,) music has individual "characters" in a story situation by virtue of the solo or prominent instruments' voices, those instruments are the chief source for a work's (nonpropositional) "events." Such a supposition does not require that we treat each and every instrumental line as prominent in the creating of the "events," although all will make a contribution: just as on the stage, there will be leading roles and minor parts, a supporting and accompanying cast that creates the background against which the main figures stand out. The analogy is less satisfactory in relation to chamber music, where arguably all roles are major ones: here, in theory at least, there would seem to be no residue that can be conceived of as the narrative background or setting, which "does not move."

A describable background or setting that is in part a cause of movement in others, but does not itself move, is a feature of some verbal and visual (imagistic) narratives. But arguably, it is not a necessary feature of narratives. At any rate, there seems no possibility of the creation of a narrative-like background in the account I have just sketched, of those respects in which music can be conceived as having several narrative-like properties (characters, events, sequence, situation-creation, perceptible change, resolution). There's something paradoxical about this since in our discourses *about* music, lay or professional, people routinely refer to what is in the background in a particular symphonic movement, or talk of particular instruments' parts as establishing a setting.[2] In piano sonatas of the classical period, what the left hand produces often strikes the listener as a background or setting for melodic "action" performed by the right hand. Likewise in orchestral music, the rhythms and chord-based sequences produced by the lower instruments often provide a frame or background (always the lower instruments, it seems, the ones whose "voices" are mostly pitched so low that they are more distant, or a greater transformation away, from the pitches of the human voices that the higher instruments can more closely match). But this background or setting is not fixed and unchanging, as in a painting. The preceding remarks cannot remove a mention of *sequences,* of the fact that the apparent background created by a ground bass of a held note or chord remains *in movement* (even if the note or chord is held, as a "background," for the entirety of the piece: it is still moving

---

2. The word *setting* is widely used in musicology, albeit in a sense close to what narrative analysts would call *adaptation.*

through the time of the performance). So perhaps such "voices" as a ground bass or similar recurring but advancing pattern should be conceived not as fixed setting but as a background character, not without potential for moving into the foreground and becoming an actor or cause of action in others. And perhaps the logic of this could be extended to other forms of narrative, thus deconstructing the character/setting distinction in favor of a recognition that all introduced entities or individuals have the potential to be agentive (or *instrumental*, to redeploy this term now in its nonmusic-related sense) in the developing sequence.

Plot/sequence seems still to be criterial in the definition of narrative (e.g., as a perceived sequence of nonrandom events, usually involving a human or quasihuman protagonist from whom we "learn" and even with whom we empathize). But we have long doubted that the related events of a narrative are invariably or even mostly *causally* related. There seems to be abundant contingency, coincidence, happy or disastrous interrelation, in much modern fiction (music, on the other hand, seems unsuited to the carrying of plot).

Some will still maintain, however, that causation is critical to narrative, or "high-narrativity" narratives, whereas it is hard even for musicologists, let alone the lay listener, to perceive causation in the progressions from one bar to the next, one section to the next, one movement to the next, in a music composition. There are some norms of harmonic progression, with related keys (C major and A minor, from C major to the key based on its dominant, namely G major, and so on). But these are more like features of genre, or formal frameworks; there is no requirement for a composer to follow these well-travelled roads. On the other hand, looking again at literary narratives, it is open to question whether the sequence of main events in a story need or even should be causally related (or whether a lower standard, such as nonrandom connection, is sufficient and even preferable); in many stories, key developments and turning points seem not to be *caused* by a set of existing conditions, in the sense of "necessary consequence." Much more common is "contingent consequence"—a first event "causes" a second event when and only when a whole host of circumstances (specified and unspecified) combine with the occurrence of that first event.

This brings us back to where I started, with *events*, where it seems perfectly possible to argue that music, especially language-less instrumental music, in addition to temporal extension and sequence, has something akin to "events," albeit events hard to associate with any notional character's or narrator's *plan*. Here I agree with Seaton, in his response to Nattiez (64, fn1), that "musical events are real events—in an important sense more real than the events referred to in a fictitious story—and they raise and sometimes frustrate real expectations in the listener." Certain kinds of sequence-fixity seem inescapable in music: it would be unconscionable to play the movements of a sonata out of their ordained order. There are thus unquestionably certain kinds of development and progression in musical pieces: like language-using narratives, they have beginnings, middles, and, most difficult of all, ends. But a beginning-middle-end structure, or a generalized arc of desire, frustration, and final satisfaction are insufficient albeit common features of true narratives, which is why we need to consider whether the presence (in some sense) of other defining elements—situation, character, and event—is attested to by music-lovers.

In summary, I can see listeners apprehending events of a sort, in sequence, undergone by characters of a sort, over time, in symphonies and other instrumental music. The hardest thing to see, it seems, is the presence or achievement, in the course of those performances or our reception of them, of something describable as plot. But I would reserve judgement at this point: on the one hand, there will be some who doubt that plot is a necessary condition for something to be deemed a narrative. On the other hand, where plot is itself defined as a recognized developmental progression through a sequence of interconnected events, it might be hard to deny such a description to various kinds of instrumental music (not just program music such as Strauss's *Till Eulenspiegel's Merry Pranks*.) Taking the latter approach much further and more creatively is what Baroni proposes ("Tensions et resolutions"), redefining plot as a play of gap-provoked tension and expectation, followed by its resolution. This, Baroni argues, is also the conception of narrative dynamics long argued for by Sternberg, Phelan, and others, and in doing so, he is replacing a formal conception of plot by a functional one. My own sense is that there is more continuity than sharp difference between these conceptions and that, for example, even the Proppian triggering functions of absence and lack do not exclude the creation of gaps and delays of the kind that generate Sternbergian suspense, curiosity, and eventual surprise. It seems to me that in Sternberg and others, the tension-and-expectation generating narrative gap is cognized by the addressee/recipient: they can state it in words and discuss it with a fellow filmgoer, for example. That is the kind of verbalizable specificity that, those who are skeptical about music narratology argue, is not possible with untexted music. Baroni's proposal opens up an old concept to radically new instantiations, but it also locates the putative narrativity of music at a level of abstraction that means it cannot be tested or falsified by recourse to the commentaries of lay informants. Perhaps he is saying just that in his conclusion, when he writes:

> If nevertheless there remains a fundamental difference between musical sequence and narrative sequence, it is because the former emerges at a level of greater abstraction than the latter. ("Tension et résolution" 10)

In any event, a conception of plot as gap-based tension-and-expectation can be interestingly contrasted with a more conventional and lay-oriented one that sees plot as a complex term that abstracts or summarizes the interaction of characters and events. The latter conception remains attractive to me, in the interest of continuing the discussion, in terms presumably congenial to them (those deeply skeptical about musical narratology). I would rather engage with those who argue that a sonata cannot be a narrative because it has no characters or events by reflecting upon the ways in which listeners to a sonata report the presence of characters and the occurrence of events than abandon the criteria of eventhood and characterhood altogether.

As for suspense and surprise, frequent features in narratives, these are surely encountered in music, albeit their particulars differ from those of their instantiation in novel and film; and the broader phenomenon of tension (Baroni, *La tension narrative*) is deeply embedded in musical form. But if "narrative sequence" denotes a succession of events (at least one) applied to a situation accepted as an *initial* situation (as per Aristotle, although at some distance: a phase that is the start of something, a phase that we *accept* as not requiring disclosure of an antecedent event or situation as needful causal source), such events causing change or transformation so that the final situation is related to but different from the initial one, then it is arguable that the final movement of a symphony or string quartet represents a related but different situation from the opening one. Through a range of nonobvious (surprising, creative) modulations, variations, reworkings, answerings, and developments, an initial theme and instrumental setting might be movingly changed by the time we reach the final moments.

I would therefore subscribe to a good deal of what Barthes brilliantly and enigmatically says at the close of his *Introduction à l'analyse structurale des récits*:

> The function of narrative is not to "represent"; it is to put together a scene which still retains a certain enigmatic character for the reader, but does not belong to the mimetic order in any way. The "reality" of a sequence does not lie in the "natural" order of actions that make it up, but in the logic that is unfolded, exposed, and finally confirmed, in the midst of the sequence. To put it another way, the origin of a sequence is not the observation of reality, but the necessity to vary and to outgrow the first form that man ever

came by, namely repetition: a sequence is essentially a whole within which nothing is repeated. (271)

My only discomfort is with Barthes's final maxim here: "*Nothing* is repeated" (for me, repetitions *of a kind* are central to artistic form, music more than most, and in art we vary them but never fully outgrow them). So I am pleased to find that the translation is a little more absolute than the 1966 original, which runs: "Une séquence est essentiellement un tout au sein duquel rien ne se répète" [a whole *at the core of which* nothing is repeated: my emphasis].

FROM ALL OF THE ABOVE it is clear that the present essay leans toward the constructivist rather than the mimeticist perspective, to adopt the terms for characterizing a main contrast in the epistemological grounds of narrative theorizing that Franco Passalaqua and Federico Pianzola propose in their insightful conclusion to this volume.

Much depends on representationality (or "aboutness"), relative to an art form that, by contrast with written narrative, is nonpropositional and, if referential at all, not stably so—thus also in contrast with film narrative, which is usually straightforwardly referential and usually offers a mimetic presentation of characters, actions, and settings that are amenable to intersubjectively agreed upon propositional descriptions. The H. C. Anderson story of the girl who trod on a loaf that the musicologist Susan McClary cites has the advantage of incontrovertibly being about a girl and a puddle and a loaf of bread, whatever else it is "really" about. Whereas the aboutness McClary identifies in the Schubert *Impromptu* op. 90, no. 2, an aboutness that registers a character and events, has no such community-ratified status. Her identification of "a blithe little tune" that "commits a fatal blunder" that "unleashes unexpected violence" (20) and leads to "annihilation" (29) will be regarded by some as fanciful personification. It is not the story I get from the *Impromptu,* or not how I would describe what its narrative is about, insofar as I understand its narrative. But I would defend her—and everyone's—right to make such narrativity claims. McClary is ambitious in her argument that much eighteenth- and nineteenth-century instrumental music enacts a shared narrative of individualism absorbed back into society. She also leans heavily on the idea of the narrativity of tone or key progressions, and of melodic line as character (conventionally deployed frequently, but used in unexpected ways in the Schubert impromptu she discusses); it is not clear that these arguments are intended to serve as more than analogy and metaphor. Rather than equate melody or theme with character, I have proposed above that instruments or orchestral sections, playing particular lines, might be characters in the narrative that a symphony or concerto relates, and that collectively the orchestra establishes that essential of narrative, a situation. Keys, inversions, and modulations are important resources for the marking of sequence or progression, but so too are changes of rhythm, tempo, volume, dominant pitch, orchestration, and melodic elaboration without change of key. The piano or violin sonata might present the orchestral "instrument equals character" equation with a problem, if the latter is assumed to imply that all sonatas carry narratives about just one or, at most, two characters. But that is not a necessary assumption: the pianoforte, especially, often impresses us as a "small orchestra," with timbres and pitches and contrasts of the legato and the percussive so varied that we "hear" different instruments being played in the course of a great sonata.

While some of McClary's narrativizing might not compel the widest agreement, it seems impertinent, pointless, and constricting to suggest that she and many other listeners who hear stories in instrumental music have "got it all wrong." As it happens, she is quite decided about the limit points of palpably narrativized Western European music, music with what she calls "independent narrative coherence" (21): it begins for her around 1700 and crumbles soon after 1900. So one can certainly adopt a more radically inclusive position than McClary's on what is evidently a continuum of opinions, with Ryan further along in the exclusionist direction, allowing some story-descriptivist powers to program music, but not judging it to possess full narrativity. What seems to be involved here, finally, are different regimes of reception and interpretation: from Ryan's point of view, listeners' reports about the "characters" and "events" they detect in the course of a sonata are just so many mnemonic and usually idiosyncratic metaphors, much too impressionistic to be the basis of a narrative analysis. As she writes in her introduction to the "Music" section of *Narrative across Media*, "In the absence of specific semantic content and spatial dimension [of the kind that verbal narratives are said to carry], the deep narrativity of music is an essentially metaphorical phenomenon" (268). Except—as her introduction also notes—there are musicologists such as Tarasti who have taken the idea of the listener's narrativizing of the music they hear as an intellectual challenge, that of identifying the musical properties and features that prompt such interpretations. And as Neubauer implicitly argues, a "listener-response" criticism might not want to ignore the mental and verbal narrativizing that so many people report doing, in the course of comprehending musical sequences.

How imaginative in one's representational claims one chooses to be might need to be addressed on a case-by-case basis—as real addressees or recipients of narratives, we assess "aboutness" one case at a time. Is *Middlemarch* really about Dorothea Brooke living in the early nineteehth century rather than, say, George Eliot's own frustrations as a woman in the late nineteenth century? If we are willing to say that there is a powerful illusion of a person called Dorothea Brooke in *Middlemarch,* and not just a complex arrangement of sentences in which the words *Dorothea, Miss Brooke,* and so on occur, might we not similarly accept some listeners averring that in the course of the slow movement of Beethoven's op. 18, no.1 the story of anguished lovers is being told? If we reject such imaginings, we might also want to reject any suggestion that Mahler's 2nd Symphony is a representation of the composer's despair at the finality of death, masked as an assertion of resurrection., We might prefer a storyless description of it, as a complex, absorbing, moving, thought-triggering, quasimathematical working-through of musical possibilities, everywhere and endlessly *suggesting* things, but nowhere and never unambiguously *saying* or representing anything. This seems a political or ethical question (allowing people to be moved by maths, but not death), not a scientific one.[3]

WORKS CITED

Baroni, Raphaël. *La tension narrative: Suspense, curiosité, surprise.* Paris: Seuil, 2007.
———. "Tensions et resolutions: Musicalité de l'intrigue ou intrigue musicale?" *Cahiers de Narratologie* 21 (2011): 2–13. URL: http://narratologie.revues.org/6461.
Barthes, Roland. "An Introduction to the Structural Analysis of Narrative." Translated by Lionel Duisit. *New Literary History* 6, no. 2 (1975): 237–72. Translation of "Introduction à l'analyse structurale des récits." *Communications* 8 (1966): 1–27.
Crozier, Daniel. *Program Note for 2010 Bach Festival Society Performance of* Fairy Tale, *a Composition for Orchestra.* 2002. URL: http://www.bachfestivalflorida.org/wp-content/uploads/2010/06/BeethovenLanierWEB.pdf.
Halliwell, Stephen. "Diegesis—Mimesis." In *Handbook of Narratology,* edited by Peter Hühn, John Pier, Wolf Schmid, and Jörg Schönert, 129–37. Berlin and New York: de Gruyter, 2009.
Hutcheon, Linda, and Michael Hutcheon. "Narrativizing the End: Death and Opera." In *A Companion Narrative Theory,* edited by Peter Rabinowitz and James Phelan, 441–50. London: Blackwell, 2006.
Langer, Susanne K. *Philosophy in a New Key: A Study in the Symbolism of Reason, Rite, and Art.* 3rd ed. Cambridge, MA: Harvard Univ. Press, 1957.
Lemco, Gary. Online review of CD recordings of Bruckner, Symphony No. 3 and Mahler Symphony No. 2 "Resurrection" by F. Charles Adler . n.d. URL: http://audaud.com/2013/01/bruckner-symphony-no-3-mahler-symphony-no-2-resurrection-anny-felbermeyer-sop-sonja-dreksler-alto-austrian-radio-choir-vienna-sym-orch-f-charles-adler/

---

3. I am most grateful to Peter Rabinowitz and to Raphaël Baroni for their comments on earlier versions of this essay; and to Marie-Laure Ryan for an essay that greatly stimulated my own thinking.

McClary, Susan. "The Impromptu That Trod on a Loaf: Or How Music Tells Stories." *Narrative* 5, no. 1 (1997): 20–35.

Meelberg, Vincent. *New Sounds, New Stories: Narrativity in Contemporary Music.* Leiden, NL: Leiden Univ. Press, 2006.

———. "Sounds Like a Story: Narrative Traveling from Literature to Music and Beyond." In *Narratology in the Age of Cross-Disciplinary Narrative Research*, edited by Roy Sommer and Sandra Heinen, 245–61. Berlin: de Gruyter, 2009.

Murray, Joddy. *Non-discursive Rhetoric: Image and Affect in Multimodal Composition.* Albany: SUNY Press, 2009.

Nattiez, Jean-Jacques. "Can One Speak of Narrativity in Music?" *Journal of the Royal Musical Association* 115 (1990): 240–57.

Neubauer, John. "Tales of Hoffmann and Others: On Narrativizations of Instrumental Music." In *Interart Poetics: Essays on the Interrelations of the Arts and Media*, edited by Ulla Britta Lagerroth, Hans Lund, and Erik Edling, 117–36. Amsterdam: Rodopi, 1999.

Rabinowitz, Peter. "Music, Genre, and Narrative Theory." *Narrative across Media: The Languages of Storytelling*, edited by Marie-Laure Ryan, 305–28. Lincoln: Univ. of Nebraska Press, 2004.

Ryan, Marie-Laure. "Narration in Various Media." In *Handbook of Narratology*, edited by Peter Hühn, John Pier, Wolf Schmid, and Jörg Schönert, 468–88. Berlin and New York: de Gruyter, 2014.

———, ed. *Narrative across Media: The Languages of Storytelling.* Lincoln: Univ. of Nebraska Press, 2004.

Seaton, Douglas. "Narrative in Music: The Case of Beethoven's 'Tempest' Sonata." In *Narratology beyond Literary Criticism*, edited by Jan Christoph Meister, 65–88. Berlin: de Gruyter, 2005.

Stedman, Kyle D. *Musical Rhetoric and Sonic Composing Processes.* PhD diss., Univ. of Southern Florida, 2012. URL: http://scholarcommons.usf.edu/cgi/viewcontent.cgi?article=5425&context=etd.

Tarasti, Eero. "Music as Narrative Art." In *Narrative across Media: The Language of Storytelling*, edited by Marie-Laure Ryan, 283–304. Lincoln: Univ. of Nebraska Press, 2004.

Vickers, Brian. "Figures of Rhetoric/Figures of Music?" *Rhetorica* 2, no. 1 (1984): 1–44.

Wolf, Werner. "Das Problem der Narrativität in Literatur, bildender Kunst und Musik: Ein Beitrag zu einer intermedialen Erzähltheorie." In *Erzähltheorie. Transgenerisch, intermedial, interdisziplinär*, edited by Vera Nünning and Ansgar Nünning, 23–104. Trier DE: WVT, 2002.

CHAPTER 9

Narrativizing the Matrix

EMMA KAFALENOS

THE TERM *MATRIX*, when it was introduced in mathematics in the middle of the nineteenth century, denoted a two-dimensional rectangle containing elements arranged in rows and columns. The relationship among the elements is not fixed. Each element is related in one way to the other elements in its column, related in a different way to the other elements in its row, and may also be related by symmetry to an element in another row or column. This property of the mathematical matrix—that each element is related to more than one other element and in more than one way—is retained in the contemporary idea of the matrix.

But whereas the elements in a mathematical matrix are numbers or symbols, the elements in a matrix as it is popularly defined are events and the people involved in those events. Also, the orderly two-dimensional pattern of rows and columns of the mathematical matrix is replaced in the contemporary idea of the matrix with a vast complex that includes a temporal dimension and in which any element can conceivably be related to any other element occurring anywhere at any time.[1] The matrix in the contemporary sense in which

---

1. Definition 4.a. in the *Oxford English Dictionary* corresponds to my use of the term: "The elements which make up a particular system, regarded as an interconnecting network. Freq. with distinguishing word, as *political matrix, social matrix*, etc." Interest in locating possible relationships between any element and any other elements is illustrated by software designed by

I am using the term represents the global interconnectedness of the world in which we live.

A *narrative,* as I define it, is a representation of a process that produces change, whether in a fictional world or our world. Even the most minimal narrative, according to Gerald Prince's definition, represents a situation and an event that changes it (58). Narratives that (a) represent change and (b) take as their topic events in our world are my focus in this essay. As we all know, narratives about events in our world often differ tremendously one from another, and often contradict each other. Using the tools that as narratologists we have at our disposal, I want to analyze the process of narrativizing events in our world and explore how and why the stories about events in our world that individuals and groups construct can differ as much as they do.

As early as 1969, in his study of the *Decameron,* Tzvetan Todorov described what he called "ambiguïté propositionnelle" [propositional ambiguity: 64–65], a form of ambiguity that arises when one event is considered in two or more sequences of events. Todorov provides two examples in a story that he summarizes about sisters living in Crete (66). In the first example, the ambiguous event is Ninette's poisoning of her husband. In the sequence of events Ninette is considering, her husband has been unfaithful, and her poisoning him is punishment for that. In the sequence of events that the ruling Duke is considering, Ninette's poisoning her husband is murder; he has Ninette imprisoned and sentences her to death. One event—Ninette's poisoning of her husband—is interpreted both as a punishment for a crime and as a crime for which the perpetrator is to be punished.

In Todorov's second example from this story, the ambiguous event is the sexual encounter between Ninette's sister Madeleine and the Duke. In the sequence of events that Madeleine is considering, her sister has been sentenced to death. To free her sister, she offers herself to the Duke, who, after the encounter, releases Ninette and sends her home. In the sequence of events that Madeleine's husband is considering, his wife commits adultery, for which he kills her. The encounter between Madeleine and the Duke is interpreted both as an act to save Ninette's life and as adultery.

Describing Todorov's account, Shlomith Rimmon-Kenan writes: "Propositional ambiguity is the result of the inclusion of one proposition in two or more sequences at the same time. Thus, the proposition 'X kills Y' can become an act of punishment in one sequence and a misdeed in another" (39).

Palantir Technologies, which, according to Siobhan Gorman writing in the *Wall Street Journal,* "can scan multiple data sources at once . . . That means an analyst who is following a tip about a planned terror attack, for example, can more quickly and easily unearth connections among suspects, money transfers, phone calls and previous attacks around the globe."

The phenomenon that Todorov calls "propositional ambiguity" seems to me identical to what Lubomír Doležel, in his analysis of Vladimir Propp's *Morphology of the Folktale*, terms "functional polyvalence." Functional polyvalence names the attribute of the event that Doležel recognizes that Propp discovered: the event is subject to interpretations that shift according to the context of other events in relation to which it is perceived (Doležel 144).

In my own work on functional polyvalence, I have emphasized that the shifts in interpretation that occur when a given event is viewed first in the context of one set of events and then in the context of another set of events are shifts in interpretation of causal relations between the given event and other events. For instance, in an ongoing feud between two families, which is an example I have used (*Narrative Causalities*, 207n10), each murder is interpreted by one family as a successful form of revenge (function I in both Propp's model and mine) and by the other family as a crime to be revenged (function A in both Propp's model and mine).[2] The family that interprets the murder as a form of revenge considers some previous crime as the cause and the murder as an effect. The family that interprets the murder as a crime considers the murder the cause for which some subsequent punishment will be the effect.

In the example of Ninette's poisoning of her husband, the two very different interpretations are possible because Ninette and the Duke interpret her action in two different sequences of events. In one sequence, the husband's infidelity precedes and causes the poisoning. In the other sequence, the poisoning precedes and causes Ninette's imprisonment. Also, in the example of Madeleine's sexual encounter with the Duke, the two very different interpretations are possible because Madeleine and her husband interpret the encounter in different sequences of events. In one, Ninette's imprisonment precedes and causes the sexual encounter. In the other, the encounter precedes and causes Madeleine's husband to kill her.

Both Todorov and Propp are analyzing the polyvalence of events in fictional narratives. But events in our world are similarly open to interpretations that shift from cause to effect or from effect to cause, depending on the selection of the other events in relation to which they are interpreted. The functional polyvalence of real events is the reason that the causality of events in the matrix can be interpreted in such different ways. My title "Narrativizing the Matrix" names the process of selecting events in our world that one sees as related, organizing the selected events in chronological sequence, and interpreting the causal relations among those events.

---

2. For Propp's model, see his *Morphology of the Folktale*. For my model, see chapter 1 of *Narrative Causalities*.

The stories that individuals and groups of people construct by assembling events in the matrix are extraordinarily varied. As a first example let us consider the death of Osama bin Laden on May 1, 2011.[3] During the hour between the announcement of bin Laden's death and President Obama's report to the nation, speakers on the *ABC* television special news report anchored by George Stephanopoulos interpreted the death both as closure for the relatives of the victims of the September 11, 2001, terrorist attacks in New York City and Washington, DC, and as an event that could trigger retaliatory attacks. Like Ninette's poisoning of her husband, Madeleine's sexual encounter with the Duke, and a murder in the course of any feud, bin Laden's death was interpreted so differently because it was being considered in relation to different other events. Bin Laden's death can be seen as an appropriate resolution if considered in relation to the anguish caused by the events of September 11, 2001. But his death can also be seen as an incitement for violence if considered as the cause of potential subsequent events.

Thus far we have looked at relatively simple two-event narratives that were created by considering two events selected from a set of three events. If Event A precedes Event B, and Event B precedes Event C, then, as we have seen, one narrative can include Events A and B and another narrative can include Events B and C. Event B, which is included in both narratives, can have a very different meaning in one narrative than in the other. But now I want to look at a more complex set of events. As my first example, I return to September 11, 2001. For people in the United States and most Western countries, the events of 9/11 were extremely shocking. The strong emotional response was in part the result of the magnitude of the death and destruction. But another reason for the strength of the response was the element of surprise. The United States was not at war with another country. No nongovernmental entity had previously caused equivalent damage. In addition, since World War II the United States had regularly contributed technical and financial support to other countries, allowing U.S. citizens to think of their country as generous and to assume that their country was as appreciated abroad as benefactors want to think they deserve to be.

News coverage in the weeks and years after 9/11 drew attention to efforts to avert future events similar to 9/11 and to punish Al Qaeda for the attack. It is in the context of these efforts that Bin Laden's death can be interpreted

---

3. Because this essay was initially written for the colloquium "Redefinitions of the Sequence in Postclassical Narratology," coorganized by Françoise Revaz and Raphaël Baroni, which attracted an international audience, I chose as examples events that I assumed would be familiar to everyone attending. The colloquium took place in May 2011, after the death of Osama bin Laden and before the death of Muammar el-Qaddafi.

as a resolution. But the news coverage since 9/11 has also taught people in the United States and other Western countries that the popular opinion generally known as the "Arab street" strongly objected to the presence of the Great Satan (i.e., the United States) in Kuwait, to U.S. support for inefficient and corrupt governments in Africa and the Middle East, to U.S. military bases scattered throughout the region, to U.S. support for Israel, and so on. We can now construct a chronological sequence of events that begins decades before 2001 and continues up to and after bin Laden's death in 2011. Given that everyone around the world who is paying attention to global events is informed about all these events, how is it possible that the Arab street can continue to see the United States as the Great Satan while people in the United States can continue to see bin Laden as the Devil incarnate?

Here is a place where the tools of narratology can be of use. Meir Sternberg posits, correctly I think, that the feature that most clearly distinguishes narrative from other modes of communication is the interplay in narrative between its two temporalities: the *sjuzhet* or "discourse" and the *fabula* or "story" ("How Narrativity Makes a Difference"). In this essay, I use the Russian terms, referring to the *sjuzhet* that is given and the *fabula* that I see as constructed by readers, listeners, and viewers in response to a *sjuzhet*. Sternberg has extensively studied the effects of the sequence of the *sjuzhet* in relation to the sequence of the *fabula*. Already in his *Expositional Modes and Temporal Ordering in Fiction*, he draws attention to the importance of the choice of the first scene in a work of fiction: "The author's finding it to be the first time section that is 'of consequence enough' to deserve full scenic treatment turns it, implicitly but clearly, into a conspicuous signpost, signifying that this is precisely the point in time that the author has decided . . . to make the reader regard as the beginning of the action proper" (20).

In earlier work (chapter 6 of *Narrative Causalities*), I have shown that one of the effects of the choice of the first event in the *sjuzhet* is that readers, listeners, and viewers interpret causal relations initially among the events initially revealed. These first interpretations of causal relations among events also guide our initial judgements about the characters who perform or are affected by those events. As subsequent and prior events are revealed, we insert them into the chronological *fabula* we are constructing, which we are generally able to construct accurately. I have speculated, however, that the sequence of the *sjuzhet* continues to influence our interpretations of causality even after we have constructed the entire *fabula*. My hypothesis is that our first interpretations of causal relations among events and our resultant judgements about characters remain with us and color our attitudes toward those events and characters, even if these interpretations are flatly contradicted by the logic of the completed *fabula*. If my hypothesis is correct, all narratives shape their readers' (listeners,' viewers') causal interpretations, not only those narratives that begin *in medias res*, because all narratives, including narratives told chronologically, reveal some events before they reveal other events.

In earlier work I have taken my examples from fiction available in print, where it is easy to distinguish between the *sjuzhet* that we read and the chronological *fabula* that we construct in response to what we read. In fact the terms "sjuzhet" and "fabula" were introduced by the Russian Formalists into the vocabulary of narratology as a means to analyze the effect of written accounts of fictional events. Moreover, the term *narrative* itself denotes a representation of events. How can we use the terms *sjuzhet* and *fabula* in analyzing interpretations of events in the matrix?

This is the parallel that I draw: The *sjuzhet* of a novel, a story someone tells, a play, or a film determines the information we receive and the sequence in which we receive it; in response to that information we construct a *fabula*. In our world, our personal interests and the availability of information in the time and place where we are, function in the same way that a *sjuzhet* does to determine the information that we receive from the matrix and the sequence in which we receive it. Because the matrix includes among its elements not only events and the people involved in those events but also the dates when events occur, we can generally order the events we learn about chronologically just as we order events in a *sjuzhet* to construct a *fabula*. Although I recognize that the narrative-like structures we construct to explain our world to ourselves are representations that are perceived only by the person who constructs them, I am nonetheless calling them "narratives." I also use the term *sjuzhet* to denote the sequence in which we learn about events in our world that we consider related and *fabula* to denote those events arranged in chronological sequence.

If my hypothesis is correct that the information initially revealed in a *sjuzhet* not only determines our first interpretation of causal relations and judgements about characters but that our first interpretation tends to remain with us even if we later receive contradictory information, then the sequence in which information from the matrix reaches us presumably also shapes our interpretations. I have chosen 9/11 as an example because the terrorist events of that day were experienced simultaneously by millions of people in the United States and Western Europe as the initial events in a *sjuzhet*. Like all *sjuzhets*, this one needed to be interpreted by constructing a chronological sequence and interpreting causal relations. But for many people, the only additional information available was that bin Laden claimed to be the mastermind. These people judged bin Laden as the great criminal and constructed a *fabula* that, like the *sjuzhet,* began with the events of 9/11, followed by potential subsequent events: preferably finding bin Laden and punishing him.[4]

With the greater knowledge the intervening ten years have given us, we know that the behavior of the United States in the Middle East has been anything but irreproachable and that some of the goals of Al Qaeda are understandable, even if the methods are not. In other words, we now have the necessary information to construct a *fabula* that begins decades prior to 9/11 and continues for a decade after. But the approval—almost joy—expressed in the United States at the death of bin Laden would seem to support my hypothesis that our interpretations of the first events we learn about and our initial judgments of those who perform them remain with us even after we receive information about subsequent and prior events.

While the narratives that we read (or hear or view) control the sequence of the *sjuzhet,* where and when we happen to be largely determines the sequence in which we learn about events in the matrix. In the extreme case of 9/11, for millions of people the events of that day were the first event in their *sjuzhets.* Usually there is somewhat more variation in the sequence in which individuals learn about the events they come to consider related. But the effects of place and time—and the sociopolitical and economic aspects of that place and time—generally ensure that sufficiently similar initial information is available to people in a given culture that interpretations of the initial information are broadly shared within a society or social group. These initial interpretations of events and the people who perform or are affected by them, like the interpretations in the West of 9/11, also seem to endure even after further information is acquired.[5]

---

4. I am emphasizing, perhaps overemphasizing, a lack of attention to the details of international affairs that is entirely too prevalent in the United States. In contrast, in comments on an earlier version of this essay, Peter Rabinowitz correctly points out that there were in fact many well-informed people in the United States who were familiar with—and could interpret 9/11 in the context of—the history of relations between the United States and the Middle East.

5. Patrick Colm Hogan, as I do, chooses the events of September 11 to illustrate the effect of the first event in a narrative on interpretations of causality. Like me, he assumes that most Americans, if asked what gave rise to the War on Terror, will point to the terrorist attacks on September 11. Like me, he recognizes that this response is illogical: "To say that the World Trade Center bombings gave rise to the recent wars is, implicitly, to suggest that these wars did not develop out of preceding U.S. policy. It also involves treating the bombings themselves as if they were uncaused" (46). But Hogan and I look in different—and complementary—directions for our explanations. Whereas I turn to narrative theory to understand the effect of the sequence in which we learn information, and develop that theory to analyze the narratives we tell ourselves, Hogan turns to cognitive theory to understand the effect of human emotions on interpretations of causality, and does not distinguish between the narratives we read (or hear or view) and those we tell ourselves. For Hogan, "Insofar as they involve strong emotions, our spontaneous attributions of causality may remain at least partially impervious to our knowledge about

Let us take as another example the events in Libya. Whether we initially knew only about the Lockerbie bombing in 1986 that killed the passengers on Pan Am flight 103, or our initial information included other state-sponsored terrorist activities under the aegis of Libya's ruler, Muammar el-Qaddafi, logically our judgements of Qaddafi should have changed for the better when we learned that he later accepted responsibility for the Lockerbie bombing, paid reparations to the families of the victims, and ended his nuclear weapons program. Yet in early 2011, when protests broke out in Libya, which then turned into a civil war, the first response of the West was to sympathize with the insurgents and interpret their actions as those of patriots risking their lives to bring about a much-needed change in their government. And when we were informed that Qaddafi's forces were firing on Libyans, NATO forces authorized by the United Nations Security Council intervened. Again in this example, our interpretations of the initial events we learn about and our initial judgements of the people who perform or are affected by those events seem to remain with us, even if we learn about subsequent events that might seem to contradict those first interpretations.

But I choose Libya as an example in part because an interview in the *New York Times* with Qaddafi's daughter, Aisha el-Qaddafi, offers a glimpse of how differently events can be interpreted by people for whom the first events they learn about in the set of events they consider related are very different. Ms. Qaddafi is described in the article as "36, a Libyan-trained lawyer who once worked on Saddam Hussein's legal defense team" and the mother of three young children (Kirkpatrick A1). In her comments to the interviewer she rules out dialogue with the Libyan insurgents, "dismissing them as 'terrorists' who 'are just fighting for the sake of fighting'" and she expresses doubt that Qaddafi's forces had shot at unarmed demonstrators: "'I am not sure that happened,' she [is quoted as saying]. 'But let's say that it did: it was limited in scope'" (Kirkpatrick A8).

These citations demonstrate that Ms. Qaddafi's view of events is very different from views typical in the West. But yet another statement she makes helps us understand how she narrativizes the matrix: "Under her brother Seif's unofficial leadership, she said, the Libyan government had been on the verge of unveiling a constitution as a step toward democratic reform when

---

actual causal relations.... This results from two complementary factors. First, our emotional responses may usurp working memory, thus the very inferential processes that should inhibit our spontaneous causal attributions. Second, our lack of emotional involvement with alternative analyses ... means that these alternative analyses receive no further attentional focus or elaboration and thus are unlikely to engage inhibitory processes" (57). I am grateful to Brian Richardson for bringing to my attention Hogan's essay.

'this tragedy happened and spoiled things'" (Kirkpatrick A8). This citation would seem to indicate that in Ms. Qaddafi's narrativization, the status of Libyans had gradually improved under Qaddafi's reign and was about to move toward democracy through peaceful means when the rebellion unfortunately occurred. The near-term introduction of a constitution, which is included in the subset of events that Ms. Qaddafi narrativizes, is not included in the subset the West typically narrativizes. On the one hand, Ms. Qaddafi apparently has information that people in the West do not have. On the other hand, she is more willing to believe that her father would support a move toward democracy than people in the West typically are. We can hypothesize that her initial information about her father and resultant judgements continue to influence her present judgements, just as the initial information and resultant judgements of Qaddafi in the West continue to influence judgements in the West.

My analyses are not—and are not meant to be—a detailed investigation of international relations. My purpose is to investigate what narratology can teach us about how and why the causality of events in the world can be interpreted in so many ways. I have used very broad brush strokes in order to illustrate both a similarity and two differences in how we interpret causality in response to the narratives we read (or hear or view) and the narratives we tell ourselves about the events in the matrix.

The similarity is that both the narratives we read (or hear or view) and the matrix offer us information sequentially, piece by piece. Thus we always receive some information before we receive other information. In response to the initial information we receive, whether from a narrative or from the matrix, we construct an initial chronological *fabula* in relation to which we make our first interpretations about the causality of events and resultant judgements about the people who perform or are affected by those events. If my hypothesis is correct, that these first interpretations remain with us and are very difficult to change, it applies equally to narratives we read (or hear or view) and to the narratives of events from the matrix that we tell ourselves. In the world, if my hypothesis is correct, the results of initial interpretations that are difficult to change may include nationalism, patriotism, prejudice, political and economic choices, and religious beliefs. The various perspectives on the world that children are taught surely affect the narratives that as adults they construct from the matrix.

The first difference is that the narratives we read (or hear or view) determine for us which events to consider as related. In response to the matrix, in contrast, individuals select the events they consider to be related. At the beginning of this essay, in relation to Todorov's examples, I looked at two-event narratives and noted how very differently the causality of Event B would be interpreted depending on whether it was considered in relation to Event

A or Event C. The very size of the matrix, because it offers so nearly infinite subsets of events for individuals to narrativize, helps to explain how causal relations among events in the world can be interpreted so differently. Where one might hope that global communication would facilitate people's understanding each other, instead, I fear, the more there is that we can know, the more difficult it becomes for us to reach agreement about causality.

But the second difference is that the narratives we read (or hear or view) are finite. In response to the matrix, in contrast, individuals may add events they consider to be related for as long as they remain conscious and able to perceive. Changes in the events one considers to be related, as we have seen, can change one's interpretations of causality. Thus it is possible for an individual to rewrite a previously constructed narrative in a way that alters the causal logic. It may even be possible for individuals whose interpretations of events disagree to recognize—and revise by extending—the narratives that underlie their conflicting views. Admittedly, renarrativizing the matrix is not likely to lead to global peace. But at least on the very local level, among friends and family, colleagues and acquaintances, perhaps it is possible for two people to understand why they disagree by considering the differences in the subset from the matrix that each is narrativizing and recognizing differences in the initial elements in the matrix that each person happened to learn.

WORKS CITED

Doležel, Lubomír. *Occidental Poetics: Tradition and Progress.* Lincoln: Univ. of Nebraska Press, 1990.

Gorman, Siobhan. "How Team of Geeks Cracked Spy Trade." In *The Wall Street Journal* 4 September 2009. URL: http://online.wsj.com/article/SB125200842406984303.html.

Hogan, Patrick Colm. "Stories, Wars, and Emotions: The Absoluteness of Narrative Beginnings." In *Narrative Beginnings: Theories and Practices,* edited by Brian Richardson, 44–62. Lincoln: Univ. of Nebraska Press, 2008.

Kafalenos, Emma. *Narrative Causalities.* Columbus: The Ohio State Univ. Press, 2006.

Kirkpatrick, David D. "From Qaddafi Daughter, Glimpses of the Bunker." In *New York Times* 27 April 2011, natl. ed.: A1+.

"Matrix." *Oxford English Dictionary.* URL: http://www.oed.com.libproxy.wustl.edu/view/Entry/115057?rskey=3.

Prince, Gerald. *Dictionary of Narratology.* Lincoln: Univ. of Nebraska Press, 2003 (1987).

Propp, Vladimir. *Morphology of the Folktale.* 2nd ed. Translated by Laurence Scott. Revised by Louis A. Wagner. Austin: Univ. of Texas Press, 1968 (1928).

Rimmon-Kenan, Shlomith. *The Concept of Ambiguity—The Example of James.* Chicago: Univ. of Chicago Press, 1977.

Sternberg, Meir. *Expositional Modes and Temporal Ordering in Fiction.* Baltimore: Johns Hopkins Univ. Press, 1993 (1978).

———. "How Narrativity Makes a Difference." *Narrative* 9 (May 2001): 115–22.

Todorov, Tzvetan. *Grammaire du Décaméron.* The Hague: Mouton, 1969.

PART IV

Unnatural and Nonlinear Sequences

CHAPTER 10

Unusual and Unnatural Narrative Sequences

BRIAN RICHARDSON

THE NEW LINEARITY

THE LATTER PART of the twentieth century and the first years of the twenty-first have seen an explosion of innovative developments in the possibilities of the *sjuzhet*; every aspect of the sequencing of the narrative text is in the process of being reconstructed. Narrative theory has not fully caught up with many of the more unusual and extreme cases; in what follows, I will attempt to identify the most interesting adventures of narrative sequencing and go on to offer some supplemental theoretical formulations where needed. My essay will therefore be conceptually situated in this anthology between those of Raphaël Baroni and James Phelan, on the one hand, and Emma Kafalenos and Marie-Laure Ryan, on the other, and it is in dialogue with Eyal Segal's essay on endings.

THE NEW LINEARITY

A new linearity is emerging in which authors explore chronological sequencing in original ways. Daniel Glattauer's novel, *Gut gegen Nordwind* [*Love Virtually*], is a transcription of a sequence of email messages between a man and a woman. The temporality of this unswerving linearity is often identified to the second that successive email messages were sent. This produces a keen attention to chronology, as emails fly almost instantaneously or as each correspondent wonders in print why the other has not responded to the latest message. This practice updates, intensifies, and speeds up the kinds of interactions between correspondents present in the eighteenth-century epistolary novel. It also produces a virtually disembodied narrative; all the protagonists have to work with are each other's email messages.

A more radical play with linearity can be found in Eva Figes's 1981 novel, *Waking*. It recounts the thoughts of a woman as she wakes over the course of seven mornings, each separated by about a decade. Such a practice foregrounds the tenuous nature of personal identity over time, as well as residual characteristics that resist time's effacement. Another work that employs a comparable technique is David Nichols's *One Day*, which narrates the story of two people on a single day, July 15, each year over the course of two decades. Since there is no summary or contextualizing material between each chapter, the reader is left with a powerful sense of pure sequence as the story leaps ahead, year after year. We also recognize the transitory nature of many seemingly important events when viewed from a greater temporal distance and note, as well, persistent character traits that endure over the years.

Linearity can move in either direction, however, and a number of authors have sequenced episodes in an antichronological order; they move backward into the past as the reader moves forward in the text. Elizabeth Howard's *The Long View*, a novel about the demise of a marriage, is composed of five parts that respectively present the events of the years 1950, 1942, 1937, 1927, and 1926. The antichronological arrangement imbues the trajectory of events with a powerful sense of fatality. Similarly constructed works include C. H. Sisson's *Christopher Homm*, Julia Alvarez's *How the Garcia Girls Lost Their Accents*, and, barring a couple of scenes, Harold Pinter's play, *Betrayal*. In these works, each segment is set deeper into the past; at the unit of the chapter or scene, the order of the *sjuzhet* is thus the opposite of the order of the *fabula*. Watching a performance of *Betrayal* produces a curious kind of suspense, as the audience keeps waiting to see the beginning of the story, wondering when it will see the enactment of the crucial scene that is frequently remembered by the characters, what revelations will be divulged concerning the early events of the story, how the affair really began, and even, "When will the playwright stop giving us backstory?" Seymour Chatman and Per Krog Hansen have recently published stimulating articles that discuss in-depth the nature, effects, and reception of such texts, while Mieke Bal reveals an ancient (if brief) precedent for such strategies by pointing out that the opening passages of the *Iliad* narrate the development of the wrath of Achilles in a largely antichronological order (83–84).

Others have gone on to combine these two kinds of linearity by alternating chronological with antichronological progressions. Christopher Nolan's 2000 film, *Memento*, intersperses linear segments of a chronological narrative with a narrative whose segments are presented in reverse chronological sequence; the former are presented in black and white, the latter in color shots. The beginning of the film includes additional chronological play as a short sequence is run in reverse. The *Memento* (limited edition) DVD set also offers the viewer the additional option of playing the entire film in a purely chronological sequence where the *sjuzhet* can be resequenced to reproduce the order of the *fabula*.

Tom Stoppard provides a number of creative deployments of his *sjuzhets*; his play *Indian Ink* alternates two linear plot lines that are separated by several decades, and *Arcadia* does the same with stories that are nearly two hundred years apart in time but which take place on the same physical space, an old English country house. His most playful *sjuzhet* construction is no doubt *Artist Descending a Staircase*. In it, each scene moves progressively further into the past until it reaches the middle of the *sjuzhet*; then the play is presented in chronological segments that lead back into the narrative present as each chronologically earlier scene is returned to and continued; the *fabula* is thus presented in the sequence 6, 5, 4, 3, 2, 1, 2, 3, 4, 5, 6. The sense of narrative progression and closure are particularly powerful as the work moves forward toward the resolution of the mystery and by the completion of the symmetrical pattern of temporal representation. A similar trajectory informs David Mitchell's *The Cloud Atlas*, a series of six nested narratives that extend progressively into the future and then return in reverse order to the previously represented time period.

Still more elaborate is the sequencing of Jim Crace's novel, *Being Dead*, an account of the deaths of a husband and wife, both biologists, on a deserted beach. Three narrative strands are interwoven here into a strangely compelling totality: the chronological narrative of the decomposition of the corpses, day by day, during the period just after the murders; the linear account of the first meeting of the two and the daily development of their relationship thirty years previously; and the account of the last day of their lives, told in an antichronological order that starts with their deaths and moves back in time hour by hour.

THE UNLIKELY *SJUZHET*

The *sjuzhet* is usually defined as the way the story is presented in a narrative text. Some ingenious authors, however, have played with this convention and offered a seemingly nonnarrative text from which a story is able to be derived.

This strategy, at least in its more extravagant forms, seems to have originated with Vladimir Nabokov's *Pale Fire* in which a 999-line poem and over two hundred pages of ostensible and often wayward commentary produce a narrative of a deluded critic's life and fantasies. A number of recent experimental works present an ostensibly nonnarrative text from which a compelling story can be derived; there is no doubt a greater range of such texts than is generally recognized. These forms are varied and include a dictionary, a catalogue of an art exhibition, and liner notes to a music disk: respectively, Milorad Pavić's *Dictionary of the Khazars: A Lexicon Novel*; Stephen Millhauser's "Catalogue of the Exhibition: The Art of Edward Moorash" in *Little Kingdoms,* and Christopher Miller's *Sudden Noises from Intimate Objects: A Novel in Liner Notes*. In his story, "Problems," John Updike utilizes the form of the standard arithmetic test problem to produce a clever story. Thus, the third problem reads:

> *A* has four children. Two are in college, two attend private school. Annual college expenses amount to $6,300 each, those of private school to $4,700. *A*'s annual income is *n*. Three-seventh's (3/7) of *n* are taken by taxes, federal and state. One-third goes to *C*, who is having the driveway improved. Total educational expenses are equivalent to five-twenty-firsts (5/21) of *n*. The cost each week of a psychiatric session is $45, of a laundromat session, $1.10. For purposes of computation, consider these *A*'s only expenses.
>
> PROBLEM: How long can *A* go on like this? Round to the nearest week. (169–70)

Sjuzhets arranged in an alphabetical sequence include such varied works as Roland Barthes's book, *Roland Barthes par lui même*; Michèle Roberts's "Un Glossaire / A Glossary" in *During Mother's Absence*; Rick Moody's "Primary Sources," an annotated list of the books in the narrator's library, which constitute a kind of autobiography; and J. G. Ballard's story "The Index," a narrative in the form of the index to an autobiography (in *War Fever*). How exactly are the events disclosed in such unusual texts? Sometimes, the unconventional arrangement reproduces a largely linear temporal progression, as when the circumstances surrounding the birth of the protagonist of "The Index" are revealed, respectively, in an entry beginning with the letter "A" ("Avignon, birthplace of HRH, 9–13"), and his final days are disclosed by the entries, "Young husband, Lord Chancellor" and "Zielinski, Bronislaw." Lists are also sometimes presented as implicit narratives, such as "Receipt Found in Parking Lot of the Super Walmart" by slam poet Big Poppa E (Eirik Ott) that includes the following items: "Anniversary Hallmark card. Flowers. Candles. Matches. Incense. . . . Block of white chocolate. Bottle of white wine. Barry White's Greatest Hits cd.... Honey. Box of condoms, 32 count, extra large." (45).

VARIABLE *SJUZHETS*

In a typical work, the *sjuzhet* is the narrative in the sequence that it appears in the text: it is usually coextensive with its presentation, whether page by page or, in an oral narrative, word by word. It is widely affirmed that narrative and its reception are sequential processes and that simultaneous events must therefore be presented and processed sequentially, not simultaneously. In works with multiple storylines, the *fabula* has to be presented in more than one discrete segment, as happens in the first part of Virginia Woolf's *To the Lighthouse,* since independent acts of simultaneous perception or depictions of concurrent chains of events cannot be presented at the same time. We may refer to this as the "meanwhile, back at the ranch" principle. This is usually the case for most fiction, but some experiments have suggested the possibility of a multiple presentation of such events. Joyce Carol Oates alters the physical layout of the standard printed page to create a "simultaneity effect" by using two parallel columns to disclose the thoughts of separate individuals in her story, "The Turn of the Screw." Harold Pinter uses three playing spaces on the same stage to indicate simultaneous events at two locations in his play, "The Collection." Film occasionally uses a split screen to achieve the same effect, as found throughout Hans Canosa's *Conversations with Other Women.* Mike Figgis's *Timecode,* where the screen is split in four, is an even more extreme example. The audience thus helps choose some of the arrangement of the *sjuzhet.*

The text of J. M. Coetzee's *Diary of a Bad Year* is, for the most part, divided into three segments on each page. The uppermost contains nonnarrative essays on an assortment of topics; the middle consists of a diary-like narrative that records the narrator's fascination with a young woman named Anya; and the final segment of the page contains Anya's narrative of the relationship. At several points, the two linear narratives approach simultaneity, or at least different perspectives on the same events shortly after they occur. For much of the work, the two narratives diverge as one moves ahead of the other in its disclosure of different periods in the same overall *fabula.* The reader typically starts processing the text left to right and top to bottom, but soon is tempted, seemingly irresistibly, to continue on with one or both of the narratives as their events become increasingly dramatic.

Among narrative theorists, it is widely believed that the *sjuzhet* of a work is always linear. In the words of Shlomith Rimmon-Kenan, "The disposition of elements in the text . . . is bound to be one-directional and irreversible, because language prescribes a linear figuration of signs and hence a linear presentation of information about things. We read letter after letter, word after word, sentence after sentence, chapter after chapter, and so on" (45). For the most part, she is correct: the *sjuzhet* of a text is simply the sequence of pages you hold in your hand or experience in performance. However, as Jukka Tyrkkö has noted, this principle can be abrogated in classic novels; authors like Cervantes and Sterne "engaged readers by means of metanarratives giving instructions to skip certain 'irrelevant' chapters or to reread some previous ones" (279). Dave Eggers has recently extended this tradition in the note, "Rules and Suggestions for Enjoyment of this Book," which precedes his narrative, *A Heartbreaking Work of Staggering Genius*, where he notes the various pages and sections that an impatient reader might want to skip, some of them rather considerable: "Many of you may want to omit much of the middle, namely pages 239–351, which concern the lives of people in their early twenties, and those lives are very difficult to make interesting" (vii).

There is still greater freedom when the *sjuzhet* is alterable. In some lexicon novels, like Richard Horn's *Encyclopedia*, one may either follow the alphabetical sequence of entries or skip from one item to another that expands on it; the entry "Bishop's Cope" concludes with the invitation to see the entries "Doom" and "Papageno" (21–22). An extreme example of a variable *sjuzhet* is B. S. Johnson's "novel-in-a-box," *The Unfortunates*, which is composed of individually bound chapters that may be read in any sequence (though here one chapter is to be read first and another last). Readers are informed that the sections appear in a random order; if they don't like the arrangement, they are invited to place the segments in their own random sequence. The book, if one may call it that, describes the sensations and memories of a sports reporter who revisits the town where a close friend of his had died some time before. Each chapter primarily records one of two sets of events: poignant memories from the past or the meaningless events in the reporter's day. A few sections combine both temporal frameworks, but for the most part, they situate themselves in one or the other period, each indicated by a different tense of narration, the past tense for the memories and the present tense for the current day's account. What is interesting is that nearly all the chapters in the two sets can be situated within the earlier or later chronological sequence—there are no iterative accounts (e.g., "Year after year, we would . . .") and surprisingly little *achrony*, or temporally indeterminate events. Like a bound modernist novel, most of these segments can be placed within a normal *fabula;* the question that arises is why does Johnson forgo sequencing his *sjuzhet*? The answer lies, I believe, in the irrelevance of any possible sequence to the grieving narrator.

It does not matter where he situates the account of his lunch or where he places his memory of hitchhiking with his friend. The former event is utterly unimportant and so is its placement; the latter event can appear anywhere, just as it will appear in a different sequence when it is remembered again.

Some texts go still further. Marc Saporta's *Composition No. 1* consists of a box of unnumbered, self-contained pages. Saporta invites the reader to take the pages and shuffle them as one might a deck of cards: "Le lecteur est prié de battre ces pages comme un jeu de cartes" [first printed page, unnumbered]. Saporta goes on to claim that the sequence that emerges determines the fate of the characters since, as he points out, it makes a considerable difference whether the protagonist met his mistress, Dagmar, before or after his marriage began. Thus, the author concludes, time and the order of events control a man's life more than the occurrence of the events themselves. Here the *fabula* might be somewhat variable, and the *sjuzhet* is entirely so.

Drama also has interesting examples of unfixed or variable *sjuzhets*. Charles Ludlam's *The Grand Tarot* enacts these possibilities. The play contains twenty-two scenes. Before each performance, tarot cards were dealt out to determine the sequence in which the scenes would be presented. Every performance was different and incorporated the play of chance into the presentation of events. Ludlam claimed that the story was never the same twice. From our vantage point, we might say instead that the *fabula* was constant (all twenty-two scenes were always performed) though the *sjuzhet* was always different. Here we have a fixed *fabula* with an entirely variable *sjuzhet*. It is worth noting that this unpredictable sequencing proved so difficult that Ludlam later established a fixed order of presentation for subsequent productions.

Milorad Pavić's *Landscape Painted with Tea* (1990) is a novel in the shape of a crossword puzzle and can be read either "across," in the conventional sequence of numbered pages as the narrative intersperses one storyline with another, or "down," as each separate storyline is read from beginning to end. The narrator provides an informative gloss on this arrangement that no doubt points toward one of the motivations for constructing unusual and unnatural stories and texts: "Why now introduce a new way of reading a book, instead of one that moves, like life, from beginning to end, from birth to death?" He responds, "Because any new way of reading that goes against the matrix of time, which pulls us toward death, is a futile but honest effort to resist this inexorability of one's fate, in literature at least, if not in reality" (185–86).

Other forms of narrative may have unfixed *sjuzhets*. Narrative paintings, in which several scenes of the life of an individual are depicted on a single canvas, can be read in many possible sequences. Graphic novels can employ several different reading progressions, including top to bottom, left to right, and even right to left, as well as unmoored sequences. As Thomas A. Bredehoft explains, Chris Ware's *Jimmy Corrigan: The Smartest Kid on Earth*, presents a page of images delineating the crucial backstory of the *fabula* that can be read in different ways. "Ware's page-layout, which on one level enforces right-to-left reading [of the recounting of events before the narrative present tense], also demands a left-to-right reading of the same sequence of panels for a different narrative line" (878). The most familiar narratives with an indeterminate *sjuzhet* are of course hyperfictions, including those that seem to have a fixed, determinate *fabula*.

RECONSTRUCTING THE MATERIAL BOOK

The adventures of the *sjuzhet* continue in the physical layout of the material book. The traditional *sjuzhet* is so entrenched that its contravention can be quite disconcerting. When one opens Ishmael Reed's novel, *Mumbo Jumbo*, one finds just inside the front cover the first page of the first chapter. At the end of this chapter, there are the conventional pages that almost invariably precede the text of any novel—that is, the epigraphs, list of other works by the author, title page, copyright page, and dedication—before returning to the second chapter of the novel proper; the story frames its own antetext and thereby seems to defy any prior framing by paratextual material. Another fascinating *sjuzhet* construction occurs in William Gibson's early hypertext, *Agrippa: Book of the Dead*.[1] The text was constructed so it would encrypt itself after its original viewing and thus become unreadable afterward. It materially destroys itself. If anyone misses a key line, there is no going back. The work thus uses a post-Gutenburg technology to approximate the typical irretrievability of oral narration.

More radical experiments involve the physical shape of the book. Armine Kotin Mortimer notes that "Jean Ricardou, in *La Prise de Constantinople*, invented a form to redefine beginnings and endings by giving his novel a second entry: the back cover looks exactly like the front cover, except that the title is *La Prose de Constantinople*," (385). As Ricardou explains:

> This book is laid out a bit like those movie theaters where you go in under a brilliant marquee but go out at the back, down some shadowy adjacent street, by way of the discreet back cover of the book. . . . Once the single entrance is passed, the reader is called upon to follow the corridor out to the single

---

1. See http://agrippa.english.ucsb.edu.

exit, at the very end. Bringing this underlying ideology of the book to light by contesting it amounts to establishing a reverse course: setting up a second entrance against the first. (qtd. In Mortimer 385)

Hélène Cixous's 1976 novel, *Partie,* is composed of two parts that are in reciprocal relation to each other. The book has two front covers, each of which is an inverted image of the other, and each of which is upside down in relation to the other. Thus one can read the book from one beginning point until one comes to page 66 (90).

Carol Shields's *Happenstance: Two Novels in One about a Marriage in Transition* is another book that can be read linearly from either direction. It narrates the story of a changing marriage from both the husband's and the wife's perspectives. Both have thirty chapters; the book has two front covers; one is blue, the other pink. Due to an inverted binding, neither one has the place of being the first version or the last word; it all depends on how the reader holds the physical volume. Needless to say, each narrative position essentially stands the other on its head. This allows the author, incidentally, to dedicate the book to two different people, one on each side of the volume. There are no instructions for use, and the *sjuzhet* can be constructed in a number of ways. A reader may read first one and then the other half *in toto,* or since each covers the same time period from different perspectives, the reader may read a few chapters of one version and then turn the book upside down and read a chapter or two of what is literally the other side of the story.

More recently, Mark Danielewski has produced a similar kind of text, *Only Revolutions.* This volume, too, has two covers and two sets of front matter: both beginnings of the book have the copyright information. One side, with a green cover, is the story as told by Sam, while the side with the gold cover is the same story as told by his lover, Hailey. The top of each page contains one story, while the bottom contains the other narrative, printed upside down; each has the same number of words. Up to this point, I have scrupulously resisted the great temptation of every narratologist: the coining of obscure neologisms. To describe the kind of books that can be read in either direction, however, I feel we need a special term. I will employ a very old one: *boustrophedonic,* which is used to describe ancient systems of writing that move first left to right, then right to left, the way one plows a field.

A final and particularly poignant example of the creative utilization of the material book comes at the end of Jonathan Safran Foer's 2005 novel, *Extremely Loud and Incredibly Close.* This is a narrative about a boy's search for his father, who is believed to have been killed in the attack on 9/11. The narrator states that he took photos of a man falling from the top of one of the Twin Towers to his death below. The photos, however, are arranged in reverse sequence: "I reversed the order, so the last one was first, and the first was last. When I flipped through them, it looked like the man was floating up through the sky" (325). The narrator goes on to speculate that had time been inverted, the figure in the picture, who might have been his father, "would have left his messages backward, and the plane would have flown backward away from him, all the way to Boston" (325). Then, "Dad would have gone backward through the turnstile, then swiped his Metrocard backward, then walked home backward as he read the *New York Times* from right to left" (326). The book ends with the photos in reverse order, which the reader can physically flip to make the falling man seem to return to the top of the building, as the effects of time and death are temporarily vanquished by what I have elsewhere called *antinomic temporality*.

VARIABLE *SJUZHETS*, MULTIPLE *FABULAS*

Ana Castillo's *The Mixquiahuala Letters* suggests other possible ways of constructing a *sjuzhet*. It is both a postmodern epistolary novel and an act of homage to Julio Cortazar's *Hopscotch*. The text itself consists of forty undated letters. At the beginning of the work, the reader is warned not to read the book in the usual sequence, but rather to follow "one of the author's proposed options" (9); these are partial sequences of most of the letters designed, respectively, for the conformist, for the cynical, or for the quixotic personalities. Thus, the conformist is to begin with letters 2, 3, 6, 7, 9, 11, and 12, while the quixotic will read letters 2 through 10 and then skip to letter 12. The conformist is the only one who reads letters 39 and 40, only the cynic reads letter 38, and the first letter is intended only for the quixotic, and it is to be read after all the others. Each reading constructs a different *sjuzhet* and each yields a different story with a different resolution.

The metaphor of the deck of cards is made literal in Robert Coover's recent story, "Heart Suit," which is printed on thirteen oversized, glossy playing cards. The author states that the cards may be shuffled and read in any order, though the introductory card is to be read first, and the Joker is to be read last. Each card begins with the continuation of a sentence that describes the adventures of an unnamed individual, and each card ends with a new sentence beginning with the name of an individual. Thus, the Five of Hearts card begins with the words, "—pent up with self-righteous anger, burst in upon the King of Hearts, who has fallen fast asleep on a kitchen maid, to complain that someone has penned a scurrilous accusation against him in the latrine."

If the preceding card was the Deuce of Hearts, then the text identifies the intruder as the king's royal chaplain. If, instead, the previous card was the Eight of Hearts, then the intruder would have been the ambitious Viceroy. The construction of the work (as well as the kingdom) indicates that any of the depictions could be predicated of any of the male principals. This kind of variability of identities is particularly problematic when one reaches the Three of Hearts card, which begins, "—is the thief who actually stole the tarts," a statement that can be believed of any of the characters but proven of none, since the internal evidence is always inconclusive—and, for that matter, the deck can always be shuffled again. The king is determined to have an answer and decides to torture all the suspects, but the tactic fails: all of them confess. The interchangeability of the figures in the drama is metafictionally indicated in the Eight of Hearts card: "The King feels lashed by uncertainty. Actions are known . . . but the actors are interchangeable, the perpetrators' varied and manifold motivations best understood as a collective one, a swarm of intent, from which can be snared only a faint glimmering of a general truth."

DELAYED VARIATIONS

Some unnatural authors wait until the ending of a work to tamper with its *sjuzhet*. There is the ending that returns, Ouroboros-like, to the beginning of the story and continues to repeat itself indefinitely. The last sentence of *Finnegans Wake* is also its first sentence; similarly, the last sentence of Nabokov's "The Circle" begins, "In the first place," (384) which leads directly back to the story's first sentence, "In the second place," (375) as the text seems to continue itself perpetually (see Richardson 48).

More outrageous is the text that negates itself and, after providing one ending, goes on to offer another equally possible conclusion, as John Fowles does in *The French Lieutenant's Woman*. The death of Shiva is similarly denarrated at the end of Salman Rushdie's *Midnight's Children*. In these works, the original *sjuzhet* is violated and threatened with negation as an alternative ending is allowed to replace the text that was presented earlier. This "negated *sjuzhet*" is also evident in Malcolm Bradbury's story, "Composition." This narrative tells the story of a new teaching assistant at a Midwestern university during the Vietnam War. After completing his course on composition (but before turning in the final grades), he is invited to party with two of his female students. The evening itself is fairly innocent, though some extremely compromising photos are taken. The next morning, the instructor receives a sample Polaroid and a request for a higher grade for a third student who has neglected composition in order to more fully engage in political struggles; he has to decide what to do, knowing that if the pictures get circulated he is sure to lose his position. The earlier sections of the work are numbered 1 through 4; the final section offers three different resolutions, designated 5A, 5B, and 5C. In the first option, the instructor quietly raises the grade and saves his job. In the second, he corrects the grammar of the letter, sends it back to the blackmailers, and defiantly turns in the correct grade of F. In the third, he agrees with the student that grades are crap and all words are inadequate; he destroys the grade sheet and abandons the college in order to devote himself to life and love. The text offers no indication of which of these possibilities will be (or has been) actualized; each has a certain plausibility. The text thus ends with a series of options that the reader is implicitly invited to adjudicate, only one of which can be the actual *sjuzhet,* the others merely being unactualized possible sequences of events. As the instructor is informed by one of the other characters, "You have to write your own ending" (141).

The same is true of many hyperfictions, in which the *sjuzhet* is always changing. Espen Aarseth observes that the hypertext structure of nodes and links allows for one kind of reading, which he calls hyperlinear, or "the improvised selection of paths across a network structure" (79). Elsewhere in this volume, Eyal Segal has argued that "the image of a work with alternate endings comes to reside, at least to a certain extent, in the totality of these endings and the different options or perspectives they provide. On a higher level yet, this problematizes the sometimes too-facile notion of the artwork as an 'organic whole,' in which every detail is necessary and irreplaceable" (page 84). Segal's statement is a good summary of some of the key issues at play in such works; I would also add that it deconstructs the idea of a fixed, preexisting *fabula.*

Together, these texts should give a good sense of the wide range of creative play present in unexpected, unprecedented, and unnatural *sjuzhets,* and indicate how the physical sequencing of the actual text has become a powerful medium of artistic representation in its own right, where dominant themes are creatively embodied. Finally, we should modify existing theoretical formulations to include three subcategories to describe increasingly prominent experiments: (1) the variable *sjuzhet,* to account for texts whose fixed stories are presented in a nonlinear manner that the reader must organize (e.g., Johnson's *The Unfortunates* or Shields's *Happenstance*); (2) multiple *sjuzhets* present in works from which the reader selects one of the textual units that make up a story and leaves aside other possible *sjuzhets* (Castillo's *Mixquiahuala Letters*); and (3) negated *sjuzhets*: textual sequences presented as the arrangement of the story that turn out to be merely possible or unactualized sequences

(Fowles's *The French Lieutenant's Woman*). With such extensions of existing models, we can bring narrative theory effectively into the twenty-first century.

WORKS CITED

Aarseth, Espen. *Cybertext: Perspectives on Ergodic Literature*. Baltimore: Johns Hopkins Univ. Press, 1997.

Bal, Mieke. *Narratology: Introduction to the Study of Narrative*. 3rd ed. Toronto: Univ. of Toronto Press, 2009 (1985).

Ballard, J. G. *War Fever*. New York: Farrar, Straus and Giroux, 1990.

Bradbury, Malcolm. *Who Do You Think You Are? Stories and Parodies*. New York: Penguin, 1993 (1976).

Bredehoft, Thomas A. "Comics Architecture, Multidimensionality, and Time: Chris Ware's *Jimmy Corrigan: The Smartest Kid on Earth*." *MFS* 52, no. 4 (2006): 869–90.

Castillo, Ana. *The Mixquiahuala Letters*. New York: Doubleday, 1992.

Chatman, Seymour. "Backward." *Narrative* 17, no. 1 (2009): 31–55.

Coover, Robert. "Heart Suite," Narrative playing cards affixed in sleeve of *A Child Again*. San Francisco: McSweeney's, 2005.

Eggers, Dave. *A Heartbreaking Work of Staggering Genius*. New York: Simon and Schuster, 2000.

Foer, Jonathan Safran. *Incredibly Loud and Extremely Close*. New York: Houghton Mifflin, 2005.

Hansen, Per Krogh. "Backmasked Messages: On the *Fabula* Construction in Episodically Reversed Narratives." In *Unnatural Narrative—Unnatural Narratology*, edited by Jan Alber and Rüdiger Heinze, 162–86. Berlin: de Gruyter, 2011.

Horn, Richard. *Encyclopedia: A Novel*. New York: Grove, 1969.

Mortimer, Armine Kotin. "Connecting Links: Beginnings and Endings." In *Narrative Beginnings: Theories and Practices*, edited by Brian Richardson, 213–27. Lincoln: Univ. of Nebraska Press, 2008.

Ott, Eirik R. "Receipt Found in Parking Lot of the Super Walmart." In *Greatest Hits: Poems to Read Out Loud*. Austin, TX: Sanctum Sanctorum Productions, 2007.

Pavić, Milorad. *Landscape Painted with Tea*. Translated by Christina Pribićević-Zorić. New York: Random House, 1990.

Richardson, Brian. "Beyond Story and Discourse: Narrative Time in Postmodern and Nonmimetic Fiction." In *Narrative Dynamics: Essays on Time, Plot, Closure, and Frames*, edited by Brian Richardson, 47–63. Columbus: The Ohio Univ. Press, 2002.

Rimmon-Kenan, Shlomith. *Narrative Fiction: Contemporary Poetics*. New York: Methuen, 2002 (1983).

Saporta, Marc. *Composition No. 1*, translated by Richard Howard. New York: Simon and Schuster, 1963.

Tyrkkö, Jukka, "'Kaleidoscope' Novels and the Act of Reading." In *Theorizing Narrativity*, edited by John Pier and José Ángel García Landa, 277–306. Berlin: de Gruyter, 2008.

Updike, John. *Problems and Other Stories*. New York: Knopf, 1979.

CHAPTER 11

Sequence, Linearity, Spatiality, or: Why Be Afraid of Fixed Narrative Order?

MARIE-LAURE RYAN

WHETHER IT IS conceived as an order inherent to the events of a story or as the order in which these events are presented by discourse, narrative sequence is a basically linear phenomenon. In contemporary literary theory, linearity is generally regarded with contempt, because its one-dimensionality suggests lack of complexity, and complexity tends to be praised as an inherently desirable property of artistic texts. In this chapter, I propose to investigate the sources of this rejection of linear sequence as well as the fortune of attempts to create narratives that do away with it.

The postmodern suspicion toward sequence can be traced back to Roland Barthes's *S/Z* and to its famous opposition between the *scriptible* (writerly) and the *lisible* (readerly). *S/Z* was written in the aftermath of the events of 1968, a period when many French intellectuals aspired to some kind of political relevance, which meant the adoption of a Marxist vocabulary. Barthes observes that the institution of literature is based on an opposition between producer and consumer. Blatantly ignoring the complexity of the reading process, he associates the *lisible* with a product that turns us into passive consumers who mindlessly devour the text until no page is left:

> Notre littérature est marquée par le divorce impitoyable que l'institution littéraire maintient entre le fabricant et l'usager du texte, son propriétaire et son

client, son auteur et son lecteur. Ce lecteur est alors plongé dans une sorte d'oisiveté, d'intransitivité, et, pour tout dire, de *sérieux:* au lieu de jouer lui-même, d'accéder pleinement à l'enchantement du signifiant, à la volupté de l'écriture, il ne lui reste plus en partage que la pauvre liberté de recevoir ou de rejeter le texte: la lecture n'est plus qu'un *referendum.* (10)

Our literature is characterized by the pitiless divorce which the literary institution maintains between the producer of the text and its user, between its owner and its customer, between its author and its reader. This reader is thereby plunged into a kind of idleness—he is intransitive; he is, in short, *serious:* instead of functioning ["playing" would be a better translation] himself, instead of gaining access to the magic of the signifier, to the pleasure of writing, he is left with no more than the poor freedom either to accept or reject the text: reading is nothing more than a *referendum.* (English version, 4)[1]

To the conception of literature as a product to be consumed, Barthes opposes the vision of literature as a *travail,*[2] which means as a process:

Pourquoi le scriptible est-il notre valeur? Parce que l'enjeu du travail littéraire (de la littérature comme travail), c'est de faire du lecteur, non plus un consommateur, mais un producteur du texte. (10)

Why is the writerly our value? Because the goal of literary work (of literature as work) is to make the reader no longer a consumer, but a producer of the text. (4)

If the *scriptible* is a process, not a product, it cannot be embodied in any actual text. "Le texte scriptible n'est pas une chose, on le trouvera mal en librairie.... Le scriptible—c'est nous en train d'écrire" (11) [The writerly text is not a thing, we would have a hard time finding it in a bookstore.... The writerly text is *ourselves writing*] (5). The consequence of this purely mental nature of the *scriptible* is that it cannot be described, since the activity of the writing mind is largely inaccessible to observation (or if it can be observed, it is through its products). In order to formulate an aesthetics, which is the point of the whole discussion, Barthes replaces the binary opposition *scriptible-lisible* with

---

1. This idea of referendum has become literalized with the use of the "Like" button in certain social media Web sites, such as YouTube or Facebook.
2. It is ironic that while Barthes, the would-be political activist, describes literature as work, Barthes, the hedonist, uses the metaphor of play, the exact opposite of work.

a concept that tolerates various degrees of actualization: the concept of *texte pluriel* [plural text]. The more plurality a text possesses, the more it will turn the reader into a producer. The description of full plurality has become an enduring manifesto of postmodern aesthetics:

> Posons d'abord l'image d'un pluriel triomphant, que ne vient appauvrir aucune contrainte de représentation (d'imitation). Dans ce texte idéal, les réseaux sont multiples et jouent entre eux sans qu'aucun puisse coiffer les autres; ce texte est une galaxie de signifiants, non une structure de signifiés; il n'a pas de commencement; il est réversible; on y accède par plusieurs entrées dont aucune ne peut être à coup sûr déclarée principale; les codes qu'il mobilise se profilent *à perte de vue,* ils sont indécidables (le sens n'y est jamais soumis à un principe de décision, sinon par coup de dés); de ce texte absolument pluriel, les systèmes de sens peuvent s'emparer, mais leur nombre n'est jamais clos, ayant pour mesure l'infini du langage. (12)

> Let us first posit the image of a triumphant plural, unimpoverished by any constraint of representation (of imitation). In this ideal text, the networks are many and interact, without any one of them being able to surpass the rest; this text is a galaxy of signifiers, not a structure of signifieds; it has no beginning; it is reversible; we gain access to it by several entrances, none of which can be authoritatively declared to be the main one; the codes it mobilizes extend *as far as the eye can reach,* they are indeterminable (meaning here is never subject to a principle of determination, unless by throwing dice); the systems of meaning can take over this absolutely plural text, but their number is never closed, based as it is on the infinity of language. (5–6)

To this image of a total or "triumphant pluralism," Barthes opposes a structure that limits the infinity of language and is therefore typical of the "classical" or "readerly" text. This structure is narrativity:

> Tout cela revient à dire que pour le texte pluriel, il ne peut y avoir de structure narrative, de grammaire ou de logique du récit; si donc les unes et les autres se laissent parfois approcher, c'est *dans la mesure* (en donnant à cette expression sa pleine valeur qualitative) où l'on a affaire à des textes incomplètement pluriels, des textes dont le pluriel est plus ou moins parcimonieux. (12)

> All of which comes down to saying that for the plural text, there cannot be a narrative structure, a grammar or a logic; thus, if one or another of these are sometimes permitted to come forward, it is *in proportion* (giving this

expression its full quantitative value) as we are dealing with incompletely plural texts, texts whose plural is more or less parsimonious. (6)

Why can the *texte pluriel* not have a narrative structure? To see this, let's return to Barthes's description of full pluralism. Following Barthes's image of the *réseau*, we can represent this pluralism as a distributed network (figure 11.1a). In contrast to a line, a network requires two dimensions: it is therefore a spatial object. The fundamental property of a network, compared to a tree diagram (figure 11.1b) or a vector, is that it has no root node, and it allows loops. There is consequently no entry point, and there are many different ways to reach a given node. Once they enter the network, explorers must make a decision every time they reach a node that is connected to many other nodes. It is this constant need to make decisions that elevates, in Barthes's view, the reader of plural texts from a passive consumer to an active producer. Since there is a virtually infinite variety of routes through the network, which means an infinite number of potential interpretations, it is impossible to produce a reading that exhausts the meaning of the text. Narrativity conflicts with Barthes's vision of a triumphal pluralism for at least three reasons. First, Barthes regards unrestricted pluralism as incompatible with "imitation," or the constraints of representation.

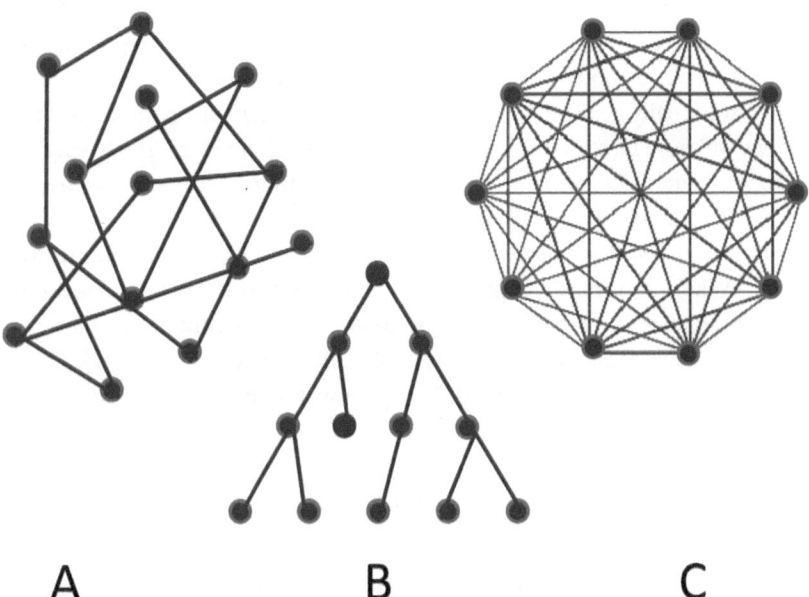

FIGURE 11.1. Types of networks: (a) distributed network, (b) tree, (c) complete graph

I don't know if by "imitation" he means "imitation of something that exists in the real world," such as a horse, or simply the ability to evoke the mental representation of a familiar object, whether real or imaginary, in which case imitation could concern a unicorn. At any rate, when readers regard a group of words as the evocation of a particular object, they reduce the polysemy inherent to each word by focusing on the meaning that relates to the kind of object that is being described at the expense of the other meanings conventionally encoded in that word. Since narrative is a fundamentally mimetic form of discourse, it cannot avoid this limitation of potential meanings. Poetry, being far less mimetic, is much more respectful of polysemy. Barthes was indeed writing in a time when poetry was regarded as the model of literary meaning and though he was never particularly interested in the lyric, he was certainly supportive of theories that regarded the practice of literary art as letting language speak for itself by liberating the multiple meanings inherent to each word.[3]

Second, while a network is a spatial structure, narrativity is a fundamentally temporal structure. This is not to say that space does not play a role in narrative: stories concern a world that functions as a spatial container for existents; thanks to the actions of these existents, the world undergoes changes. Following a story means building a mental simulation (Oatley 13–14) of the changes that take place in a world and of the processes that occasion these changes. Bakhtin expressed this inseparability of space and time through the concept of *chronotope*. But space and time have fundamentally different properties. Because space has more than one dimension, one can go from one point in space to another through several routes. But time is one-dimensional; it is traditionally represented by images such as the river or the flight of an arrow, which suggests a unidirectional movement along a line. If we represent a story through a diagram, there will be only one trajectory that goes from the world of time 1 to the world of time 2: changing the order of the events will result in the best cases in a different story, and in the worst case in no story at all.[4] When a narrative sequence involves causality, it cannot be inverted, because an inversion would mean that the effect precedes the cause—an order that most philosophers regard as logically impossible (e.g., Tooley). Moreover, if time could be represented through a spatial network, the loops of the

---

3. I am thinking here of New Criticism, or of thinkers such as Heidegger or Maurice Blanchot, who interrogated poets, especially Hölderlin, Trakl, Rilke, and Mallarmé, for the essence of literary language.

4. I am talking here about major events that have an impact on the story. On the level of minor or routine events, order may be inverted without significant consequences. For instance, a character may go to the doctor and then to the supermarket, or vice-versa, since there is no causal relation between these events.

network would mean that it is possible to return to an earlier time. It could be argued that time-travel stories involve temporal loops; but these stories are notorious for creating all sorts of logical paradoxes (cf. Nahin).

The network structure of the plural text leads to the third reason why Barthes's vision of triumphant pluralism cannot take narrative form: narrative, as Aristotle taught us, has a beginning and an end; but networks, because of their loops, allow endless wandering. Barthes is dreaming of a text that renews itself constantly and holds the reader forever fascinated—which means forever captive—in stark contrast to the consumerist page-turners that we read for the plot, driven by the desire to find out how it ends.

Barthes must have found sufficient pluralism in narrative texts to entertain himself, because his critical work is entirely devoted to "readerly" stories, whether these stories come from popular culture or classical literature. Yet his conception of the ultimate text as a network created by the infinity of language reflects a general trend in twentieth-century literature and criticism that Fredric Jameson has called the *spatial turn*. Jameson claims that "our daily life, our psychic experiences, our cultural languages are today dominated by categories of space rather than by categories of time" (64). I find this claim hyperbolic; recent art and literature play with time as much as they play with space. But because time is usually represented in language through spatial metaphors, and because it is conceptualized through spatial diagrams, experiments with narrative time often involve new types of spatial organization.

The spatial turn is a broad-ranging movement that covers a wide variety of phenomena. In criticism, it has inspired the school known as "spatial form" (inspired by Joseph Frank), which focuses on synchronic relations between the parts of the text rather than on the diachronic relations between constituents. This focus, which is also typical of structuralism and of the Geneva school of criticism, has led to an emphasis on individual themes and to a neglect of both plot and the dynamics of storytelling.[5] In practice, the spatial turn has produced forms of narrative composition that break down narrative sequence and deemphasize causality through compositional devices such as fragmentation, montage of disparate elements, and juxtaposition of parallel plot lines. Here, I will restrict my investigation of the spatial turn to one type of phenomenon: the attempt to build stories based on the two-dimensional structure of the network rather than on one-dimensional sequences.

The elements—or nodes—of a network can be more or less densely connected. In a loosely connected network, there are long stretches of linear

---

5. See Rousset for a critical program that respects both spatial form and diachronic sequence.

sequences; in a densely connected network, there is a wide choice of paths of navigation. Maximal connectivity occurs when every node has a path that leads to every other node. This is known in graph theory as a complete graph (figure 11.1c). A text that relies on a complete graph is Marc Saporta's novel *Composition No. 1*, which was printed on a deck of cards and produces a different sequence of discourse with every reshuffling. In this type of structure, the text can start with any card, and any card can succeed any other card. This represents a literal implementation of Barthes's vision of a text that can be entered through multiple points and where meaning is created by chance—what he calls *un coup de dés*—rather than by a rational principle of decision. In such a text, the author has no control over narrative sequence, and the reader has no reason to choose one path rather than another. The question, of course, is whether the total randomness of the system can really produce anything worth calling meaning. It certainly cannot create narrative meaning, because narrativity is based on an asymmetric relation between cause and effect: if A causes B, A must precede B; but a random shuffling can generate the sequence AB as well as the sequence BA.

The idea of the narrative text as a set of loose leaves has had no progeny, beyond a few imitations of *Composition No. 1* in various languages: it was one of those experiments whose artistic value lies entirely in their novelty, and which are not worth repeating once they lose this novelty.[6] But in the mid-eighties, the development of digital technology inspired a new type of play with network structure. This new type is known as hypertext. Rather than allowing free passage from any node of the network to any other node, as was the case with the complete graph of Saporta, hypertext is based on a limited system of built-in links between individual units of text.[7] The user passes from one unit to another by clicking on a hot spot that activates the link. Through the placement of links, the author can control which units follow each other, but if the network is densely connected, she cannot control lon-

---

6. For Umberto Eco, *Composition No. 1* embodies the problematic nature of experimental art: "I recently came across *Composition No. 1*, by Marc Saporta. A brief look at the book was enough to tell me what its mechanism was, and what vision of life (and obviously, what vision of literature) it proposed, after which I did not feel the slightest desire to read even one of its loose pages, despite its promise to yield a different story every time it was shuffled. To me the book had exhausted all its possible readings in the very enunciation of its constructive idea" (170–71). Eco might not be giving a fair chance to *Composition No. 1*, but if Saporta's narrative experiment does not inspire him to read it, even less would a work that borrows Saporta's original idea.

7. For an example of what a hypertext network might look like, using the software Tinderbox, see David Kolb, *Sprawling Places* (http://www.dkolb.org/sprawlingplaces/images/fullsize/themapof.jpg).

ger sequences. When the reader has no specific reason to make one choice rather than another, and when the choices offered to her are too numerous to be anticipated by the designer, progression through the network becomes a random process.

The literary applications of the hypertext principle were promoted by early theorists as "a vindication of postmodern theory" (Bolter 24) or as "the convergence of contemporary critical theory and technology," which is the subtitle of George Landow's work, in which we read: "Hypertext embodies many of the ideas and attitudes proposed by Barthes, Derrida, Foucault, and others" (91). Barthes's description of the plural text in *S/Z* played a particularly prominent role in this theorization. Just as Barthes argued that the plural text elevates the reader from passive consumer to active producer of meaning, the early advocates of hypertext (e.g., Landow) claimed that the system of choices of hypertext turns the reader into a writer. But if the choice of links to follow is purely random, which means if the user's exploration of the network is a blind navigation, then the user's activity is no more worthy of being described as "writing" than the automatic act of turning the pages of a book. The only difference that elevates the so-called reader-author of hypertext over the consumerist reader who is driven by the desire to find out how it ends is that his reading experience never ends: hypertext is a "garden of forking paths,"[8] in which readers can loop forever, unable to tell how far along they are in the text, since the text resides in the invisible memory of the computer, rather than in the visible volume of a book.[9] According to the advocates of hypertext, this impossibility to conceive reading as a progress toward a goal encourages the attitude toward the text that Baudelaire described as *flânerie*. In contrast to the traveler who moves from one point to another and regards the space between these two points as an obstacle to overcome, the *flâneur* wanders for the pure pleasure of the journey, open to whatever discoveries the vagaries of his itinerary will bring, and he develops an aesthetic relation to space. By analogy, the reader who has been freed from the pull of narrative toward its outcome—from what Raphaël Baroni calls *la tension narrative*—is supposed to develop an appreciation of the text as an open space of signification.

Yet without a plot to give the reader a global view of the text, it becomes very difficult to keep its elements in memory and to imagine meaningful

---

8. Title of a short story by Jorge Luis Borges, which was very inspirational for hypertext authors, especially Stuart Moulthrop, who created a hypertext extension of it (unpublished; mentioned in Wardrip-Fruin and Montfort, 691).

9. A point made by Shelley Jackson in her hypertext fiction *Patchwork Girl*.

connections between these elements, unless of course the text is as short as a poem. The cognitive value of narrative, together with its universal appeal, might explain why the proponents of hypertext were not ready to accept Barthes's claim that narrativity is incompatible with triumphant pluralism. Hypertext was widely promoted as the novel of the future, and the texts that are now regarded as the classics of the genre all retain some kind of narrative structure. I am thinking here of texts such as Michael Joyce's *afternoon: a story* and *Twelve Blue*, Stuart Moulthrop's *Victory Garden*, and Shelley Jackson's *Patchwork Girl*. These texts tell about characters who are engaged in certain situations, who perform actions, who interact with other characters, who experience changes in their world, and who are emotionally affected by these changes. For hypertext to retain some degree of narrativity, there must be limitations on the connectivity of the network: by this I mean that there must be reasonably long stretches of nodes with a linear connection, so that they can be interpreted as a chronological and causal sequence. But for the hypertext mechanism to be justified, these linear sequences must occasionally intersect; in other words, there must be decision points. This raises the problem of the meaning of the reader's choices.

Since narrative consists of both story and discourse, the choices can be given two interpretations: they can be seen as a way to generate different stories taking place in different storyworlds, or as a way to generate different discourse sequences that describe the same world and tell the same story. According to the first view, the contents of the nodes are events, the links stand for temporal and causal relations, and the task of the reader is to imagine connections between the events encountered during his traversal of the network that give narrative meaning to the sequence. For instance, out the elements listed below, at least three stories can be constructed (I let the reader imagine the causal connections that turn the sequences into meaningful narratives):

John is rich
John marries a movie star
John gambles
John is poor
John's wife divorces him

John is poor
John's wife divorces him
John gambles
John is rich
John marries a movie star

John marries a movie star
John is rich
John's wife divorces him
John gambles
John is poor

Here I have somewhat cheated by using a nondefinite description for John's wife: in stories 1 and 3 she is the same person as the movie star, but not in story 2. However, if hypertext authors are going to produce systems that generate different stories with each run, they will have to play such tricks. These three stories can be represented by the network of figure 11.2. For this system to generate well-formed stories that come to closure, however, a rule must be included specifying that every node must be visited and visited only once.

Although hypertext has occasionally been praised as a story-generating machine, it has not been used in the generative way I have just suggested, because it would be too difficult to design a network that produces well-formed

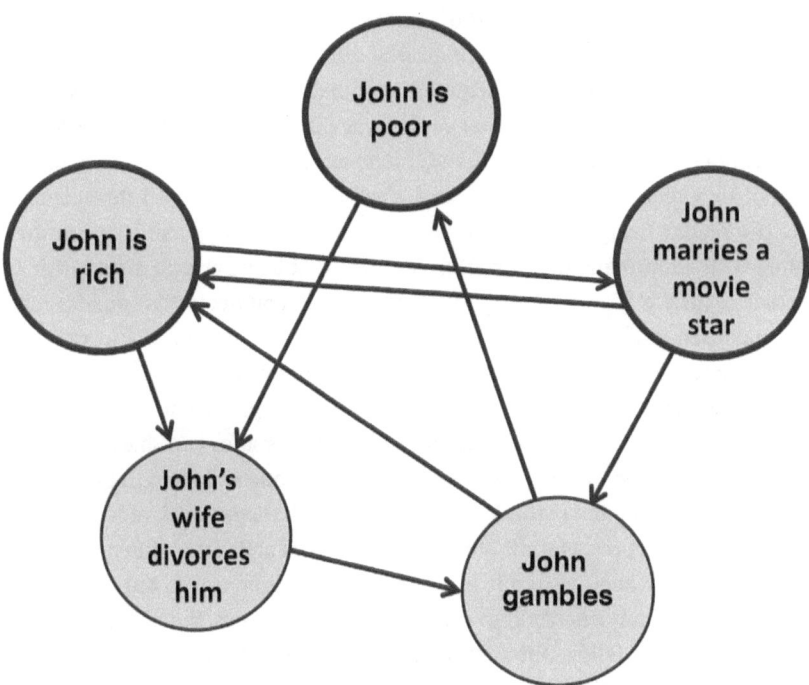

FIGURE 11.2. Generative network for the sample stories. Rule: Every node must be visited and visited only once.

stories, nothing but well-formed stories, and emergent stories—that is, stories that have not been foreseen by the author. If a story-generating system does not fulfill these three conditions, it will not be considered significant from a computational point of view: it would be just too easy to create a system that generates a handful of well-formed stories and a thousand strings of nonsense, or a system that generates nothing more than the stories anticipated by the designer. I am not even mentioning the aesthetic quality of the output, which has remained, so far, the most elusive property of computer-generated stories.

An alternative conception that also operates on the level of story consists of regarding hypertext as a way to explore the various possibilities that can develop out of a given situation. Normally the exploration of such possibilities would take the form of a tree-shaped diagram (figure 11.1b). Since trees do not have loops, each branch can be kept separate, and the succession of nodes can be associated with a linear time flow without creating the problem of time travel; but this linear flow also prevents the endless play of signification that Barthes associates with the network. When the reader reaches the end of a branch, she reaches the end of the story associated with that branch, and she must start again from the root node to explore another possibility. This explains why hypertext authors have avoided tree-diagrams in favor of a structure that makes the representation of different possibilities intersect with each other and in which, consequently, the reader can loop forever. Michael Joyce's *afternoon* focuses for instance on an accident that the narrator observes. He wonders if the victims of this accident were or were not his ex-wife and son, if they died or are still alive, and whether or not he caused the accident. As the reader navigates the text, she is taken from one version to another, often without noticing the transitions and without being able to distinguish an actual sequence corresponding to the facts from counterfactual possibilities. To make sense of the text, and to avoid logical contradiction, she might conceive the text as the flow of a mental activity that contemplates various possibilities, and she will associate some nodes with one particular possible world and some nodes with another. But since different versions can share some elements, it might be impossible to sort out every node as belonging to this or that version. When the reader's navigation through the network of hypertext is conceived as a representation of the flow of mental activity, a return to a node that has already been visited is not interpreted as time travel, but as a return of thought to a certain event. In different runs of the text, the narrator's mind will consequently follow different paths and visit different memories. I find the mentalist interpretation the most satisfactory way to give narrative significance to hypertext; but its availability depends on the thematics of the work and on how the author handles the system. Michael Joyce is a master of this art.

One may wonder whether the representation of multiple entangled possibilities truly requires the interface typical of hypertext. Consider Robert Coover's print short story, "The Babysitter." It consists of 107 numbered and linearly ordered paragraphs representing the various events that can occur between the moment a couple leaves for a party, entrusting its three children to the care of an attractive babysitter, and the moment the couple returns home (figure 11.3). In one version, the babysitter is murdered, in another she is raped by her boyfriend and his buddy, in another the baby drowns in the tub, and in yet another the father leaves the party under the pretext that he needs to check on the children, while he is really driven by the hope of having sex with the babysitter. The rigid order of appearance determined by the print medium does not prevent the reader from trying to construct different stories by sorting out the paragraphs and assigning them to different narrative sequences (figure 11.4). But this sorting remains approximative. A precise mapping of the text into distinct scenarios—for instance, by assigning paragraphs 1, 3, 13, 24, and 107 to one possible scenario, and paragraphs 1, 6, 12, 19, 32, and 107 to another—would exceed the cognitive abilities of the reader, because many paragraphs are compatible with different versions.[10] The inextricable entanglement of these versions becomes obvious when 107, the last paragraph, asserts events that belong to multiple alternative sequences: "Your children are murdered, your husband gone, a corpse in your bathtub, and your house is wrecked. I'm sorry. But what can I say?" (239). Coover's story has been called a "print hypertext," but "The Babysitter" is much more respectful of chronological sequence than network-based hypertext narratives. While it might not be cognitively feasible to arrange the segments into precise sequences, the linear progression of the text corresponds roughly to the passing of time that takes place in the storyworld: just as in a narrative that adheres to chronological order, early in the text means early in the evening, and late in the text means late in the evening. The loops of network-based hypertexts would prevent this sense of progression. I also think that the print story's ability to combine multiple possibilities with a sense of temporal progression could not be efficiently realized in digital hypertext, because in print the presentation of several possible developments in round-robin fashion allows the reader to watch them progress more or less simultaneously, even if this means in a scrambled order, while in hypertext, she must make a choice among different possibilities. Once a possibility has been selected, the others

---

10. Given sufficient time and effort, it would certainly be possible to map "The Babysitter" in terms of possible sequences of events, but it would take a writing system that makes it easy to erase and correct. I tried mapping the text with pencil and paper, but I gave up after many false starts, discouraged by the sheer number of possibilities.

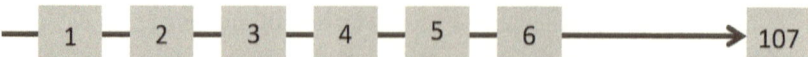

FIGURE 11.3. The linear discourse structure of Robert Coover's "The Babysitter"

become inaccessible until she returns to their point of divergence, a return that might or might not happen.

So far I have considered naturalizations of the hypertext mechanism that operate on the level of story. The alternative is to regard all the nodes as the representation of the same storyworld and to interpret the variability of the sequences generated by the system as a discourse phenomenon. In this case, every sequence generated by the reader will represent a different itinerary across the storyworld. This conceptualization would be unproblematic if storyworlds consisted of space exclusively, since you can always travel through a territory by taking different routes. But because storyworlds are made of time as much as they are of space, these different itineraries involve a more or less arbitrary disruption of narrative sequence. I say arbitrary because, as I have argued, the order of presentation cannot be fully controlled by the author. In this conception, the text is a jigsaw puzzle whose pieces come to the reader one by one in order to be assembled into a coherent picture. We can also compare this process to the game of Tetris: chunks of story appear on the screen in an order blindly specified by the user's choices, and she tries to fit these chunks into a global narrative pattern, just as the player of Tetris tries to fit the pieces that fall from the top of the screen into a solid row. If we conceive narrativity as a type of content located exclusively on the level of story—that is, as a sequence of events involving characters and leading to changes in the storyworld (cf. Ryan, "Toward a Definition of Narrative")—then this conception of hypertext can be compatible with a narrative interpretation. But if we adopt Meir Sternberg's more dynamic and more rhetorical definition of narrative, which regards storytelling as a presentation of information about worlds, existents, and events that generates specific responses, such as suspense, curiosity, or surprise,[11] then the randomization of sequence that inevitably occurs in hypertext is incompatible with any of these basic narrative effects. Suspense, curiosity, and surprise are highly dependent on a controlled management of

---

11. "I define narrativity as the play of suspense/curiosity/surprise between represented and communicative time (in whatever combination, whatever medium, whatever manifest or latent form). Along the same functional lines, I define narrative as a discourse where such play dominates: narrativity then ascends from a possibly marginal or secondary role to the status of regulating principle, first among the priorities of telling/reading" (Sternberg 529).

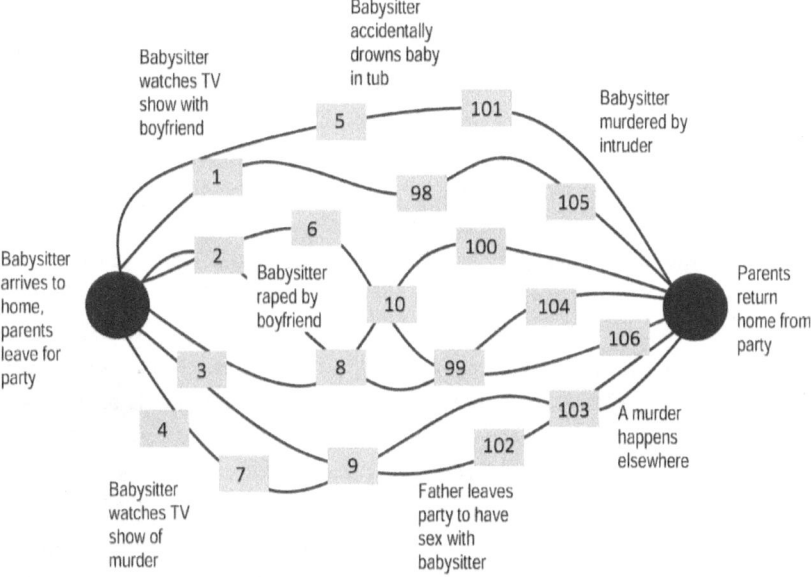

FIGURE 11.4. What the reader's mental map of "The Babysitter" could look like, if the reader had perfect memory of the text

information that determines what the reader knows and does not know when he reaches a certain point in the story. With a hypertext based on a network, however, the reader might reach a certain node through different routes: in one case, he might learn the identity of the murderer before discovering the body; in another case, he first finds the body and then learns who did it; and in yet another case, he might tire of operating the system after a few nodes and never find the body. It could be argued that a well-designed hypertext should exercise sufficient control over the reader's path and maintain sufficient interest to avoid such problems. But if the reader's narrative satisfaction depends on top-down control and on carefully planned discourse sequences, why bother with hypertext at all, since the main reason for adopting this interface is to challenge top-down control?

I am not saying that hypertext is a useless device. It is after all the principle that organizes the gigantic bank of information that we call the Internet. But surfing the Web and reading hypertext fiction are very different experiences. When we surf the Web, we go for specific pieces of information contained in individual locations, not for a global textual experience that covers many nodes. The buttons of a well-designed Web site display text labels that tell the user what kind of information the next page will offer. Like the signs at an intersection of roads, these labels allow the traveler to make the kind of rational decisions that, according to Barthes, would restrict the pluralism of the literary text. And while the Web as a whole is a network of incredible complexity, most of its individual sites are organized as wheels (a configuration formally equivalent to a tree), with a home page serving as a hub for clearly distinct branches that remain neatly separate so that the designer can control the user's progression along these branches.

In the literary domain, hypertext has been most successful as the representation of stream-of-consciousness or of dream worlds, in which images flow into each other and undergo incessant transformations.[12] In dream realities, events occur and they create change, but these changes do not need to observe the laws of nature, so that A causes B is just as possible as B causes A. Hypertext could also be very useful in representing an experience of space typical of twentieth-century literature, especially of literature that represents the city: the experience of being lost in a maze. Alain Robbe-Grillet's *Dans le labyrinthe*, or Claude Simon's *La Route des Flandres*, with their frequent returns to the same images, would fare reasonably well in hypertext format. But the argument can be turned around: if print narrative, with its fixed discourse sequence, can give the impression of wandering in circles, why do we need hypertext? Here I will play the devil's advocate by saying that with print texts we know how far along we are in our reading and that we will eventually get out of the maze, but with hypertext we may run in circles forever and truly experience the frustration of going nowhere.

The end of the hypertext adventure in pluralism is well known. Far from becoming the dominant form of narrative that its advocates anticipated, hypertext has faded away and is now regarded as a form typical of the nineties. Scholarly activity about the genre (e.g., Bell) still focuses heavily on the same group of classics (Michael Joyce, Stuart Moulthrop, Shelley Jackson, and a few others), all dating back to the same period. Traditional novels, based on fixed sequence, have lost none of their popularity to narrative with variable sequence, and digital textuality has taken two directions. First, with the development of the multimodal capacities of computers, we have seen more and more works in the tradition of concrete poetry, visual poetry, and surrealist experiments with aleatory writing (cf. Ryan, "What Has the Computer Done for the Word?"). These works dismantle language into its basic elements—words and letters—, make them dance on the screen, and perform quite literally the play with signifiers that Barthes regarded as the trademark of the *scriptible*—I would say a little bit too literally, because a pure play with

---

12. I am thinking here of Michael Joyce's hypertext, *Twelve Blue*.

signifiers loses sight of the signifieds. Turning language into pure spectacle, these experiments do away with sequence, mostly on the intersentential level but also occasionally on the level of syntax.[13] The few recent works of digital literature that remain focused on storytelling, such as Kate Pullinger's *Inanimate Alice*, are combinations of words, images, and animation that minimize interactivity and revert to a linear organization.

The other branch of digital textuality is the wildly popular domain of video games. Here, sequence is all-important, since the player's progression in the game depends on the pursuit of specific goals, and the achievement of these goals depends on a causal chain: for instance, before you can open a door, you must find the key; before you can start a car, you must fill the tank with gas. But the fixed sequences written into the design of the game often combine with a freedom to wander through the game world and a choice of ways to solve a certain problem. Games are spatial and temporal texts on a very literal level, the level of the world being represented, rather than on the level of the organization and succession of the signifiers, as was the case with hypertext. Their underlying structure is not a network but a combination of flowchart and tree (figure 11.5): a flowchart when there are many different ways to solve the same problem; a tree when the actions of the player steer the plot in different directions, for instance, by offering different endings. On this type of diagram, one of the two axes stands for temporal progression, and the other stands for different possibilities of action. (In the networks that map hypertext, by contrast, both axes stand for possible transitions, without taking semantics into consideration.) If video games have turned into the most successful form of digital entertainment, despite their lack of variety on the level of plot,[14] it is because their creators understand the importance of designing the experience of the player as a journey through a fictional world that offers opportunities for adventures, dangers, interesting encounters, and surprises, a world that rewards players with a sense of achievement for every level passed, rather than frustrating their need for closure and coherence. The difference between a network narrative with largely randomized sequence and a well-designed flowchart narrative with built-in sequences is the difference between holding the

---

13. See the *Electronic Literature Collection*, vol. 1 (http://collection.eliterature.org/1/) and vol. 2 (http://collection.eliterature.org/2/). I am thinking particularly of works by John Cayley, Giselle Beiguelman, Jason Nelson, Judd Morrissey, Edward Falco, and Brian Kim Stefans.

14. This lack of variety can be explained by the fact that due to the difficulty for computers to process language, interaction with game worlds is largely limited to physical actions such as moving, picking up objects, and using them. This limitation predisposes games to superhero plots focused on the solving of problems and the defeat of enemies at the expense of plots concerned with the evolution of human relations.

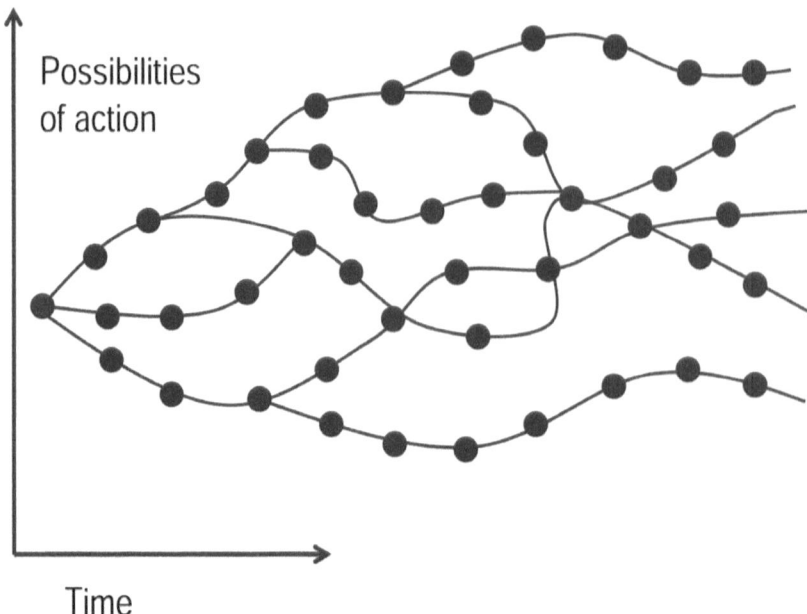

FIGURE 11.5. Structure of a typical computer game showing a combination of flowchart and tree

user captive in a labyrinth and creating a captivating storyworld. It is a safe bet that the top-down control of the author or designer over narrative sequence will outlast all attempts to do away with it.

This does not mean that Barthes's dream of the plural text should be abandoned. The spatiality of the network is fully compatible with the temporality of narrative sequence, if we think of narrative sequence as one of the many lines that traverse the network. The various points on this line can be interconnected through a complex web of relations—for instance, the beginning foreshadowing the end, or parallelism and oppositions between themes and situations that occur at different moments on the narrative time line. The logical line of the plot can also serve as a support for digressions, descriptions, imagery, opinions, and evaluations that expand the text's patterns of signification. Far from being a restriction of pluralism, narrative sequence is both an intrinsic source of pleasure—the pleasure of being taken along for a ride toward a point of view from which everything will ideally make sense—and a mnemonic structure that provides the reader with a global view of the text, for it is much easier to remember information when it is narratively—that is, temporally and causally—connected. In a longer text, it is the global view afforded by narrative sequence that enables readers to detect and follow the multiple threads of signification that weave together its aesthetic texture.

WORKS CITED

Bakhtin, Mikhail. "Forms of Time and of the Chronotope in the Novel." In *The Dialogic Imagination: Four Essays by M. M. Bakhtin*, edited by Michael Holquist, translated by Caryl Emerson and Michael Holquist, 84–258. Austin: Univ. of Texas Press, 1981.
Baroni, Raphaël. *La tension narrative: Suspense, curiosité et surprise*. Paris: Seuil, 2007.
Barthes, Roland. *S/Z*. Paris: Seuil, 1970, English translation: *S/Z*. Translated by Richard Miller. New York: Farrar, Strauss and Giroux, 1974.
Bell, Alice. *The Possible Worlds of Hypertext Fiction*. New York: Palgrave-Macmillan, 2010.
Bolter, Jay David. "Literature in the Electronic Writing Space." In *Literacy Online: The Promise (and Perils) of Reading and Writing with Computers*, edited by Myron C. Truman, 19–42. Pittsburgh: Univ. of Pittsburg Press, 1992.
Coover, Robert. "The Babysitter." In *Pricksongs and Descants*, 206–39. New York: Plenum Books, 1969.
Eco, Umberto. *The Open Work*. Cambridge, MA: Harvard Univ. Press, 1989.
Frank, Joseph. *The Idea of Spatial Form*. New Brunswick, NJ: Rutgers Univ. Press, 1991 (1945).
Jackson, Shelley. *Patchwork Girl, or, a Modern Monster*. Watertown, MA: Eastgate Systems, 1995.
Jameson, Fredric. "Postmodernism, or, the Cultural Logic of Late Capitalism." *New Left Review* 146 (1984): 53–92.
Joyce, Michael. *afternoon: a story*. Watertown, MA: Eastgate Systems, 1987.
———. *Twelve Blue*. URL: http://www.eastgate.com/TwelveBlue/
Landow, George. *Hypertext 2.0: The Convergence of Contemporary Critical Theory and Technology*. Baltimore: Johns Hopkins Univ. Press, 1997.
Moulthrop, Stuart. *Victory Garden*. Watertown, MA: Eastgate Systems, 1991.
Pullinger, Kate. *Inanimate Alice*. URL: http://collection.eliterature.org/1/works/pullinger_babel _inanimate_alice_episode_1_china.html
Nahin, Paul J. *Time Machines: Time Travel in Physics, Metaphysics and Science Fiction*. New York: Springer, 1993.
Oatley, Keith. *Such Stuff as Dreams: The Psychology of Fiction*. Malden, MA: Wiley-Blackwell, 2011.
Rousset, Jean. "Toward a Reading of Form." *Style* 29, no. 1 (1995): 132–48.
Ryan, Marie-Laure. "Toward a Definition of Narrative." *The Cambridge Companion to Narrative*, edited by David Herman, 22–35. Cambridge: Cambridge Univ. Press, 2007.
———. "What Has the Computer Done for the Word?" *Genre* 41, no. 3–4 (2008): 33–58.
Saporta, Marc. *Composition No. 1*. Paris: Seuil, 1961.
Sternberg, Meir. "Telling in Time (II): Chronology, Teleology, and Narrativity." *Poetics Today* 13 (1992): 463–541.
Tooley, Michael. *Time, Tense and Causation*. Oxford: Clarendon Press, 1997.
Wardrip-Fruin, Noah, and Nick Montfort. *The New Media Reader*. Cambridge, MA: MIT Press, 2003.

CONCLUSION

Epistemological Problems in Narrative Theory

Objectivist vs. Constructivist Paradigm

FRANCO PASSALACQUA and FEDERICO PIANZOLA

THIS BRIEF CONTRIBUTION is aimed at the elaboration of some critical questions often addressed within the contemporary debate in narrative theory. The specificity of the subject at issue in this anthology—narrative sequence—has added to the coherence of our remarks by encouraging the authors to keep their attention on problems concerning the definition of narrative, a crucial step in the growth of the discipline.

Over and above the theoretical interest of such a focused perspective, we regard the task of defining narrative as an important preliminary path to be followed in order to reflect on broader issues concerning the role of narrative studies, both within the humanities and with respect to other disciplines (cognitive sciences, psychology, pedagogy, etc.). We reckon that a reflection on the epistemological grounds of narrative theory is among the most important duties in the field because we think that many incompatibilities and frictions between terminologies, models, and theories are often underestimated. Such reflection is important to the extent that lack of comprehension can negatively affect the debate or even thwart acknowledgement of the specificity of the concepts used in narrative theory.

In the light of the considerations above, we are focusing here on the dubious theoretical effectiveness of the classical/postclassical distinction and on the proposal of a different dichotomy; on the different scopes of various definitions of *narrative sequence*; on the epistemology of the two paradigms indicated by the *objectivist/constructivist* dichotomy; and on the evaluation of the pros and cons of the two paradigms outlined. Our aim is to show that every theory is built upon assumptions that necessarily shape the theory itself, and we argue, all in all, for the advantages of adopting a constructivist epistemology, inasmuch as it renders explicit such presuppositions and consequently helps in the confrontation and possible integration between concepts, models, and theories.

CLASSICAL AND POSTCLASSICAL

The distinction between classical and postclassical theories and methodologies in narrative studies is currently a widely accepted dichotomy. Since 1997, when David Herman proposed it for the first time in his article "Scripts, Sequences, and Stories: Elements of a Postclassical Narratology," many scholars have had their say on the topic, expressing contrasting opinions, either endorsing or questioning the differentiation. Various criteria and formulations have been proposed in order to distinguish what appears to be a succession of two distinct narratological phases;[1] nevertheless, acknowledging this difference in the field of narrative theory is sometimes considered a problematic issue. According to Meir Sternberg, for instance, putting incompatible research programs together under the same label is a misleading effort ("Reconceptualizing Narratology" 35). An interesting alternative has been proposed by Raphaël Baroni,[2] who notably conceives the dichotomy as a performative distinction, the purpose being to point out the plurality of voices and the scientific attitude that has come to characterize narratology in the last thirty years.

We think that the problems that arise with the classical/postclassical distinction can hardly be resolved by refining the dichotomy in any particular way and that there are limits to its theoretical soundness and applications. Indeed, the features that qualify the difference between classical and

---

1. "Postclassical narratology contains structuralist theory as one of its 'moments' but enriches the older approach with research tools taken from other areas of inquiry. The result is not simply new ways of getting at old problems in narrative analysis but a rearticulation of those problems, including the root problem of how to define stories" (Herman, "Scripts, Sequences and Stories" 1057).

2. "It might be useful, within some institutional contexts, to underline that narratology is a discipline which is still living and that it is not limited to only one epistemological approach" (*Rapport*; our translation).

postclassical are also markers of the problems encountered by such a distinction: (1) definitional looseness of the terms; (2) lack of theoretical insight (Prince; Richardson).

Despite its different uses, the concept of *classical narratology* often shows a noticeable aporia, namely that, whatever the criteria adopted to discern a classical party in narratology, we are inevitably led to accept one of two negative consequences: either (1a) we limit the scope of the category to French structuralism; or (1b) we extend its inclusiveness to the detriment of theoretical effectiveness in order to specify what is typical of classical narratology. Such a flaw is not strictly dependent on the criteria chosen to determine what is classical, be it temporal (work dating from the late 1960s until the early 1980s), geographical (work done in France), or theoretical (work that can be ascribed to the structuralist-semiological framework). With respect to (1a), it is difficult to argue for the exclusion of narrative research that was contemporary to French structuralism and had interesting relations with it, whether relations of affinity or of opposition (the Tel Aviv school, the Neo-Aristotelian school of Chicago). In contrast, option (1b) tends to include in the same category proposals that are grounded on incommensurable theoretical and epistemic assumptions (like formalism and functionalism, realism and constructivism), or proposals that could be defined as classical as well as postclassical (see Prince), thus making their grouping questionable.

The concept of *postclassical narratology* presents analogous problems, namely the fact that it is often used as an umbrella term, which can comprise almost all the proposals of the last twenty years. Jan Alber and Monika Fludernik identify four generic parameters that distinguish postclassical studies ("Postclassical Narratology" 3); however, even though such a broad definition might be correct, it does not seem very satisfactory, since it does not include discriminating features that would grant a convincing definitional quality to the term. It is generally recognized that a major reconfiguration of narrative studies occurred through methodological and theoretical reflections of pragmatic fashion with the aim of taking into account many more aspects of the narrative process, but even more preferable would be a methodology that elucidates the peculiar differences between postclassical theories, since there is not much point in collecting a wide number of new approaches and studies[3] under the same label without offering the possibility of a systematic differentiation among them (Kindt; Lamarque). The flaw, hence, does not lie so much

---

3. See Nünning ("Narratology or Narratologies?") for a survey of recent narratological models and theories.

in the way we define the term so much as it does in the usefulness of the term itself, as loose as it has proved to be.

This obvious downside of the classical/postclassical distinction is its inability to state the theoretical differences between the two parties. Surprisingly, the opposition does not highlight the theoretical and methodological discontinuities that, in the last decades, have led to significant changes to the epistemology of narratology, aspects that have been spelled out on only a few occasions (Sternberg, "Narrativity"; Patron; Alber and Fludernik 12). Below, we will try to identify some discontinuities, suggesting the use of an alternative dichotomy that is not anchored to the prefix *post-* but rather focused on the epistemology that underlies the theories: either *objectivist* or *constructivist*.[4] The purpose is to offer an alternative to the classical/postclassical distinction by drawing on the objectivist/functionalist distinction extensively commented on by Sternberg ("Narrativity").[5] What moves us is the need to develop concepts that will help in a transversal comparison between different theories and methodologies and thus add to a reflection on the epistemology of a field of study that crosses the boundaries of disciplines.

WHAT IS A DEFINITION OF NARRATIVE?

One of the issues that animate the narratological debate concerns the conditions underlying the possible definition of narrative. It is quite common to deal with this question by relying on the three levels of division (syntactic, semantic, pragmatic) that pertain to any semiotic object, a division we adopt as a parameter for our remarks about the epistemology of narrative theories. This is quite helpful, since definitions of narrative are traditionally bound to two sequences (e.g., *fabula/sjuzhet, story/discourse*, etc.), which, in one way or another, are regarded as semantic and/or syntactic levels of narrative, more or less combined with a pragmatic dimension. However, resorting to syntax alone is rarely considered a viable option in order to define narrative, and "even those narratologists who would prefer to characterize sequences in syntactic or 'formal' terms often do not altogether avoid recourse to semantic or 'content' features" (Prince, "On Narrative Sequence" 13 in this volume). Consequently, we will focus on semantics and pragmatics, commenting on

---

4. For an introductory work on this long-standing opposition in philosophy, see Ernst von Glaserfeld.

5. See also Pier's chapter in this volume ("The Configuration of Narrative Sequences") for an application of the insights offered by Sternberg's distinction.

each level as the basic and necessary one for the definition. In this section we will anticipate some remarks about the particularities of the objectivist and constructivist paradigms, which will be dealt with in detail in the section "Different Paradigms."

At the *Réseau Romand de Narratologie* (RRN) conference, Raphaël Baroni noted that "the speakers underlined the importance of giving a new dynamism to the narrative sequence with an approach that stresses the cognitive abilities of the interpreters and the interpretive performances that actualize the narratives. From such a perspective, new questions can be addressed about the nature, function, and functioning of narrative sequences" ("Rapport" 1, our translation). Questions that pertain to narrative theory surely concern all three such aspects—the nature, function, and functioning of narrative. However, what is often regarded as essential for the definition of narrative is only its nature, that is, the elements of which it is composed. Peter Hühn's contribution to the present volume deals with this matter in a very detailed way, reflecting on the concept of *eventfulness*. It will be interesting to analyze the difficulties that can arise out of conceiving narrative as a sequence of events.

Semantics

Almost all definitions of narrative deal with semantics, that is, with the representational function of narrative. However, definitions of narrative commonly specify a *semantic content* ("what" narrative represents), not a *semantic function* ("how" narrative represents):[6] narrative represents certain "things," and pointing out what properties such represented things have is often supposed to be essential in order to define narrative—at least, this is what *objectivist theories* assume to be necessary for the definition. The fundamental things that narrative can represent are, among others: "a possible world," "protagonists of anthropomorphic nature," "time," "space," "actions" (Fludernik, *Introduction to Narratology* 73); "characters," "a changing world" (Ryan); or "world," "time," "space" (Sternberg, "Ordering the Unordered" 6).

Accordingly, what characterizes many definitions is the role attributed to the referents of narrative: in most cases, the presence of certain elements and/or of some of their properties is a necessary and sufficient condition for the definition of what narrative is. What complicates the theoretical duty is that

---

6. Cf. Gérard Genette's distinction between "thematic" narratology and "modal" narratology (*Narrative Discourse Revisited* 16).

all the terms mentioned are negotiable and present us with further definitional tasks that entail assumptions about complex entities such as "time," "space," and "events." In this respect, it can be helpful to rely on established linguistic theories like *possible worlds semantics, situation semantics,* or *event semantics*. But in any case, defining narrative in terms of situations, events, or other semantic entities raises further questions and problems regarding how we use language to refer to things. The debate about semantics is very intense in linguistics and philosophy, and within these disciplines, many conflicting positions can be found. Since narrative is considered a discursive phenomenon, narrative theories are necessarily based upon a semantic theory, be it explicit or implicit, formalized or naïve. In this regard, our interest is to understand what the pros and cons are of postulating a semantic content as an ontological primitive that qualifies narrative as such.

Concepts like *event, situation, state, action, change,* and so on are often used without much concern for definitions—there being a widespread tendency to assume that by virtue of common sense we all have a satisfactory knowledge of what these terms indicate. In contrast, Hühn is very precise on this matter, defining an event as a "decisive, unexpected, and surprising turn within the sequence of elements, a significant departure from the normal or expected course.... Events are changes of states that fulfill the additional requirement of special significance" ("The Eventfulness of Non-Events" 37 in this volume). Since the concept of event is a constant and recurrent element in the definition of narrative, it will be interesting to take a closer look at Hühn's proposal and to examine the properties of the concept and the role it plays in the definition.[7]

We think that Hühn's concepts of *event* and *eventfulness* are the best elaborated so far in narrative studies, to the extent that he takes into consideration their limits and possible uses, therefore highlighting a few decisive aspects that concern all narrative theories.[8] It is noteworthy that Hühn defines the core (necessary) element of the narrative sequence, relating it to a process of meaning-attribution, a judgment: change in the sequence is "decisive," "unexpected," "surprising," "significant" only with regard to an interpreter who can evaluate whether there is a change and whether it is significant. This ability to evaluate is influenced by the cultural, historical, and literary context. Hühn's examples of "eventful non-events" show how the concept of event is strictly connected to language (or other media) use: in fact, it can be defined

---

7. Special thanks to Emma Kafalenos, whose objections helped us to rethink and clarify our remarks about Hühn's proposal.

8. See also Hühn, "Functions and Forms of Eventfulness in Narrative Fiction."

in terms of meaning-attribution without including other features of change. Thus, in order to define an event, it is only necessary to specify what a *change* is and how it can be *significant*.

First, Hühn's definition of event requires a *change:* it is assumed that there is a variation that is somehow part of our experience of narrative. Second, eventfulness (the property of being a *significant* change) is a necessary requirement for the tellability of a story (39–40). Interestingly, according to Hühn, even a *non-event*—either (ne1) the failure of an expected significant change to occur, or (ne2) the nonsignificance of a particular expected change—can be eventful if, for instance, the virtual/actual change is foregrounded. To be more specific, "Non-events usually refer to the sequence of happenings on the *histoire* level as represented by the text. But non-events can also occur in the mediation process of a story, as negative equivalents to presentation events" (40).[9] Hence, if we need to specify how we experience both a change and its being significant, we need, in addition to the "standard" case, a definition that, for (ne1), includes the possibility of a variation that does not actually occur in the *histoire*; and for (ne2), an account of how a significant role is attributed to a change that is not significant for the *histoire*.

According to Hühn, there is also another restriction that has to be considered in the definition of narrative: "Narration as a discourse-type is distinguished from other discourse-types, such as argumentation or description, by the temporal organization of a sequence of happenings on the level of *histoire* constituted and mediated in a text" (37). He is thus stating that narrative is defined by virtue of the temporal properties of the *histoire*. Still, it needs to be clarified whether or not how the *histoire* is "constituted" by the mediation process is relevant. Moreover, with respect to the concept of non-event, further interesting questions arise: Given that a change can be eventful either if a *temporal* variation actually occurs or (ne1) if it is only virtually possible and somehow expected, to what extent does the constitutive process affect our experience of time? Given that a change can be eventful either if the (actual/virtual) temporal variation is decisive for the *histoire* or (ne2) if it is significant for other reasons, to what extent does the constitutive process affect our judgment of significance?

---

9. Presentation events are "decisive changes in the *narrator*'s position, attitude, or consciousness in the course of telling a story" (39), hence a matter of mediation (point of view, focalization, reported speech and thought, etc.). "If a narrator tells of horrifying deeds committed by formerly law-abiding friends without changing his or her approving attitude toward them, this would be experienced as a non-event" (40).

Non-events can occur both in the sequence of happenings and in the presentation sequence. However, Hühn states, "Non-events are ultimately located on the *histoire* level," since "the term non-event refers to the phenomenon that an incident, especially one that is expected, actually does *not* happen" (40n4). Therefore, a discourse that generates the expectation of a change that concerns exclusively the level of presentation—cannot be defined as narrative by virtue of this feature alone.[10] Hühn's proposal is very thought-provoking, but the latter condition seems to tie the definition of event to the *histoire* level only, limiting the process of meaning production within the realm of referential semantics. In order to avoid such a controversial restriction, a revision of his definition is possible: either assuming that events are elements of the *histoire* only, or excluding "significance" from the definition of presentation events. However, the former case would lead to defining narrative by virtue of its reference whereas the latter would result in using—for the definition of the concept of event—criteria that are different according to the sequence to which the change belongs: for the *histoire*, an account of (significant) virtually possible outcomes is necessary, while for the presentation sequence, it is not needed.

Although according to Hühn, non-events are more likely to pertain to the *histoire* only, it seems more advisable to us that the definition of event be grounded on *both* narrative sequences: *histoire* and *discours*. Otherwise, given that narrative is defined as a specific process of meaning attribution—that is, a significant "change of state or a succession of such changes" (37)—we have to justify on what grounds we are not considering as narrative-specific change and significance that concern the *discours*. Having said that, the question is whether it is possible to develop a solution for which change and significance are somehow related to both sequences. In addition to the interest of answering such a question, we think that, despite Hühn's thorough consideration of the role of pragmatics, a serious shortcoming in his proposal is the assumption that there is a semantic basic element that is necessarily present in every narrative: a change in the *histoire*, be it actual or virtual.[11] This is an attitude that consequently might affect the possibility of giving a satisfactory account

---

10. Cf. Segal for a different perspective on expectations generated by narrative: "Any operative convention (or system of conventions) may be viewed—just like an event or any other narrative world-element—as a means of achieving the fundamental rhetorical end of manipulating and controlling narrative interest. (For example, observance of a convention could then be explained as regulating suspense, or a breach of a convention as producing surprise)" ("Ending Twice Over" 82–84 in this volume).

11. Even considering *histoire* in terms of cognitive schema theory or using Lotman's semiotic model, as Hühn does, semantics remains the key level for the definition of the concepts of event and eventfulness. See Hühn, "Functions and Forms of Eventfulness in Narrative Fiction."

of the role that syntax and pragmatics have in the composition of narrative discourse, since they are regarded as dependent on the semantic level.

Pragmatics

We can find some help with these issues in the contributions by Raphaël Baroni and John Pier. Baroni ("Virtualities of Plots") argues that the virtual actions outlined by the story and sketched by the readers who progress in the text tend to become as important as the actions actually told. Baroni's proposal is relevant to the extent that it underlines the interdependency of the two sequences, particularly with respect to the role of the audience. "The narrative construction of an enduring *pathos* does not rely only on some sort of identification with the character. . . . It also depends on the non-actualized virtualities of the story, which are nevertheless actualizable as interpretive hypothesis" ("Rapport" 4, our translation). "Non-actualized virtualities" and non-events are very similar, except that Baroni conceives actual and virtual actions as something functional to the construction of the narrative tension; in other words, semantics is subordinated to a pragmatic effect. Interestingly the sequence of events (plot) is conceived as a "narrative construction" taking into account "non-actualized virtualities" and "interpretive hypotheses," as well—namely, not considering an event as something strictly anchored to the semantic level.

In a similar way, John Pier's approach

> characterizes sequence as *prototypical*, on the one hand, and as *intersequential*, on the other. This means, among other things, that sequences are constituted in the course of narration as a communicative process: rather than a stable entity or a "deep structure" manifested on the textual surface, they play out in a "more-or-less" fashion in relation to other textual and discoursive categories but also in relation to the various other instances or exemplifications of discourse. (21 in this volume)

Referring to Pierce's semiotic model, Pier conceives of "sequence as prototypical, serving as a diagram in the semiotic sense of an implicit regulating principle rather than as an immanent structure" (34), and both the *fabula* and the *sjuzhet*—the actional and communicative sequence in Sternberg's terms, quoted by Pier—are equally important for the prototypicality of the narrative sequence (34). While Hühn focuses on the *fabula* in defining the concept of event, for Pier both the actional and the communicative sequences intervene in the operations of abductive reasoning typical of narrative; for his part, Baroni gives special attention to the tension between the two sequences, since this is what generates all narrative effects.

Two other contributions included in this volume implicitly challenge the usual conception of semantics as a criterion for the definition of narrative. Brian Richardson, noting that "the latter part of the twentieth century and the first years of the twenty-first have seen an explosion of innovative developments of the possibilities of the sjuzhet," argues for new theoretical formulations that would include "variable sjuzhet," "multiple sjuzhet," and "negated sjuzhet" ("Unusual and Unnatural Narrative Sequences" 174 in this volume). And according to Michael Toolan, "Music, especially language-less instrumental music, in addition to temporal extension and sequence, has something akin to 'events,' albeit events hard to associate with any notional character's or narrator's *plan*" (44).

It is also worth mentioning an example of how semantic content might be considered in a broader framework. The rhetorical approach advocated by James Phelan claims that "in order to explain the principles underlying the movement of narratives from beginning through middle to ending, we need to go beyond plot dynamics to include telling dynamics and readerly dynamics" ("Privileged Authorial Disclosure about Events" 56 in this volume). Any experience in reading is primarily a function of textual phenomena and shaping by the author: "Characters, events, and temporality, though crucial to a narrative's progression and effects, are themselves ultimately subordinated to the implied author's relationship with the audience" (53). Hence, semantics is subordinated to pragmatics: "There are multiple facts and multiple ways of construing facts" (*Narrative as Rhetoric* 17).

Many other examples might be taken into consideration, but these are enough to cast reasonable doubt on the role semantics has in the definition of narrative. If identifying a semantic content is a controversial and unstable interpretative process, to what extent can we assume a specific type of semantic content to be a necessary requisite of narrative? Not all the authors of the proposals discussed above would subscribe to such a thorny question, but their considerations lead to reflection as to how crucial it is to understand the role that the concepts we use play in our ontological commitment, in our representation/construction of the narrated reality. We think that special attention must be devoted to the role attributed to each of the semiotic levels—also including the "syntactic" organization of discursive elements—and, accordingly, to the role of the two sequences that can define narrative. This is a critical but decisive point with regard to the degree of compatibility among different theories. For instance, as noted by Sternberg, "Merely acknowledging that the genre requires two sequences means little, as witnessed by the two-make-one fallacy. The fallacy may even involve a claim or practice of alternative sequential focusing" ("Narrativity" 635). Along the line of this remark, we will try now to draw a distinction between two main epistemological paradigms in narrative studies, with the aim of bringing out the different attitude that theories have toward the narrative object and its semantics.

DIFFERENT PARADIGMS: OBJECTIVIST VS. CONSTRUCTIVIST[12]

An important preliminary remark is that the identification of two narratological paradigms does not have an all-embracing scope: our aim is to show and clarify two main tendencies that concern the theoretical assumptions of all narrative theories. We hope that our analytical gaze may spur some insights toward issues that are often neglected but are nonetheless critical in all fields of research, namely: (i) the ontological status of the object studied; and (ii) the relationship between the object and the theoretical framework that informs our experience of it (epistemic level).

Reflecting upon (i) means investigating what kind of object narrative is and, if any, what conditions or elements (events, causal relations, change, agents, etc.) are necessary for its existence. Reflecting upon (ii) leads to an evaluation of the quality and consistency of the theoretical frameworks, of their concepts and methodologies, and of how their use affects the object studied. To put it another way: how to define narrativity? Is it a property immanent to the object or something we attribute to it, or does narrativity perhaps arise out of the cooccurrence of various semiotic conditions? How are narrativity and narrative sequence linked? And to what extent does the theoretical framework affect our knowledge and awareness of what narrative is?

Showing how objectivist and constructivist theories address such questions, we will focus on two basic steps of every theory, based on the scientific method: the detection of recurrent features within the corpus considered (narrative constants); and the abstraction and codification of invariable elements

---

12. Sharing a similar purpose, this proposal is inspired by the distinction between *objectivist* and *functionalist* adopted by Sternberg ("Narrativity"). Our terminological choice is due to the will to link our remarks to a broader philosophical tradition, reflecting on the epistemic relation between theory and object, and can thus be considered as an elaboration of Sternberg's dichotomy for the purpose of understanding whether the concepts, models, and definitions that we use are fit for the different phenomena we want them to describe. See page 212 and Pier's chapter in this volume.

or constitutive principles, while also considering the methodology used in such operations (methodological norms) (cf. Margolin, "Response").

The Objectivist Paradigm

With the term "objectivist paradigm," we refer to those narrative theories characterized by the following conditions:

(i) Ontological level: narrative is an entity that has an immanent and specific ontological status, an object that we can recognize thanks to its essential qualities, which are differential features. In general, certain syntactic and/or semantic properties are assumed to be the predicative basis of the narrative object.[13]

(ii) Epistemic level: the identification and description of narrative relies on the possibility of the *recognition* of those features that are considered to be typical of all and only narratives. The process of knowing that an object is a narrative is an act of detection of the narrative properties of the object, without any influence on its ontology due to the process of knowing it or to the extra-objectual domain.

Narrative Constants

In a discourse, the invariable properties that can be identified as narrative features are located in the object of study—that is, they are objective. This is due to the fact that the ontological level is logically antecedent to the epistemic level: it is the case that an object has some elements and/or properties, and only then can we determine its relationships with the framework of knowledge, with the pragmatic level. What follows from this epistemic orientation is the notion that objectivist narrative theories postulate the existence of narrative constants, which are abstracted in various concepts and terms (event, *fabula, sjuzhet,* plot, etc.), sometimes subsumed under labels such as "narrative sequence," "basic plot structure," "minimal narrative," and the like. The structure or configuration of narrative is usually determined by syntactic and

---

13. Predication is the ascription of attributes to an entity, and the predicative basis is constituted by the existents (attributes and entities) that we can associate through predication (Kahn 3–4).

compositional properties and/or with respect to its semantic content; pragmatic elements come into play only for the role they have in the recognition of those immanent properties. Hence, pragmatic elements do not have any ontological and epistemic value that affects the postulation of narrative constants.

Methodological Norms

Within the objectivist paradigm, the methodological norms that guide the theoretical activity comply with a unidirectional principle:[14] either univocal, one-to-one (within a given domain, each element is linked to one and only one element/function of another domain); or plurivocal, one-to-many (each element of the given domain can be linked to multiple elements/functions, each link defining a unique concept). This is because the given domain—usually a combination of syntactic and/or semantic elements—is assumed to be immanent to the object, hence logically primitive in comparison to other (narrative) elements. These essential elements are assumed as the predicative basis for the definitions and a logical constraint is entailed, namely the subordination of extra-objectual elements to immanent factors. An example of univocal definition is as follows: "Narrative sequences represent linked series of situations and events" (Prince 12 in this volume), narrative sequence thus being the output of a syntactic combination (somehow "linked") of semantic elements ("situations and events"). But Prince also shows a plurivocal attitude in stating that a sequence of events can be either a description or a narrative (12).

The Constructivist Paradigm

With the term "constructivist paradigm," we refer to those narrative theories characterized by the following conditions:

(i) Ontological level: the ontological status of being narrative is not a datum of (the perception of) reality, but it rather depends on the occurrence of certain pragmatic conditions. An object is not narrative in itself but becomes narrative in a particular semiotic situation. Hence, narrativity is the result of a process of construction and combination of

---

14. See Sternberg ("Proteus in Quotation-Land") and other references in Yacobi ("Package Deals in Fictional Narrative" 228n1).

certain processes and properties whose specificity is also dependent on extra-objectual factors: it is a construction that is the outcome of the audience-discourse relationship.

(ii) Epistemic level: the possibility of knowing/experiencing something as narrative strictly depends on the presence of specific pragmatic conditions. The perceiving subject and the discursive context (information about the author, paratext, genre specific conventions, etc.) play a key role in the constitution of the narrative object. The possibility of knowing/experiencing an object as narrative requires a particular act, a specific disposition on the part of the subject in relation to the object in a particular context.

Narrative Constants

Within a constructivist paradigm, pragmatics is the very condition of possibility of discourse, such that syntax and semantics alone do not have specific properties that can qualify a discourse as narrative. Any definition within the constructivist paradigm must specify a particular combination of pragmatic features, and only afterwards, syntactic and semantic elements correlated and subordinated to them can be taken into consideration. It is worth noting that in order not to get drawn into a slippery relativism for which anything goes as a definition, a constructivist theory still has the burden of specifying the invariable constitutive principles of the "narrative relationship" between audience and discourse.[15]

To quote two examples, both Sternberg and Monika Fludernik locate the narrative constants in the contextual and pragmatic domain: in their theories, it is the subject's attitude toward the discourse in a particular context that enables the process of narrativization. They ground the necessary conditions for narrativity in the extra-objectual domain, but in different ways. According to Sternberg:

Narrative rules [are] distinctive, universal roles of sequence which govern (at will assimilate, "narrativize") all other elements and patterns found in discourse at large. These generic master roles (to be called, in shorthand, "suspense," "surprise," "curiosity," each with its proper dynamics between the telling and the told) are alone constant as a threefold set; everything else

---

15. For more about a theory based on a constructivist epistemology, see the comments about Sternberg's work in Passalacqua and Pianzola (28–31).

(including established favorites apart from time, such as perspective, space, character, verbal medium, or linear form) turns out to be variable, because nondistinctive by itself, if not dispensable, yet always narrativizable in the generic process. ("Telling in Time (II)" 472)

Sternberg firmly anchors his constructivism in the teleological aspect of the Proteus Principle: "We always (de)narrativize for a reason—if only the wish to read for, or against narrativity/narrative in a certain shape and context" ("Narrativity" 639). In contrast, Fludernik seems to promote a different version of constructivism, less bounded by a specific teleology since narrativity is obtained in the cognitive process of perceiving a "mediated experientiality" (consciousness), but instead, anytime "the mere decision to read something as a narrative can override the lack of material or appropriate story matter [i.e., experientiality]" ("A Reply to Nilli Diengott" 209):

> Not only do readers construct the narrativity of a given text, thereby superseding any inherent or essentialist understandings of narrativity, but they also construct narrativity on the basis of the real-world cognitive parameters (handled in a flexible manner), and they even enforce narrative readings for texts that have no evident experiential core. (The "real world," in turn, is of course a primary-level construct.) Narrative texts are therefore, first and foremost, texts that are read narratively, whatever their formal makeup, although the fact that they are read in a narrative manner may be largely determined by formal and, particularly, contextual factors. ("A Reply to Nilli Diengott" 235)

Methodological Norms

The analytical instruments developed within a constructivist paradigm must account for the links between narrative features whose ontological status is context-dependent. In other words, there is no basic domain with predetermined elements to which functions and effects can be associated in order to describe what narrative is and how it works. The most widely known principle that rules the identification of narrative constants is called the Proteus Principle, a guiding norm brought to narrative theory by Sternberg ("Proteus in Quotation-Land"). According to this principle, the links between the properties of discourse and its functions are not univocal or unidirectional, but can be described only as connected through a many-to-many relationship: a certain function can be accomplished by different discursive forms, and a certain form can accomplish many different functions. It is the contextualized occurrence of a specific relationship or network of relationships that constitutes narrative. The Proteus Principle rules every theoretical operation, not only the definition of narrative: given that there is no autonomous existence of narrative, its form varies (within certain conventional limits) according to context and to the framework of knowledge. Syntax, semantics, pragmatics—everything is dependent on interpretive hypothesis, which associates some contextually situated property of discourse with some function.[16]

EPISTEMOLOGY AND THEORY: PROS AND CONS OF THE TWO PARADIGMS

Once it is established which characteristics are particular to each of the two paradigms, it is advisable, for a thorough evaluation, to ponder how they affect the logical consistency, empirical validity, and descriptive effectiveness of the theoretical frameworks they underlie. We think that a constructivist epistemology provides the most powerful basis for narrative theories and that we should "prefer the Proteus Principle over the principle of univocity" (Jahn 384). Following are some of the theoretical arguments in favor of this claim.

Epistemic Argument

The main drawbacks of the objectivist paradigm are that it easily leads to the elaboration of objectivist theories—with all their subsequent flaws and, above all, an essentialist fallacy, for which classification is not a value-laden process—and that it thwarts a satisfactory and empirically valid account of the pragmatic elements of discourse. If the basic and invariable features of narrative are considered immanent to the object and assumed as the predicative basis of definitions, then the aim of narrative theory is merely to describe and classify the various elements of discourse, pushing aside any interest in the relationship between the object and the framework of knowledge, between discourse and hermeneutic processes. The constructivist paradigm reverses this order: what is basic—and a logical primitive—are cognitive and pragmatic processes.

---

16. For examples of application of the Proteus Principle, see Yacobi's work on unreliable narrators ("Package Deals") and Segal's work on narrative closure ("Closure in Detective Fiction" and "Ending Twice Over").

This assumption makes possible an integrated account of the semiotic process as a whole, acknowledging the centrality of the audience-discourse relationship. If pragmatics is regarded as logically antecedent to syntax and semantics, and is assumed as the predicative basis of narrative ontology, then a theory can give an epistemically grounded account of the dynamics and the cognitive processes involved in the experience of narrative. If, on the contrary, the first logical stage of theory is to detect narrative properties, and only afterward to investigate their links to and roles in cognitive processes, then the latter aspects are logically and theoretically subordinated to the former so that the theory reflects the objectivist epistemic structures underlying it, thus neglecting the shaping role of values, beliefs, and desires in every experience.

Ontological Argument

The constructivist paradigm makes possible the formulation of theories that postulate a sober ontology of the discourse, thus ruling out the necessity to justify—empirically or theoretically—the existence of many narrative elements. In a word, every narrative element is postulated only to the extent that it is justified by a specific cognitive and aesthetic experience and not, for instance, by the intuitive knowledge of what an event is. From a constructivist perspective, it is impossible to univocally identify the properties of what are usually considered to be narrative elements and forms (e.g., events, point of view, or even narrator), insofar they are not forms in themselves but become forms only if associated with *functions*. Forms are abstract terms that we use to describe the complex relationship between audience and discourse, they are the output of a function that can take different semiotic arguments within a given context.[17] Consequently, if we accept the constructivist assumptions and we accordingly develop a narrative theory that is epistemically consistent with those assumptions, then we will also reconceptualize narrative elements of more limited scope. For this reason, theories that assume narrative elements *a priori* can hardly integrate with constructivist theories, which only postulate narrative properties *a posteriori*. Herein lies the impossibility of bringing concepts and terms borrowed from structuralism into constructivist theories without a thorough rethinking of their meanings.

---

17. This is finely stated by Sternberg ("Proteus in Quotation-Land") in his explanation of the (constructivist) "Proteus Principle" as the many-to-many correspondence between forms and functions. See also Pianzola.

Logical Argument

A constructivist epistemology has the advantage of providing a sound and coherent basis for a theory that aims to describe the nature, function, and functioning of narrative. The growing attention that narrative theories have devoted to the pragmatics of discourse has rarely been accompanied by an epistemic reflection on the object studied, and this has resulted in an objectivist bias that hinders a thorough understanding of the processes involved in the narrative experience. Incoherencies surface when the epistemic assumptions of objectivist definitions—the use of syntactic and/or semantic primitives—clash with the concepts and models used to describe the functions and functioning of narrative. This is because cognitive and pragmatic elements—which in the objectivist paradigm have a role neither in the definition of narrative, nor in the ontology/postulation of primitives—intervene in, and affect, syntax and semantics.

If among the purposes of a theory there is the description of cognitive processes, narrative effects, and other pragmatic properties, the Proteus Principle grants that epistemology and theory be consistent, inasmuch as, adopting it, the ontological status of entities and the logical status of concepts are always context-dependent and thus also dependent on the audience's framework of knowledge. That is to say, given that we want a theory to do "such and such," we need an epistemology that is logically consistent with that theory. The Proteus Principle can be very helpful in this pursuit, as well as in a revision of the concepts, models, and categories of narrative theory: it is not sufficient to integrate the major classifications of "classical" narratology into new theoretical instruments, for indeed, a whole reconfiguration of the theoretical framework is needed.[18]

The toughest matter, however, is the converse issue: the logical consistency of theory with epistemology. That is to say, if we believe that narrative, semantics, or any other discursive element is a context-dependent construction, then we need a theory that is consistent with such basic beliefs. On this topic, we must refer to the thorough investigation carried out by Sternberg ("Narrativity"), which shows how objectivist biases often resurface in pragmatic and contextual theories of narrative.

---

18. But not all scholars with constructivist sympathies agree that narrative theories might be incommensurable due to their epistemic assumptions. For instance, Nünning claims, "Though it leaves the narrow confines of structuralist taxonomy, a contextual and cultural narratological framework is informed by a critical practice that only the toolbox of classical narratology and thorough training in the precise semiotic analysis of narratives can provide. Denying or ignoring the many achievements of structuralist narratology would thus be foolish, a way of throwing the conceptual baby out with the formalist bathwater" ("Surveying Contextualist and Cultural Narratologies" 61).

Empirical Argument

A constructivist theory might seem too general with respect to the set of conditions that must be satisfied in order to qualify an object as narrative, and it can therefore be regarded as empirically weak. However, it is its flexibility that makes a broader scope of applicability and predictability possible: a constructivist theory can be satisfactorily used to describe phenomena that, by common sense, pertain to its field of application, and phenomena that will possibly emerge later within that field. As suggested by Uri Margolin, an "important feature [is] a theory's elasticity or ability to accommodate, sometimes through internal modification, new unforeseen cases or ones initially ignored. This is most important in our field, since the object itself is subject to frequent major changes" ("Response" 203). And for this purpose the adoption of a constructivist epistemology is the best ground for a theory.[19]

The need to overcome "mimetic reductionism" is also underlined by Jan Alber and his colleagues, who seek to account for nonconventional narratives and criticize "the argument that each and every aspect of narrative can be explained on the basis of our real-world knowledge and resulting cognitive parameters" ("Unnatural Narratology" 115). We think that overcoming such mimetic reductionism can be achieved by adopting a constructivist epistemology for which the ontology of the narrative object is dependent on the audience's framework of knowledge. That is to say, whatever elements of narrative are considered to be its essentials, a theory cannot conceive of them as something univocally given in the discourse: these elements must be regarded as the result of a process of actualization. This process arises out of the interaction between the knowledge domain and the objectual domain: the specificity of the narrating voice, of viewpoint, of temporal sequences, and so on must be qualified in terms of the interdependence of the process of knowledge and the empirical extra-objectual domain, and not with respect to a pre-established typology that subordinates the possible configurations of the audience-discourse relationship to discursive properties that have univocally identified functions.

The scope of a theory's applicability is also determined by its ability to account for narratives constructed through media other than verbal discourse, and even for narratives constructed across media. Considering pragmatics as the necessary basis of discourse production—and, therefore, of any of its qualifications—allows us to free a theory from any constraint due to the

---

19. It is worth stressing that arguing for adaptability does not mean that the constructivist paradigm is trying to elude the falsifiability of theories (Pianzola).

particularities of any medium. Of course, even objectivist theories can account for visual and transmedia narratives, but they encounter serious epistemological difficulties when dealing with complex narratives (cf. Ryan, "Sequence, Linearity, Spatiality" in this volume) and tend to broaden the scope of their definitions to the detriment of theoretical synthesis (cf. Ryan, "Narration in Various Media").

Interdisciplinarity

A last point in favor of the constructivist paradigm concerns the relationship between different disciplines interested in the same phenomenon, that is, narrative. In this regard, the convergence of narratology and the cognitive sciences has caught the attention of many scholars. A constructivist approach, insofar as it assumes that cognitive attitudes and strategies are part of the predicative basis of narrative ontology, can serve as a bridge between narratology and the cognitive sciences, facilitating the integration of their respective theoretical instruments. The risk of pushing narrative theory toward an arguably fruitful investigation of cognitive processes typical of the narrative experience has already been stressed (Sternberg, "Universals of Narrative"); nevertheless, it is also important to bear in mind how valuable the exchange can be if disciplines share ontologies, epistemologies, and methodologies that are commensurable, notably conceiving of narrative as constructed through cognitive processes. In our opinion, the constructivist paradigm can open up the common epistemic ground needed in order to understand what contributions each discipline can bring to the other, and to what extent the discoveries of the cognitive sciences can fruitfully influence narrative theory.

CONCLUSION

The reason why we insist so much on issues that might seem very abstract and remote from any experience of narrative is that theories and "concepts are not just tools. They raise the underlying issues of instrumentalism, realism, and nominalism, and the possibility of interaction between the analyst and the object" (Bal 29).

Uri Margolin suggests that we "adopt an instrumentalist view of theories, regarding them as cognitive tools rather than ontological commitments" ("Discussion: 'Narrator'"). Adopting such an attitude, however, does not detract from the point that we want to stress here. Even if we agree that a theory does not entail any ontological commitment, an instrumental theory based on an objectivist epistemology still asserts that our cognition of narrative is due to some property of the object. As we have tried to show, the main issue is whether the hypothesis that there are some properties immanent to the object—be they real, perceived, or postulated—that are recognizable by everybody as the *differentia specifica* of all, and only narratives might somehow hinder narrative inquiry.

Adopting a constructivist epistemology within narrative theory leads to rethinking the categories elaborated so far by both classical and postclassical narratology. Even more radically, it urges us to reconfigure the theoretical principles underlying such categories: first on the list should be the adoption of the Proteus Principle and a critical reflection on the analytical method used so far in most narrative studies. The need for such an assessment should be especially acknowledged by many recent approaches in narratology to the extent that they rely on the following assumptions: (1) narrativity is not codified in discourse, but rather constructed through cognitive strategies and dispositions involved in the hermeneutic process; (2) the properties of discourse depend on the audience's expectations, encyclopedia, and teleological elements that pertain to the hermeneutic process.

> To challenge concepts that seem either obviously right or too dubious to keep using as they are, in order to revise instead of reject them, is a most responsible activity for theorists. Interestingly, concepts that don't seem to budge under the challenge may well be more problematic than those that do. Some concepts are so much taken for granted and have such generalized meaning that they fail to be helpful in actual analytic practice. (Bal 44)[20]

WORKS CITED

Alber, Jan, and Monika Fludernik. Introduction in *Postclassical Narratology: Approaches and Analyses*, edited by Jan Alber and Monika Fludernik, 1–31. Columbus: The Ohio State Univ. Press, 2010.

Alber, Jan, Stefan Iversen, Henrik Skov Nielsen, and Brian Richardson. "Unnatural Narratology, Unnatural Narratives: Beyond Mimetic Models." *Narrative* 18, no. 2 (2010): 113–36.

Bal, Mieke. *Travelling Concepts in the Humanities: A Rough Guide*. Toronto: Univ. of Toronto Press, 2002.

---

20. This essay is a newly revised version of a previous article published in the journal *Enthymema* 4 (2011). Substantial changes have been made and the present contribution offers remarks that can be considered complementary to those advanced there. For a more exhaustive comprehension of the topic here discussed, see also Sternberg ("Narrativity").

Baroni, Raphaël. *Rapport du 1er colloque international organisé par le Réseau Romand de Narratologie.* URL: http://www.narratologie.ch/Rapport colloque RRN2011.pdf.

Fludernik, Monika. *An Introduction to Narratology.* London: Routledge, 2009.

——. "Towards a 'Natural' Narratology: Frames and Pedagogy. A Reply to Nilli Diengott." *Journal of Literary Semantics* 39 (2010): 203–11.

Genette, Gérard. *Narrative Discourse Revisited.* Translated by Jane E. Lewin. Ithaca, NY: Cornell Univ. Press, 1988

Herman, David. "Scripts, Sequences, and Stories: Elements of a Postclassical Narratology." *PMLA* 112 (1997): 1046–59.

Hühn, Peter. "Functions and Forms of Eventfulness in Narrative Fiction." In *Theorizing Narrativity,* edited by John Pier and José Ángel García Landa, 141–63. Berlin, New York: Walter de Gruyter, 2008.

Jahn, Manfred. "Stanley Fish and the Constructivist Basis of Postclassical Narratology." In *Anglistentag 1999 Mainz: Proceedings,* edited by B. Reitz and S. Rieuwertsv, 375–87. Trier, DE: WVT, 2000.

Kahn, Charles H. *Essays on Being.* New York: Oxford Univ. Press, 2009.

Kindt, Tom. "Narratological Expansionism and Its Discontents." In *Narratology in the Age of Cross-Disciplinary Narrative Research,* edited by Sandra Heinen and Roy Sommer, 35–47. Berlin, New York: Walter de Gruyter, 2009.

Lamarque, Peter. "On Not Expecting Too Much From Narrative." *Mind & Language* 19, no. 4 (2004): 393–408.

Margolin, Uri. "Discussion: 'Narrator.'" In *The Living Handbook of Narratology,* edited by Peter Hühn, John Pier, Wolf Schmid, and Jörg Schönert. Hamburg: Hamburg Univ. Press, 2014. URL: http://www.lhn.uni-hamburg.de/discussion/discussion-narrator.

——. "Response." *JLT online* (20 Mar. 2009). URL: http://nbn-resolving.de/urn:nbn:de:0222-000515.

Nünning, Ansgar. "Narratology or Narratologies? Taking Stock of Recent Developments, Critique and Modest Proposals for Future Usages of the Term." In *What Is Narratology? Questions and Answers Regarding the Status of a Theory,* edited by Thomas Kindt and Hans-Harald Müller, 239–75. Berlin, New York: Walter de Gruyter, 2003.

——. "Surveying Contextualist and Cultural Narratologies: Towards an Outline of Approaches, Concepts and Potentials." In *Narratology in the Age of Cross-Disciplinary Narrative Research,* edited by Sandra Heinen and Roy Sommer, 48–70. Berlin, New York: Walter de Gruyter, 2009.

Passalacqua, Franco, and Federico Pianzola. "Continuity and Break Points: Some Aspects of the Contemporary Debate in Narrative Theory." *Enthymema* 4 (2011): 19–34.

Patron, Sylvie. "On the Epistemology of Narrative Theory: Narratology and Other Theories of Fictional Narrative." In *The Travelling Concept of Narrative,* edited by Matti Hyvärinen, Anu Korhonen, and Juri Mykkänen, 118–33. Helsinki: Helsinki Collegium for Advanced Studies, 2006.

Phelan, James. *Narrative as Rhetoric: Technique, Audiences, Ethics, Ideology.* Columbus: The Ohio State Univ. Press, 1996.

Pianzola, Federico. "Looking at Narrative as a Complex System: The Proteus Principle." [under review]

Prince, Gerald. "Classical and/or Postclassical Narratology." *L'Esprit Créateur* 48 (2008): 115–23.

Richardson, Brian. "A Postclassical Narratology." *PMLA* 113 (1998): 288–89.

Ryan, Marie-Laure. "Narration in Various Media." In *The Living Handbook of Narratology,* edited by Peter Hühn, John Pier, Wolf Schmid, and Jörg Schönert. Hamburg: Hamburg Univ. Press, 2014. URL: http://www.lhn.uni-hamburg.de/article/narration-various-media.

Segal, Eyal. "Closure in Detective Fiction." *Poetics Today* 31, no. 2 (Summer 2010): 153–215.

Sternberg, Meir. "Narrativity: From Objectivist to Functional Paradigm." *Poetics Today* 31, no. 3 (Fall 2010): 507–659.

———. "Ordering the Unordered: Time, Space and Descriptive Coherence." *Yale French Studies* 61 (1981): 60–88.

———. "Proteus in Quotation-Land: Mimesis and the Forms of Reported Discourse." *Poetics Today* 3, no. 2 (Spring 1982): 107–56.

———. "Reconceptualizing Narratology: Arguments for a Functionalist and Constructivist Approach to Narrative." *Enthymema* 4 (2011): 35–50.

———. "Telling in Time (II): Chronology, Teleology, Narrativity." *Poetics Today* 13, no. 3 (Autumn 1992): 463–541.

———. "Universals of Narrative and their Cognitive Fortunes." *Poetics Today* 24, no. 2 (Summer 2003): 297–395.

von Glaserfeld, Ernst. "Introduction to Radical Constructivism." In *The Invented Reality*, edited by Paul Watzlawick, 17–40. New York: Norton, 1984.

Yacobi, Tamar. "Package Deals in Fictional Narrative: The Case of the Narrator's (Un)Reliability." *Narrative* 9 (May 2001): 223–29.

CONTRIBUTORS

Raphaël Baroni (raphael.baroni@unil.ch) is full associate professor at the University of Lausanne. His publications on narrative theory include *La tension narrative* (2007), *L'oeuvre du temps* (2009), and *Les rouages de l'intrigue* (forthcoming). He has coedited several volumes, including *Les bifurcations du récit interactif: Continuité ou rupture?* (Cahiers de Narratologie n° 27, 2014), *Les passions en literature: De la théorie à l'enseignement* (Etudes de Lettres n° 295, 2014), *Rencontre de narrativités: Perspectives sur l'intrigue musicale* (Cahiers de Narratologie n° 21, 2011), and *Le Savoir des genres* (PUR, 2007). Baroni has published many articles in journals such as *Poétique, Littérature, Semiotica, Semiotic Inquiry,* and *Image & Narrative*. In 2010, he founded, with Françoise Revaz, the Narratology Network of French Speaking Switzerland (RRN).

Alain Boillat (alain.boillat@unil.ch) is professor at the Department of History and Aesthetics of Cinema at the University of Lausanne. His research relates, in particular, to the history of scriptwriting practices, to the study of technological imaginaries, to the relationship between comics and movies, as well as to issues concerning narrative and fiction in media productions. He has recently published *Cinéma: Machine à mondes* (Georg, 2014), *Star Wars: Un monde en expansion* (Maison d'Ailleurs, 2014), and was coeditor of *Dubbing: La traduction audiovisuelle* (Schüren, 2014), *BD-US: Les comics en Europe* (Infolio, 2015), *Loin des yeux ... le cinéma* (L'Âge d'Homme, 2015), and *Dialogues avec le cinéma: Approches interdisciplinaires de l'oralité cinématographique* (Nota bene, 2015).

Peter Hühn (huehn@uni-hamburg.de) is professor of English Literature at Hamburg University (retired since 2005). His main fields of interest are British poetry, theory of poetry, narratology, application of narratology to poetry analysis, detective fiction, and systems theory. He is the author of *Eventfulness in British Fiction* (2010) and *The Narratological Analysis of Lyric Poetry: Studies in English Poetry from the 16th to the 20th Century* (with J. Kiefer, 2005). He is also editor-in-chief and coauthor of *The Handbook of Narratology* (with J. C. Meister, J. Pier, and W. Schmid, 2nd ed. 2014).

Emma Kafalenos (emkafale@wustl.edu) is the author of *Narrative Causalities* (2007); was the guest editor of *Narrative* 9, no. 2 (2001), a special issue on *Contemporary Narratology*; and has published numerous articles in journals and edited collections. She is Honorary Senior Lecturer in Comparative Literature at Washington University in St. Louis, Missouri.

Franco Passalacqua (fr.passa@gmail.com) is a PhD candidate at the Department of Human Sciences for Education "Riccardo Massa" of the University of Milano-Bicocca and lecturer in the didactic in literature and Italian literature at the same university. He is the author of several scholarly journal articles on narrative theory and narrative teaching and translator of Meir Sternberg's works into Italian. His current research is focused on narrative learning and teaching in a school context, both exploring the role of narrative competence in learning development and the epistemological grounding of narrative teaching strategies and methodologies. He is coordinator of didactic projects, financed by an Italian private foundation centered on literary teaching and learning in primary and secondary schools.

James Phelan (phelan.1@osu.edu) is Distinguished University Professor of English at The Ohio State University and a founding member of Project Narrative. He is the editor of *Narrative* and the coeditor (with Peter J. Rabinowitz) of The Ohio State University Press Series on the Theory and Interpretation of Narrative. He is the author or coauthor of six books on narrative theory, the most recent of which are *Living to Tell about It* (2005), *Experiencing Fiction* (2007), and (with David Herman, Peter J. Rabinowitz, Brian Richardson, and Robyn Warhol) *Practicing Narrative Theory: Four Perspectives in Conversation* (under review). Phelan is also editor or coeditor of numerous books in narrative theory, the most recent of which are the Blackwell *Companion to Narrative Theory* (2005), *Joseph Conrad* (with Jakob Lothe and Jeremy Hawthorn, 2008), and *Teaching Narrative Theory* (with David Herman and Brian McHale, 2010). He is currently working on a study of the twentieth-century American novel for Blackwell's Reading the Novel series.

Federico Pianzola (f.pianzola@gmail.com) is postdoctoral research fellow at the Department of Human Sciences for Education "Riccardo Massa" of the University of Milano-Bicocca. He has an international PhD in Italian literature awarded in 2014 by the University of Florence, the Université Paris-Sorbonne, and the Rheinische Friedrich-Wilhelms-Universität Bonn, also having a co-tutelle arrangement with the University of Cambridge. He completed a dissertation on aspects of myth and fiction in the work of the Holocaust survivor-writer and scientist Primo Levi (in press). He is the author of several scholarly journal articles, interviews, and translations on contemporary Italian literature and on narrative theory, and editor-in-chief of *Enthymema*, an international academic journal of theory, critics, and philosophy of literature.

John Pier (j.pier@wanadoo.fr) is Professor Emeritus of English at the University of Tours and a member of the Centre de recherche sur les arts et le langage (CNRS-EHESS) in Paris, where he codirects the seminar "Recherches en narratologie contemporaine." Cofounder of the European Narratology Network (ENN) and past president of the ENN Steering Committee, his numerous articles on narrative theory and literary semiotics have appeared in publications in France and abroad. He is also coeditor of the book series Narratologia at De Gruyter and serves on the editorial board of a number of journals. Among the volumes he has edited or coedited are *The Dynamics of Narrative Form* (2004), *La métalepse, aujourd'hui* (with J. M. Schaeffer, 2005), *Théorie du récit: L'apport de la recherche allemande* (2007), *Theorizing*

Narrativity (with J. A. García Landa, 2008), *Narratologies contemporaines* (with F. Berthelot, 2010), *L'effacement selon Nabokov: Lolita versus* The Original of Laura (with A. Gassin, 2014), and *Handbook of Narratology* (with P. Hühn, J. C. Meister, and W. Schmid, 1st ed. 2009; 2nd ed. 2014), also available online as *The Living Handbook of Narratology*.

Gerald Prince (gprince@babel.ling.upenn.edu) is professor of Romance languages, associate faculty at the Annenberg School of Communication, and a member of the graduate groups in linguistics and in comparative literature at the University of Pennsylvania. The author of several books (including *Métaphysique et technique dans l'œuvre romanesque de Sartre; A Grammar of Stories; Narratology: The Form and Functioning of Narrative; A Dictionary of Narratology; Narrative as Theme; Guide du roman de langue française: 1901–1950*) and many articles and reviews in the fields of (narrative) theory and of modern (French) literature, Prince is a member of the editorial or advisory board of over a dozen scholarly journals (including *Diacritics, Philosophy and Literature, Narrative, Style, The French Review, French Forum,* and *Studies in Twentieth and Twenty-First Century Literature*) and is the general editor of the Stages series for the University of Nebraska Press. He is working on the second volume of his guide to the twentieth-century novel in French (1951–2000). In 2013, he received the ISSN Wayne C. Booth Lifetime Achievement Award.

Françoise Revaz (francoise.revaz@unifr.ch) is professor of French linguistics at the University of Fribourg. She has published in collaboration with Jean-Michel Adam *L'analyse des récits* (1996), and as single-author of *Les textes d'action* (1997) and *Introduction à la narratologie: Action et narration* (2009). In 2010, she founded, with Raphaël Baroni, the Narratology Network of French Speaking Switzerland (RRN). She is currently working on action theory applied to narratology and on the functions and forms of narratives in different genres and media (journalism, historiography, literature, and publicity). She is director of a project financed by the Swiss National Science Foundation, entitled "Le découpage de l'action: Analyse narratologique de périodiques de bandes dessinées (1946–1959)."

Brian Richardson (richb@umd.edu) is a professor in the English department of the University of Maryland, where he teaches modern literature and narrative theory. He is the author of *Unlikely Stories: Causality and the Nature of Modern Narrative* (1997), *Unnatural Voices: Extreme Narration in Modern and Contemporary Fiction* (2006), *Narrative Theory: Core Concepts and Critical Debates* (with David Herman, James Phelan, Peter Rabinowitz, and Robyn Warhol, 2012), and *Unnatural Narratives: Theory, History, and Practice* (2015). Richardson has edited six collections of essays on narrative theory, including the anthologies, *Narrative Dynamics: Essays on Time, Plot, Closure, and Frames* (2002), *Narrative Beginnings: Theories and Practices* (2008), and *A Poetics of Unnatural Narratives* (coedited with Jan Alber and Henrik Skov Nielsen, 2013).

Marie-Laure Ryan (marilaur@gmail.com) is an independent scholar. She is the author of *Possible Worlds, Artificial Intelligence and Narrative Theory* (1991), *Narrative as Virtual Reality: Immersion and Interactivity in Literature and Electronic Media* (2001), and *Avatars of Story* (2006). She has also edited *Cyberspace Textuality: Computer Technology and Literary Theory* (1999), *Narrative across Media: The Languages of Storytelling* (2004), and coedited the *Routledge Encyclopedia of Narrative* (with David Herman and Manfred Jahn, 2005), *Intermediality and Storytelling* (with Marina Grishakova, 2010), the *Johns Hopkins Guide to Digital Media* (with Lori Emerson and Benjamin Robertson, 2014) and *Storyworlds across Media* (with Jan-Noël Thon, 2014). Her scholarly work has earned her the Prize for Independent Scholars and the Jeanne and Aldo Scaglione Prize for Comparative Literature, both from the Modern Language Association, and she has been the recipient of Guggenheim and NEA fellowships. Her Web site is at http://users.frii.com/mlryan/

Eyal Segal (eyalsega@post.tau.ac.il) is a research fellow in the Porter Institute for Poetics and Semiotics, Tel Aviv University. He is the author of *The Problem of Narrative Closure: How Stories Are (Not) Finished* (2007, in Hebrew) and *The Decisive Moment is Everlasting: Static Time in Kafka's Poetics* (2008, in Hebrew). His articles and book chapters appeared in *Amsterdam International Electronic Journal for Cultural Narratology, Poetics Today, Current Trends in Narratology* (edited by Greta Olson, 2011), *Theoretical Schools and Circles in the Twentieth-Century Humanities* (edited by Marina Grishakova, 2015), and *Ford Madox Ford's "The Good Soldier": Centenary Essays* (edited by Max Saunders and Sara Haslam, 2015).

Michael Toolan (m.toolan@bham.ac.uk) is professor of English language in the Department of English Language and Applied Linguistics at the University of Birmingham. His single-authored books include *The Stylistics of Fiction* (1988), *Total Speech* (1996), *Language in Literature* (1998), *Narrative* (2nd ed. 2001), and *Narrative Progression in the Short Story: A Corpus Stylistic Approach* (2009). His new book, *Making Sense with Narrative Text* should appear in 2015. He has edited several collections, including *Language, Text and Context: Essays in Contextualised Stylistics* and *Language Teaching: Integrational Linguistic Approaches* (2009). Since 2002, he has been editor of the *Journal of Literary Semantics*.

INDEX

INDEX OF AUTHORS

Aarseth, Espen, 174
Abbott, H. Porter, 2
Abelson, Robert P., 117n
Adam, Jean-Michel, 12, 21-22, 24, 28-31, 72n
Alber, Jan, 197-98, 213
Aristotle, 1-2, 5, 13, 20, 24-26, 28-30, 32, 71, 146, 181
Aubert, Michelle, 112n

Bakhtin, Mikhail, 21, 29n, 33, 180
Bal, Mieke, 6, 164, 214-215
Ballard, J. G., 166
Barad, Judith, 81n
Baroni, Raphaël, 2, 5, 13, 22n, 29n, 46n, 53n, 91n, 98, 102, 127n, 145-46, 154n, 163, 183, 196, 199, 203-4
Barthes, Roland, 3, 13, 17, 25, 146-47, 166, 176-84, 186, 190, 192
Beckett, Samuel, 41-42, 44, 46
Bell, Alice, 190
Billington, Alex, 78n
Black, John B., 117n
Blanchot, Maurice, 180n
Boillat, Alain, 5, 108
Bolter, Jay David, 183
Booth, Wayne C., 5
Bousquet, Henri, 113n
Bower, Gordon H., 117n
Bradbury, Malcolm, 173
Bredehoft, Thomas A., 170
Bremond, Claude, 12, 17, 29, 88, 96
Brewer, William, 93
Brooker, Will, 82n
Brooks, Peter, 2-3, 88
Bruner, Jerome, 38
Bukatman, Scott, 81n

Candel Borman, Daniel, 94
Canemaker, John, 117n

Carroll, Noël, 92n, 102
Castillo, Ana, 172, 174
Chatman, Seymour, 164
Chemartin, Pierre, 111n
Christen, Thomas, 82n
Clivaz, Claire, 97-98, 102
Coover, Robert, 172, 187-88
Crozier, Daniel, 142

Dannenberg, Hilary P., 1-2, 4, 53n, 87n, 89-90, 96
Derrida, Jacques, 183
Dijk (van), Teun A., 117n
Doležel, Lubomír, 76, 94, 153
Dulac, Nicolas, 111n
Dupont-Roc, Roselyne, 32n

Eco, Umberto, 2-3, 29, 32, 87-88, 94n, 127, 182n
Eggers, Dave A., 168
Eisenstein, Sergueï Mikhaïlovich, 111
Eisner, Will, 107n
Escola, Marc, 101

Fludernik, Monika, 2, 11n, 197-99, 208-9
Foer, Jonathan Safran, 171
Forestier (le), Laurent, 111n
Forster, Edward M., 2, 25, 39
Foucault, Michel, 183
Fowles, John, 84, 173, 175
Frank, Joseph, 181
Frazer, John, 113n

Genette, Gérard, 11, 20, 26n, 73-74, 76n, 199n
Gennep (van), Arnold, 38n
Gerhardie, William, 41n
Gerrig, Richard, 91-92, 102
Glaserfeld (von), Ernst, 198n
Gorman, Siobhan, 152n
Greimas, Algirdas Julien, 13
Guido, Laurent, 111n
Gunning, Tom, 111-13

INDEX

Halliwell, Stephen, 135
Hansen, Per Krogh, 164
Heidegger, Martin, 180
Herman, David, 2–4, 11n, 89, 196
Higgins, George V., 69
Hogan, Patrick Colm, 157n
Horn, Richard, 168
Hühn, Peter, 2, 4, 37, 39, 41n, 94n, 132, 199–203
Hutcheon, Linda, 135
Hutcheon, Michael, 135

Iser, Wolfgang, 40n

Jackson, Shelley, 183–84, 190
Jahn, Manfred, 210
James, Henry, 41, 44–46
Jameson, Fredric, 181
Johansen, Jorgen Dines, 31
Jordan, Enoch P., 77n
Joyce, James, 39, 41–42
Joyce, Michael, 184, 186, 190

Kafalenos, Emma, 3, 5, 12, 53n, 90
Kahn, Charles H., 206n
Kerman, Judith B., 79
Kindt, Tom, 197
Kirkpatrick, David D., 158–59
Knight, Deborah, 81n
Kukkonen, Karin, 2

Labov, William, 11, 13, 15, 29n, 38, 132
Lallot, Jean, 32n
Lamarque, Peter, 197
Landow, George, 183
Langer, Susanne K., 141n
Larivaille, Paul, 12, 28
Lemco, Gary, 134
Lotman, Yuri, 38–40, 202n

Marcher, John, 44–46
Maresca, Peter, 109n
Margolin, Uri, 206, 213–14
Marsden, Jean I., 78n
McCay, Winsor, 108–9, 111–19, 123–24, 126
McClary, Susan, 147–48
McKnight, George, 81n
McLaverty, Bernard, 45n
Meelberg, Vincent, 140–41
Meister, Jan Christoph, 5
Mink, Louis O., 31–32
Montfort, Nick, 183n
Morgan, Harry, 109

Mortimer, Armine Kotin, 170–71
Moulthrop, Stuart, 183–84, 190
Murray, Barbara A., 78n
Murray, Joddy, 141n
Musser, Charles, 113n

Nahin, Paul J., 181
Naremore, James, 76n
Nattiez, Jean-Jacques, 141, 144
Neubauer, John, 148
Nünning, Ansgar, 11n, 197n, 212n
Nünning, Vera, 11n

Oatley, Keith, 180
O'Hara, John, 52–53, 57, 62–69
Ott, Eirik R., 166
Ovid, 42

Passalacqua, Franco, 3, 6, 90n, 208n
Patron, Sylvie, 52n, 198
Pavel, Thomas, 88n
Pavić, Milorad, 166, 169
Peirce, Charles Sanders, 4, 22, 31–32
Phelan, James, 2, 5, 12, 22n, 87–88, 101n, 145, 163, 204
Pianzola, Federico, 3, 6, 90n, 132, 147, 208n, 211n, 213n
Pier, John, 4, 6n, 22–23, 26, 31n, 33, 72n, 91n, 198n, 203, 205
Plato, 33
Pratt, Mary Louise, 38
Prieto-Pablos, José, 93
Prince, Gerald, 2, 4, 11n, 20, 26, 28n, 51, 53n, 72, 92, 95–96, 152, 197–98, 207
Propp, Vladimir, 3, 12–13, 25, 88, 90, 96, 145, 153
Pullinger, Kate, 191

Rabinowitz, Peter J., 54, 75n, 131, 157n
Revaz, Françoise, 5, 12, 124n, 154n
Richardson, Brian, 6, 12, 53n, 84n, 173, 197, 204
Rickman, Lance, 113n
Ricoeur, Paul, 2, 30–31
Rimmon-Kenan, Shlomith, 152, 167
Roba, Jean, 121
Rosenberg, Edgar, 77n
Rousset, Jean, 181n
Ryan, Marie-Laure, 2, 6, 12, 91–94, 96–98, 102, 133, 135–38, 148, 163, 188, 190, 199, 214

Sadoul, Georges, 113n
Sammon, Paul M., 78–79, 82n

Saporta, Marc, 169, 182
Schank, Roger C., 117n
Schmid, Wolf, 38
Schmidt, Henry J., 77n, 83n
Seaton, Douglas, 144
Segal, Eyal, 2, 5, 74n, 174, 202n
Seguin, Jean-Claude, 112n
Shanahan, Timothy, 81–82
Shen, Dan, 5
Shklovsky, Victor, 53
Smolderen, Thierry, 116–117
Sperber, Dan, 14n
Stedman, Kyle D., 142–143
Sternberg, Meir, 2–5, 12, 22–27, 32, 53n, 71–72, 83, 88–89, 113, 120, 145, 155, 188n, 196, 198–199, 204–5, 207–9, 211–12, 214–15

Tarasti, Eero, 148
Todorov, Tzvetan, 12, 27, 89n, 152–53
Tomachevsky, Boris, 1, 13, 28n
Toolan, Michael, 5, 91, 204
Tooley, Michael, 180
Torgovnick, Marianna, 74
Törnqvist, Egil, 77
Turner, Terrence J., 117n
Tyrkkö, Jukka, 168

Updike, John, 166

Vaina, Lucia, 88n
Vickers, Brian, 141n
Villeneuve, Johanne, 90

Waletzky, Joshua, 15, 29n
Walton, Kendal, 91–92, 102
Wardrip-Fruin, Noah, 183n
Warhol, Robyn R., 40
Warner, Rebecca, 81n
Wilson, Deirdre, 14n
Wolf, Werner, 141
Wolff, Tobias, 51, 53, 55, 57–61

Yacobi, Tamar, 207n
Yanal, Robert, 91–92

INDEX OF CONCEPTS

abduction 3, 32–33
adaptation, 75, 78n, 82, 143n
affect, (the), 15–16
alternative (the), 5, 32, 91–102

antichronological, 164–165
anticipation (*see also* prospection), 41, 44, 89, 118, 128
authorial audience, 5, 56
authorial disclosure, 5, 51–54, 57, 59–60, 62–67, 69

catharsis (*see also* pathos), 5, 13, 97
causality, 33, 120, 138, 153, 155, 157n, 159–60, 180–81
classical narratology, 11, 17, 107, 197, 212n
comic strip, 107–9, 116, 122–23, 128
complexity, 1, 3, 14, 47, 96, 176
complication, 13, 28–29, 55–56, 58, 60, 88, 94, 99–101, 124–25
configuration, 2–4, 6, 15, 20, 30–31, 66, 89–90, 190, 206
constructivism, 197, 209
constructivist, 3, 6, 195–96, 199, 205, 207–15
context, 4, 14, 16–18, 24, 33, 38–40, 42, 45–46, 51, 83, 112, 135, 153–54, 196n, 200, 208–12
contingency, 101, 144
conversational disclosure, 62–67
curiosity, 22–24, 28, 34, 72, 82, 89, 92, 113, 145, 188, 208

denouement (*see also* resolution), 28–29, 90, 113, 122, 128
disclosure, 5, 51–55, 57, 59–60, 62–67, 69, 72, 146, 167
disnarrated, 92, 95–97
disnarration, 51, 57, 60, 96, 98, 100–102
dynamics, 3–4, 22, 29, 55–63, 65, 67, 69, 72–73, 77, 79, 82n, 87–89, 91, 94, 97, 145, 181, 204, 208, 211

embedded narrative, 96–97, 100
empathy, 80, 93
emplotment, 2, 29n–31
eventfulness, 4, 37–40, 42, 44, 46–47, 94n, 199–202n

fabula (see also *sjuzhet*), 1, 3–5, 13, 22, 25, 53–54, 60, 88, 90, 92, 96, 102, 155–57, 159, 164–165, 167–70, 172, 174, 198, 203, 206
fear (*see also* pathos), 1, 13, 15, 59, 69, 93
fiction, 38, 41–42, 52n, 88, 94–96, 100, 135, 144, 155–56, 167, 183n, 189
formalism, 3, 88, 91, 197
formalist, 2–4, 13, 20, 87–88, 90, 141, 156, 212n

hypertext, 170, 174, 182–91

implied author, 5, 53–56, 62, 204
interpretation, 15–16, 39, 42, 46, 81–82, 90, 103, 134, 148, 153, 155–60, 179, 184, 186, 188
intersequential / intersequentiality 4, 21–24, 26n, 29n, 34, 73

linearity, 6, 163–65, 176, 214

material book, 170–71
matrix, 4–5, 89–90, 101, 151, 153–54, 156–60, 169
media, 5–6, 37, 77, 131, 137–38, 148, 177n, 200, 213–14
mimesis, 1, 31, 133, 135–36
mimetic, 24–25, 71, 136, 146–47, 180, 213
musical sequence, 146–48

narrative configuration (*see also* configuration) 6, 32–33
narrative interest, 4–5, 72–75, 78, 83–84, 88, 92, 202n
narrative progression (*see also* progression), 4–5, 22n, 53, 87n, 165
narrative tension (*see also* tension), 13, 22n, 29n, 72, 87, 89–92, 97, 102, 203
narrativehood, 18, 28n, 140
narrativeness, 18
natural narratology, 6, 213
network, 21, 107, 151n, 174, 178–87, 189–92, 210
non-event, 4, 39–42, 44–47, 200–203

path, 3, 54, 90–91, 96–97, 101, 122, 126, 174, 182, 186, 189, 195
pathos (*see also* fear; pity), 92, 99–100, 102, 203
pity (*see also* pathos), 13, 15, 77
plot, 1–6, 13, 22, 24–25, 30–31, 38, 41n, 42, 45n, 56, 73, 75, 79, 81, 87–91, 93–94, 97–98, 120, 122, 128, 133, 144–46, 165, 181, 183, 191–92, 203, 206
plot dynamics, 55–56, 59–60, 63, 79, 204
plural text, 178–179, 181, 183, 192
portrait narrative, 53, 60, 62
possible worlds, 12, 88–89, 94–96, 186, 199–200
postclassical narratology, 3–4, 11, 17, 107, 196–97
potential, 26–27, 31, 59, 92, 94, 109, 111, 130, 132, 134, 144, 154, 179, 180
pragmatics, 15, 17, 29n, 198, 202–4, 207–8, 210–12

progression, 4–5, 22n, 53–58, 60–63, 67, 88–91, 114, 133, 144–45, 147–48, 165, 169, 183, 187, 190–91, 204
propositional ambiguity, 152–153
prospection (*see also* anticipation), 22, 34, 72
prototype / prototypical 4, 21–22, 24, 28–39, 30, 33–34, 39, 203

readerly dynamics 55–57, 59–61, 65, 67, 69, 204
recognition, 22, 59, 72, 118, 144, 206–7
repetition, 57–58, 61, 87, 92–93, 94n, 97, 102, 108, 117n, 127, 147
resolution (*see also* denouement), 1, 12, 18, 32, 55–56, 58, 60, 74, 79, 88–90, 93–94, 97–98, 118, 124–25, 143, 145, 154–55, 165, 172, 174
retrospection, 22, 34, 72
rhetoric / rhetorical, 2, 5–6, 13, 16, 53–55, 56n, 71–72, 74, 76, 83, 87–89, 132, 188, 202n, 204

schema, 16, 21, 28, 30, 202n
script, 4, 16, 38, 41, 94, 116–17, 120, 123–24, 127–28, 133, 196
scriptible, 176–77, 190
sequential / sequentiality, 1–2, 4–5, 12, 21–25, 28, 37, 73, 107, 109, 116–17, 120, 122, 126, 128, 131, 133, 167, 205
sjuzhet (see also *fabula*), 1–2, 22, 53–55, 155–57, 163–74, 198, 203–4, 206
structuralism, 23, 32, 181, 197, 211
structuralist, 2–4, 34, 87–88, 196n–197, 212
surprise, 15, 18, 22–24, 28, 33, 46, 56, 61, 72–73, 80, 82, 84, 113, 122n, 145–46, 154, 188, 191, 202n, 208
suspense, 5, 15, 18, 22–26, 28, 33–34, 72–73, 79, 84, 89, 91–95, 97–98, 101n, 102, 107, 113, 118, 120, 122, 127, 133, 143, 145–46, 164, 188, 202n, 208

tellability, 18, 37n, 40, 47, 96, 201
tension, 13, 22n, 29n, 55, 60–61, 63–65, 72–73, 87, 89–92, 96–97, 99–102, 122, 127, 137, 145–46, 183, 203–4

vectorization, 109, 122–25
verbal narrative 123, 128, 138, 148
video games, 6, 191
virtual / virtuality, 5, 87–88, 90–102, 103

THEORY AND INTERPRETATION OF NARRATIVE
James Phelan, Peter J. Rabinowitz, and Robyn Warhol, Series Editors

Because the series editors believe that the most significant work in narrative studies today contributes both to our knowledge of specific narratives and to our understanding of narrative in general, studies in the series typically offer interpretations of individual narratives and address significant theoretical issues underlying those interpretations. The series does not privilege one critical perspective but is open to work from any strong theoretical position.

Narrative Sequence in Contemporary Narratology
EDITED BY RAPHAËL BARONI AND FRANÇOISE REVAZ

The Submerged Plot and the Mother's Pleasure from Jane Austen to Arundhati Roy
KELLY A. MARSH

Narrative Theory Unbound: Queer and Feminist Interventions
EDITED BY ROBYN WARHOL AND SUSAN S. LANSER

Unnatural Narrative: Theory, History, and Practice
BRIAN RICHARDSON

Ethics and the Dynamic Observer Narrator: Reckoning with Past and Present in German Literature
KATRA A. BYRAM

Narrative Paths: African Travel in Modern Fiction and Nonfiction
KAI MIKKONEN

The Reader as Peeping Tom: Nonreciprocal Gazing in Narrative Fiction and Film
JEREMY HAWTHORN

Thomas Hardy's Brains: Psychology, Neurology, and Hardy's Imagination
SUZANNE KEEN

The Return of the Omniscient Narrator: Authorship and Authority in Twenty-First Century Fiction
PAUL DAWSON

Feminist Narrative Ethics: Tacit Persuasion in Modernist Form
KATHERINE SAUNDERS NASH

Real Mysteries: Narrative and the Unknowable
H. PORTER ABBOTT

A Poetics of Unnatural Narrative
EDITED BY JAN ALBER, HENRIK SKOV NIELSEN, AND BRIAN RICHARDSON

Narrative Discourse: Authors and Narrators in Literature, Film, and Art
PATRICK COLM HOGAN

Literary Identification from Charlotte Brontë to Tsitsi Dangarembga
LAURA GREEN

An Aesthetics of Narrative Performance: Transnational Theater, Literature, and Film in Contemporary Germany
CLAUDIA BREGER

Narrative Theory: Core Concepts and Critical Debates
DAVID HERMAN, JAMES PHELAN AND PETER J. RABINOWITZ, BRIAN RICHARDSON, AND ROBYN WARHOL

After Testimony: The Ethics and Aesthetics of Holocaust Narrative for the Future
EDITED BY JAKOB LOTHE, SUSAN RUBIN SULEIMAN, AND JAMES PHELAN

The Vitality of Allegory: Figural Narrative in Modern and Contemporary Fiction
GARY JOHNSON

Narrative Middles: Navigating the Nineteenth-Century British Novel
EDITED BY CAROLINE LEVINE AND MARIO ORTIZ-ROBLES

Fact, Fiction, and Form: Selected Essays
RALPH W. RADER. EDITED BY JAMES PHELAN AND DAVID H. RICHTER

The Real, the True, and the Told: Postmodern Historical Narrative and the Ethics of Representation
ERIC L. BERLATSKY

Franz Kafka: Narration, Rhetoric, and Reading
EDITED BY JAKOB LOTHE, BEATRICE SANDBERG, AND RONALD SPEIRS

Social Minds in the Novel
ALAN PALMER

Narrative Structures and the Language of the Self
MATTHEW CLARK

Imagining Minds: The Neuro-Aesthetics of Austen, Eliot, and Hardy
KAY YOUNG

Postclassical Narratology: Approaches and Analyses
EDITED BY JAN ALBER AND MONIKA FLUDERNIK

Techniques for Living: Fiction and Theory in the Work of Christine Brooke-Rose
KAREN R. LAWRENCE

Towards the Ethics of Form in Fiction: Narratives of Cultural Remission
LEONA TOKER

Tabloid, Inc.: Crimes, Newspapers, Narratives
V. PENELOPE PELIZZON AND NANCY M. WEST

Narrative Means, Lyric Ends: Temporality in the Nineteenth-Century British Long Poem
MONIQUE R. MORGAN

Joseph Conrad: Voice, Sequence, History, Genre
EDITED BY JAKOB LOTHE, JEREMY HAWTHORN, AND JAMES PHELAN

Understanding Nationalism: On Narrative, Cognitive Science, and Identity
PATRICK COLM HOGAN

The Rhetoric of Fictionality: Narrative Theory and the Idea of Fiction
RICHARD WALSH

Experiencing Fiction: Judgments, Progressions, and the Rhetorical Theory of Narrative
JAMES PHELAN

Unnatural Voices: Extreme Narration in Modern and Contemporary Fiction
BRIAN RICHARDSON

Narrative Causalities
EMMA KAFALENOS

Why We Read Fiction: Theory of Mind and the Novel
LISA ZUNSHINE

I Know That You Know That I Know: Narrating Subjects from Moll Flanders *to* Marnie
GEORGE BUTTE

Bloodscripts: Writing the Violent Subject
ELANA GOMEL

Surprised by Shame: Dostoevsky's Liars and Narrative Exposure
DEBORAH A. MARTINSEN

Having a Good Cry: Effeminate Feelings and Pop-Culture Forms
ROBYN R. WARHOL

Politics, Persuasion, and Pragmatism: A Rhetoric of Feminist Utopian Fiction
ELLEN PEEL

Telling Tales: Gender and Narrative Form in Victorian Literature and Culture
ELIZABETH LANGLAND

Narrative Dynamics: Essays on Time, Plot, Closure, and Frames
EDITED BY BRIAN RICHARDSON

Breaking the Frame: Metalepsis and the Construction of the Subject
DEBRA MALINA

Invisible Author: Last Essays
CHRISTINE BROOKE-ROSE

Ordinary Pleasures: Couples, Conversation, and Comedy
KAY YOUNG

Narratologies: New Perspectives on Narrative Analysis
EDITED BY DAVID HERMAN

Before Reading: Narrative Conventions and the Politics of Interpretation
PETER J. RABINOWITZ

Matters of Fact: Reading Nonfiction over the Edge
DANIEL W. LEHMAN

The Progress of Romance: Literary Historiography and the Gothic Novel
DAVID H. RICHTER

A Glance Beyond Doubt: Narration, Representation, Subjectivity
SHLOMITH RIMMON-KENAN

Narrative as Rhetoric: Technique, Audiences, Ethics, Ideology
JAMES PHELAN

Misreading Jane Eyre: *A Postformalist Paradigm*
JEROME BEATY

Psychological Politics of the American Dream: The Commodification of Subjectivity in Twentieth-Century American Literature
LOIS TYSON

Understanding Narrative
EDITED BY JAMES PHELAN AND PETER J. RABINOWITZ

Framing Anna Karenina: *Tolstoy, the Woman Question, and the Victorian Novel*
AMY MANDELKER

Gendered Interventions: Narrative Discourse in the Victorian Novel
ROBYN R. WARHOL

Reading People, Reading Plots: Character, Progression, and the Interpretation of Narrative
JAMES PHELAN

www.ingramcontent.com/pod-product-compliance
Lightning Source LLC
Chambersburg PA
CBHW030110010526
44116CB00005B/187